BORN CRIMINAL

BORN CRIMINAL

Matilda Joslyn Gage, Radical Suffragist

ANGELICA SHIRLEY CARPENTER

SOUTH DAKOTA HISTORICAL SOCIETY PRESS   Pierre

Library of Congress Cataloging-in-Publication data
Names: Carpenter, Angelica Shirley, author.
Title: Born criminal : radical suffragist / Angelica Shirley Carpenter.
Description: Pierre : South Dakota Historical Society Press, [2018] | Includes bibliographical references and index.
Identifiers: LCCN 2017059085 | ISBN 9781941813188 (hardcover : alk. paper)
Subjects: LCSH: Gage, Matilda Joslyn, 1826-1898. | Feminists—United States—Biography. | Suffragists—United States—Biography. | Suffrage—United States—History—19th century. | Feminism—United States—History—19th century.
Classification: LCC HQ1413.G34 C37 2018 | DDC 324.6/23092 [B]—dc23
LC record available at https://lccn.loc.gov/2017059085

This publication is funded, in part, by the Great Plains Education Foundation, Aberdeen, S.Dak.

Printed in the United States

Text and cover design by Rich Hendel

Please visit our website at sdhspress.com

18 19 20 21 22 1 2 3 4 5

To Carolynne

✳ Contents

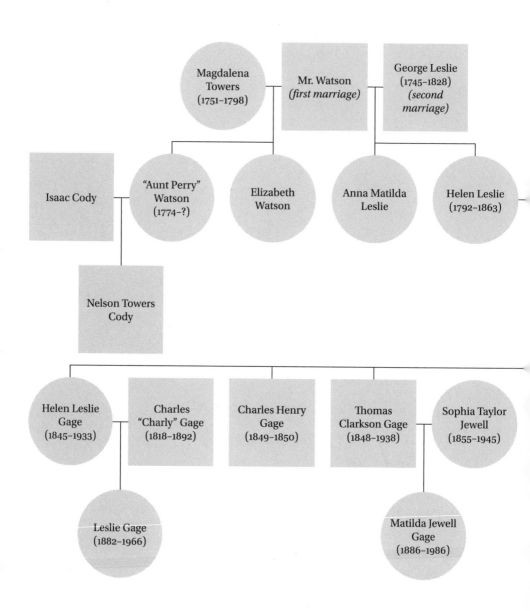

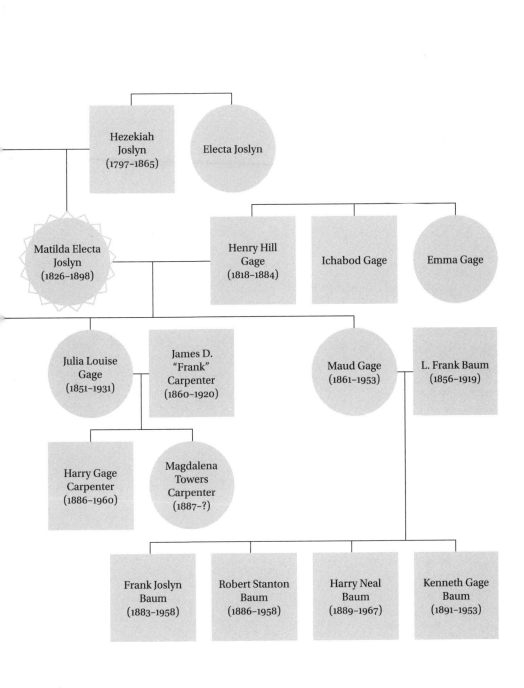

✳ Acknowledgments

Thanks to Sally Roesch Wagner, Michael Patrick Hearn, and Sue Boland for their research, knowledge, and encouragement and for reading this manuscript in various stages. Thanks to Leila R. Brammer, Mary E. Paddock Corey, Nancy Tystad Koupal, Lucia Patrick, Barbara S. Rivette, and the Matilda Joslyn Gage Foundation for documenting Matilda's life and times.

Thanks to Curt Hanson, University of North Dakota Library; Allison Cowgill and Art Mendoza, Henry Madden Library, California State University, Fresno; Peter Hanff, Bancroft Library, University of California, Berkeley; Lynda Ryan, Fayetteville Free Library, Fayetteville, New York; Rosemary Fry Plakus at the Library of Congress; and to my librarian and writer friends Kathy Haug, Christy Hicks, Carolynne Myall, Beth Olshewsky, and Ed Sullivan for many kinds of assistance.

Thanks to Matilda's great-great-grandchildren Robert A. Baum and Gita Dorothy Morena for research assistance and photos.

Thanks to the Henry Madden Library and the Society of Children's Book Writers and Illustrators, Northern California Chapter, for funding.

Thanks to authors Michael Cart, Margarita Engle, Jeri Chase Ferris, Leslie Ann Hayashi, Bonnie Hearn Hill, Kathleen Krull, Alexis O'Neill, and Susan Goldman Rubin for help with writing and marketing. Special thanks to my Fresno critique group, the Book Buds: Flora Burlingame, Vivien Cooley, Evelyne Holingue, Kelly Hollman, Claire Noland, Nancy Ralston, and Joan Schoettler.

Thanks to Rodger Hartley and Jennifer McIntyre of the South Dakota Historical Society Press, and to my copyeditor, Sarah C. Smith.

Thanks to my friends Susan Linter James, Marcie Morrison, and Kristene Scholefield for encouragement, and to my husband Richard, who has become one of Matilda's biggest fans. Listing names is risky, as I have probably forgotten some in the seven years I have been working on this book. I am truly grateful for the help I have received.

BORN
CRIMINAL

Matilda Joslyn Gage painting, 1888. Photo by L. Frank Baum. *Gage Foundation*

✳ Introduction

In 1893 a deputy sheriff knocked on Matilda Joslyn Gage's door in Fayetteville, New York. He served her with a supreme writ, court papers summoning her to appear before a judge for breaking the law.

"All of the crimes which I was *not* guilty of rushed through my mind," she wrote later, "but I *failed* to remember that I was a *born* criminal—a woman."[1]

Her crime: registering to vote. The verdict: guilty as charged.

This book describes the making of a revolutionary. As a child, Matilda campaigned against slavery. She became a famous leader in the early women's movement, working side by side with Elizabeth Cady Stanton and Susan B. Anthony. She led protests, organized conventions, and met with reformers, presidents, and reporters. She wrote about women's history in books that are still being studied.

Matilda's work changed our nation, and she expected—and deserved—to be remembered for it. But her face does not appear on our money. No parks are named after her. No marble bust of her stands in the Capitol alongside those of Susan B. Anthony and Elizabeth Cady Stanton. In fact, those so-called friends wrote her out of history. This book tells how they did it. It asks who controls history and who can change it. And it invites you to make history, too, and to write about it.

Matilda, 1876. *Gage Foundation*

1 ✳ Risking Arrest JULY 4, 1876

Matilda Joslyn Gage woke early on July 4, 1876. No one could have slept late—all the bells in Philadelphia were ringing, and guns were firing a sunrise salute. Besides, on this one-hundredth birthday of the United States, Matilda had a mission to fulfill.

Centennial parties were planned across the country all day, but the official national celebration, chaired by President Ulysses S. Grant, would be held in Philadelphia, where the Declaration of Independence had been signed a century before. And Matilda had something to give to the president, whether he wanted it or not.

To her, the centennial celebration was a farce. "The men alone of this country live in a republic," she had written, "the women enter the second hundred years of national life as political slaves."[1]

In the twenty-four years that Matilda had been fighting for women's rights, she had seen some progress, but not enough. With rare exceptions, only men could vote, and only men made the laws that limited women's choices in life. Nowhere in the nation were women full citizens with equal rights.

On July 4, 1876, the day of the centennial celebrations, Matilda planned to protest. She knew civil disobedience could get her arrested, but she was used to taking risks. Getting arrested would draw welcome attention to her cause. "We of this Centennial year must not forget that this country owes its birth to disobedience to law," Matilda had said.[2]

As usual, she dressed well—if she went to jail, at least she would look nice. The fashions of the day suited her tall, slim figure: fitted jackets worn over long skirts that were flat in front and draped behind. To protect her feet from the city pavements, she wore soft leather boots, and she pinned her hair into an upswept style with a cascade of curls in back.

Matilda had been away from her home in Fayetteville, New York, for two months, first chairing a convention in New York and then preparing for the centennial in Philadelphia. She missed her home and her family, and her family missed her, she knew, but they also took pride in her work and her fame. Her husband helped fund her efforts with profits from his store. Their four children, the youngest still in high school, advocated equal rights for women, like their parents.

Matilda, having just completed a year's term as president of the National Woman Suffrage Association ("the National"), had become the new chairman of the association's executive committee. In Philadelphia she was staying at the National's centennial headquarters, a large apartment with public parlors and sleeping rooms for the organization's officers.

After breakfast that morning, Matilda hurried to a parlor where she and her colleague Susan B. Anthony, the National's corresponding secretary, had been working for days. They were folding printed sheets of paper, tying them into bundles or stuffing them into envelopes, and hauling them off to the post office. The job was almost done.

Anthony, from Rochester, New York, was fifty-six, six years older than Matilda. Her simple way of dressing reflected her Quaker heritage. She wore her center-parted hair pulled back severely. Sharp facial features, a strong voice, and a tall, shapely physique added to her impact as a public speaker.

The document they were packing was a "Woman's Declaration of Rights and Articles of Impeachment Against the Government of the United States,"[3] written by Matilda Joslyn Gage and Elizabeth Cady Stanton. The two women were the National's primary writers. Stanton, the National's new president, had asked permission to present their declaration at the official centennial celebration.

General Joseph R. Hawley, president of the Centennial Commission, said no. After that, Elizabeth Cady Stanton decided not to attend the ceremony, but Matilda and others were "determined to do it."[4]

The others included Susan B. Anthony and Sara Andrews Spencer, who soon joined Matilda and Anthony in the parlor. Spencer, middle-

Elizabeth Cady Stanton and Susan B. Anthony, c. 1870.
Photo by Napoleon Sarony. *National Portrait Gallery, Smithsonian Institution*

aged, slight, and fair, ran a business school with her husband in Washington, D.C. A talented calligrapher, she had hand-lettered a large copy of their declaration for presentation later that morning.

Lillie Devereux Blake arrived next, wearing a light silk dress and her best hat. She was an author, lecturer, and social leader from New York City. The fifth member of their party was Phoebe Couzins, a young lawyer from St. Louis.

Grandstand behind Independence Hall in Philadelphia, July 4, 1876. *Library of Congress*

On one of the hottest mornings of the year, the women set off together through crowded city streets. They walked the mile to Independence Square, carrying heavy bundles of handbills and Spencer's three-foot scroll, tied with red, white, and blue ribbons.

Independence Square, like the rest of Philadelphia, was draped with colorful bunting. A crowd had been gathering there since before dawn, waiting for the official ceremony. Souvenir stands sold books, bandannas, Liberty Bells, and lemonade. By nine o'clock, every door, window, and rooftop overlooking the square was filled with joyous people.

"My country, 'tis of thee," they sang, waving flags to keep time, "sweet land of liberty, of thee I sing." The *New York Times* estimated the crowd at 35,000.

Matilda's parasol provided little relief from the broiling sun. Men shaded themselves with hats. The square's few trees filled quickly as boys and men climbed up, seeking a better view. Large numbers of police and military men stood ready to maintain order, but their job was easy; according to the *New York Times*, "the crowd controlled itself via patriotism."[5]

At the north side of the square, behind Independence Hall, stood a huge grandstand for the five thousand invited dignitaries—senators, congressmen, governors, Civil War generals, visiting royalty, religious leaders, and others. The highest part of the structure reached the hall's upstairs windows. Admission was tightly controlled, but Matilda and her friends had managed to obtain tickets.

Entering the hall through doors at ground level, they climbed stairs to the second floor. There they stepped through windows onto the platform, built for the occasion, that sloped down toward a podium.

The women made their way down the center aisle, their light-colored dresses glowing in the sea of men's dark suits. Some people recognized them, having heard them speak in lecture halls or at congressional hearings.

From the podium, General Hawley, the president of the Centennial Commission, watched them approach. A distinguished-looking man with a gray mustache and goatee, he wore a uniform trimmed with gold braid. It was Hawley who had denied their request to speak.

"You don't know how this inspired us," Sara Andrews Spencer said later.[6] "I never yet was forbidden by a man to do a thing, but that I resolved to do it."[7]

Hawley was also the person who could call for their arrest. He watched as the ladies found seats on the aisle, about thirty rows from the front. Their number shrank to four when Phoebe Couzins decided not to stay.

At some point the women learned that President Grant had chosen not to attend and that the acting vice president, Thomas Ferry, would preside over the ceremony. Ferry, they knew, supported the idea of votes for women. Perhaps he would let them present their declaration.

Phoebe Couzins had the same idea. She came hurrying back to them. "You must not do it!" she cried. "You must give it up."

"Why?" they asked. "What's the matter now?"

"I have just written a note to Mr. Ferry," she said, "asking if you may make the presentation, and he said, 'No.'" Then Couzins went away again, leaving the others still determined to be a part of the ceremony.[8] Nothing she said could change their minds.

"Their work was not for themselves alone," Elizabeth Cady Stanton wrote later, "nor for the present generation, but for all women of all time. The hopes of posterity were in their hands and they determined to place on record for the daughters of 1976, that their mothers of 1876 had asserted their equality of rights and impeached the government of that day for its injustice toward women."[9]

Soon the band played, and General Hawley made the opening speech. Then, still watching the women, he introduced the vice president.

Thomas Ferry praised the United States' immortal declaration that all men were free and equal.

General Joseph Roswell Hawley, c. 1865. *Library of Congress*

But to Matilda, freedom and equality had not yet been achieved.

Ferry announced that Richard Lee, whose grandfather had signed the Declaration of Independence, would read from the 1776 document. When the mayor of Philadelphia brought the original Declaration of Independence forward in a plain mahogany frame, the crowd exploded in cheers. Men tossed their hats into the air, and everyone on the platform stood to applaud.

Lee turned toward the crowd in the square to read. The women could barely hear him, but Lillie Devereux Blake caught the final words, the ones they were listening for: "our sacred honor."

"Now is the time!" she cried.[10]

"We rose," Matilda wrote later, "and pressed our way to the platform, Miss Anthony in front carrying *printed* documents, and I carrying the roll. . . . I held it before me that Hawley might not see it and forbid our approach."[11]

Blake and Spencer followed, carrying hundreds of copies of the declaration.

"There was a stir in the crowd just at the time," Blake said, "and General Hawley, who had been keeping a wary eye on us, had relaxed his vigilance for a moment, as he signed to the band to resume playing."[12]

The women moved quickly, according to one newspaper account, "Hustling Generals aside, elbowing Governors, and almost upsetting Dom Pedro [the Emperor of Brazil] in their charge."[13] The military officers on the platform could have stopped them, but instead the men drew back courteously. General Hawley did not see the women until they reached the rostrum, and by then it was too late.

"As we reached the platform," Matilda wrote later, "I gave the roll to Susan and I took from her hand the printed documents. Susan gave the roll into Ferry's hand, saying . . . 'I present this Declaration of Rights on behalf of the women citizens of the United States.' He took it, with a low bow, but as pale as he will be when dead, and we turned and went out, scattering our printed copies as we went—people [were] eager to seize them, standing on benches and asking for them."

"Order, order!" General Hawley shouted.

"It was a memorable scene," Matilda said, "and one that will live in future history."[14]

"Three cheers for the Emperor of Brazil!" General Hawley called, signaling to the band to play the Brazilian hymn.[15]

DECLARATION AND PROTEST

OF THE

WOMEN OF THE UNITED STATES

BY THE

NATIONAL WOMAN SUFFRAGE ASSOCIATION,

JULY 4th, 1876.

WHILE the Nation is buoyant with patriotism, and all hearts are attuned to praise, it is with sorrow we come to strike the one discordant note, on this hundredth anniversary of our country's birth. When subjects of Kings, Emperors, and Czars, from the Old World, join in our National Jubilee, shall the women of the Republic refuse to lay their hands with benedictions on the nation's head? Surveying America's Exposition, surpassing in magnificence those of London, Paris, and Vienna, shall we not rejoice at the success of the youngest rival among the nations of the earth? May not our hearts, in unison with all, swell with pride at our great achievements as a people; our free speech, free press, free schools, free church, and the rapid progress we have made in material wealth, trade, commerce, and the inventive arts? And we do rejoice, in the success thus far, of our experiment of self-government. Our faith is firm and unwavering in the broad principles of human rights, proclaimed in 1776, not only as abstract truths, but as the corner stones of a republic. Yet, we cannot forget, even in this glad hour, that while all men of every race, and clime, and condition, have been invested with the full rights of citizenship, under our hospitable flag, all women still suffer the degradation of disfranchisement.

Our history, the past hundred years, has been a series of assumptions and usurpations of power over woman, in direct opposition to the principles of just government, acknowledged by the United States at its foundation, which are:

First. The natural rights of each individual to self-government.

Second. The exact equality of these rights.

Third. That these rights, when not delegated by the individual, are retained by the individual.

Fourth. That no person can exercise the rights of others without delegated authority.

Fifth. That the non-use of these rights does not destroy them.

And for the violation of these fundamental principles of our Government, we arraign our rulers on this 4th day of July, 1876,—and these are our

ARTICLES OF IMPEACHMENT.

BILLS OF ATTAINDER have been passed by the introduction of the word "male" into all the State constitutions, denying to woman the right of suffrage, and thereby making sex a crime—an exercise of power clearly forbidden in Article 1st, Sections 9th and 10th of the United States Constitution.

211934
14

The document Matilda and her colleagues risked arrest to present, 1876. *Library of Congress*

"We did not know but we might be arrested," said Matilda, "but we cared not. Our work was necessary and done from principle. We went out then, through the Hall . . . and up on to a music stand, which was unoccupied during the events within. There Susan read the Declaration. I stood by her side, shading her with my parasol."[16]

Matilda was proud to hear her declaration, the words she had written with Elizabeth Cady Stanton, read aloud. It began:

> While the nation is buoyant with patriotism, and all hearts are attuned to praise, it is with sorrow we come to strike the one discordant note, on this one-hundredth anniversary of our country's birth. . . . May not [women's] hearts, in unison with all, swell with pride at our great achievements as a people; our free speech, free press, free schools, free church, and the rapid progress we have made in material wealth, trade, commerce and the inventive arts? And we do rejoice in the success, thus far, of our experiment of self-government. . . . Yet we cannot forget, even in this glad hour, that while all men of every race, and clime, and condition, have been invested with the full rights of citizenship under our hospitable flag, all women still suffer the degradation of disfranchisement.[17]

"A crowd gathered about," Matilda wrote later, "cheered the strong points and begged for copies."[18]

Well satisfied with the morning, she turned her thoughts to their afternoon project.

2 ✳ A Family Secret 1826–1836

When Matilda Electa Joslyn was a child, her parents trusted her to keep an important secret. Only a few close friends knew about certain visitors who stayed at their home in the village of Cicero, in central New York. The Joslyns' sprawling, white-pillared house was surrounded by a cedar swamp.[1] When a special person was expected, the little girl would have listened carefully for hoofbeats and for wagon wheels rattling on the road through the trees.

Next would come muffled voices as horses were tied up outside. Soon a man would enter (most of the visitors were men), usually someone she knew, bringing a dark-skinned man or sometimes a woman. These people were smuggled to the Joslyns' house in various ways: A man could be hidden under hay in a wagon. A woman might be disguised as a white lady, her face hidden under a bonnet and heavy veil, her hands concealed by gloves.

Matilda was proud that her home was a stop on the Underground Railroad, a network of people who helped enslaved men, women, and even children to escape from the South to freedom. The system used railroad terms, reflecting the popularity of new steam engines. Places where escapees could hide were known as stations or depots. People who contributed money to provide food, transportation, and disguises were called stockholders. A conductor was the person who moved a passenger from one station to another.[2] At Matilda's house, the fugitive visitors stayed until it was safe for them to move north, across the border into nearby Canada, where they could be free.

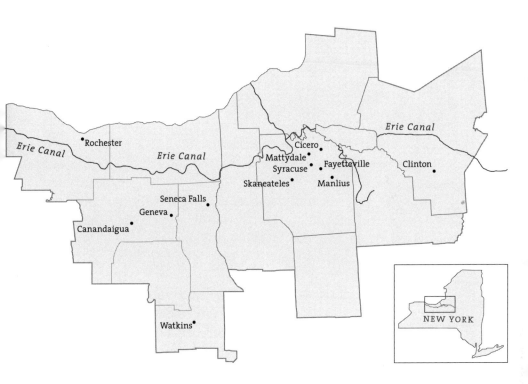

Erie Canal

Rochester

Erie Canal

Cicero

Mattydale

Syracuse

Fayetteville

Erie Canal

Clinton

Skaneateles

Manlius

Seneca Falls

Geneva

Canandaigua

Watkins

NEW YORK

Central New York

Matilda's childhood home in Cicero, New York. *Gage Foundation*

"Bless you, bless you," the escapees thanked their hosts. Some told terrible stories of the lives and families they had left behind, their sadness mixed with joy at the prospect of a new chance.

There is no record of the stories Matilda heard from the former slaves, but they likely resembled this one, told by Frederick Douglass. Douglass escaped slavery as a young man and published an autobiography. He wrote about how, at age five, he witnessed the beating of his aunt, punished by their master for seeing a young man who was also a slave.

> *[Our master] took her into the kitchen, and stripped her from neck to waist, leaving her neck, shoulders, and back, entirely naked. He then told her to cross her hands. . . . he tied them with a strong rope, and led her to a stool under a large hook in the joist, put in for the purpose. He made her get upon the stool, and tied her hands to the hook. . . . Her arms were stretched up at their full length, so that she stood upon the ends of her toes. He then said to her, "now, you d——d b——h, I'll learn you how to disobey my orders!" and after rolling up his sleeves, he commenced to lay on the heavy cowskin, and soon the warm, red*

blood (amid heart-rending shrieks from her, and horrid oaths from him) came dripping to the floor.

It was the first of a long series of such outrages, of which I was doomed to be a witness and a participant.[3]

Matilda could hardly bear to hear these stories, but she could not stop listening, either. With a freedom seeker in the house, she may have strained again to hear hoof beats, afraid that slave catchers might be following.[4] Even though New York had outlawed slavery in 1827, slave catchers were still entitled to track down escapees in the state to return them to their "owners." Apparently this never happened at the Joslyns', but the danger was always there.

The Joslyns entertained many interesting guests, including famous abolitionists (those who fought to end slavery), philosophers, and politicians. Their lively conversations heated the elegant parlor.

Whoever the guests, the little girl sat with them. No pictures of Matilda from her childhood have been found, but she was blue-eyed, brown-haired, and thin, dressed like her petite mother in a fitted bodice with long sleeves, worn over a full skirt.[5] Mrs. Joslyn's fashionable skirts touched the floor, but Matilda's were probably shorter, showing lace-trimmed pantaloons underneath.

When guests came, Matilda was allowed to stay up as late as she wanted, listening, asking questions, and offering her own opinions. It was an unusual arrangement for the 1830s, when most people believed that children should be seen but not heard. Matilda's father, Dr. Hezekiah Joslyn, insisted that his only child be included in all adult conversations.

Through long evenings, the company debated ways to make the world a better place. Their ideas were outrageous for the time: outlawing slavery, granting women rights equal to those of men, and outlawing alcoholic beverages—the temperance movement advocated this move to overcome problems caused by drunkenness. The residents of central New York, like the Joslyns, hungered for new ideas. The area provided receptive audiences for many famous radicals, especially religious leaders.

Her parents' guests spoke freely in Matilda's presence, even about ideas that were shocking and sad. In the South, she heard, again and again, black people were sold like animals, even by ministers and other so-called Christians. She heard how drunken men abused women and children. She discovered that even white women and children had no rights at all. In the North or the South, they were owned by their husbands and fathers, as slaves were.

Even when everyone talked at once, Matilda's father always made sure that she got a chance to speak. Sometimes the guests surprised her by laughing at what she said, but they always listened. If she asked a question, they answered respectfully.

Occasionally her parents took Matilda to political meetings. "I remember," she wrote later, "in my city of Syracuse . . . a large and enthusiastic anti-slavery convention . . . attended by thousands of people who all joined in singing William Lloyd Garrison's song, 'I'm an Abolitionist and glory in the Name,' and as they rang out that glorious defiance against wrong, it thrilled my very heart, and I feel it echoing to this day."[6]

Matilda's hometown of Cicero was twelve miles north of Syracuse. The area had grown quickly after completion of the Erie Canal in 1825, a year before Matilda's birth on March 24, 1826. The canal, which connected the East Coast to the Great Lakes, attracted settlers. Newcomers moved near established residents so that whites and American Indians lived closely and peacefully together around Syracuse. Local newspapers reported on events in both communities.

Men rake salt to dry in the sun in Syracuse, New York, 1895. *New York Public Library*

In those days, salt springs near Syracuse provided a product for export. Men boiled the brine, then raked the wet salt, spreading it out in the sun to dry. Lumberjacks chopped wood, which coopers made into barrels to hold salt for shipping. Farming and other businesses supported the salt workers and the boating trade on the canal. During this prosperous time, young Matilda saw houses, churches, stores, and schools being built.

The Joslyns' sprawling house was the fanciest in Cicero. Matilda's Scottish mother, Helen Leslie Joslyn, had inherited carpets and furniture from her wealthy family, including the first piano ever seen in the area. Matilda liked to hear her mother play and sing, especially her favorite song, a sad one, "Barbara Allen."[7]

When Matilda's mother took her visiting or when she entertained ladies at tea parties, the rules for the little girl's behavior changed. Then Mrs. Joslyn expected her daughter to sit quietly and listen. Matilda enjoyed seeing the women's pretty dresses, and she found their talk amusing—for a while, at least. But listening without participating soon left her bored.[8]

She preferred riding horseback, most likely on sidesaddle, with her father, the area's only doctor. He traveled a fifty-mile region on American Indian trails, and sometimes he invited her to go with him. Then they talked happily, riding through the beautiful countryside. Occasionally he even asked her to help him with patients. At a young age, she decided to become a doctor, like him.

As she learned more about the world, Matilda realized that her father was controversial. A self-made man, he had defied his own father, a farmer who wanted him to be a farmer, too. Instead Hezekiah Joslyn taught school until he earned enough money to go to medical school.[9]

Leslie family spoon. Photo by Randy Vaughn-Dotta. *Angelica Shirley Carpenter Collection*

Convinced that one person could make a difference, Dr. Joslyn spoke up for what he thought was right, and Matilda came to share his strong opinions. Her father edited a temperance newspaper. He championed the rights of women and, quite unusually for the time, children. He believed that opinions should be formed on the basis of science, logic, and reason, rather than tradition or religion, and he believed, as Matilda's mother did, in freedom for all.

Like her parents, Matilda loved to read, and as a child she wrote stories, verses, and essays; unfortunately, none has survived. Although her mother had household help, Matilda learned to sew, knit, and cook, and she polished the Leslie family silverware. Each spoon bore an engraving of the letter *L* and the head of a creature with little eyes and pointy ears.[10]

Mrs. Joslyn was proud of her background. Sometimes she showed

Matilda her white crepe wedding dress and the imitation pearls and white silk stockings that went with it. She was saving them for her daughter to wear. Occasionally they looked at old letters—notes from Mrs. Joslyn's former suitors and invitations she had received to balls. Matilda's mother had kept school papers, too, from the days when she attended the Schenectady Ladies' Seminary.[11]

The little girl sniffed happily when her mother opened a snuff box engraved with the silver initials "G. L." It had belonged to Matilda's Scottish grandfather, George Leslie. Inside were two dried vanilla beans that kept the tobacco fresh.[12]

Matilda heard more family stories from her mother's half-sister, who lived just across the road. Aunt Perry Cody's only child was a boy, six years older than Matilda, so Aunt Perry especially welcomed the company of a little girl. Uncle Isaac Cody teased Matilda when she visited and told her jokes. Matilda thought of their house as her second home.

She loved to sit in the kitchen while Aunt Perry kneaded bread and, in her gentle accent, talked of growing up in Scotland. The Leslie family had moved to New York when Matilda's mother was just two years old, but Aunt Perry, who was quite a bit older, could remember life across the sea.[13]

In Cicero, Aunt Perry had owned a store for a time, an unusual job for a married woman who had a husband to support her. Although the store had closed, Matilda enjoyed hearing about it. Aunt Perry told how she had traveled alone by stagecoach and boat to New York City to buy goods to sell, carrying the gold for payments in a belt around her waist.[14] Listening to her aunt, Matilda decided that someday she, too, would earn her own money.

Eventually Matilda's grandfather, her father's father, came to live with the Joslyns. Proudly he told Matilda how he and his brothers had fought the British in the Revolutionary War. He explained how, before the war, her great-uncle by marriage dressed as an American Indian to dump boxes of tea into the harbor at Boston.[15] The incident, known as the Boston Tea Party, protested British taxes on Americans. "No taxation without representation," the little girl learned, became a slogan for Americans fighting for independence.

As much as she loved hearing family stories, Matilda preferred playing outside. "My early life was largely spent outdoors," she wrote later, "climbing trees, racing through the fields, jumping from hillock to hill-

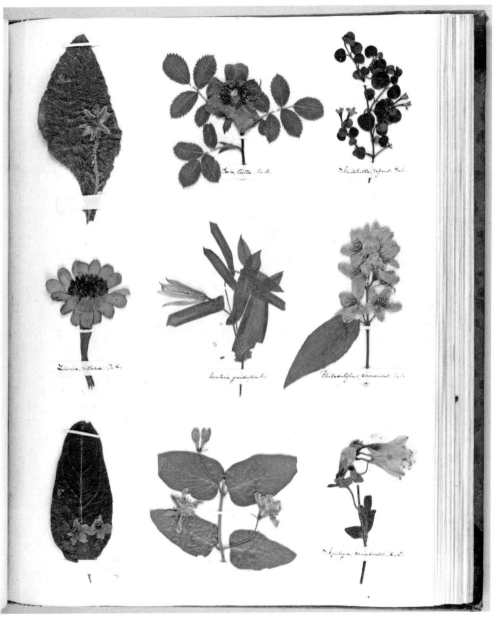

**Herbarium made by poet Emily Dickinson as a teenager,
c. 1842.** *Harvard University, Houghton Library*

ock of a swamp after flowers, or in a small rowboat penetrating its fast-nesses to see where it went."[16]

Sometimes she was naughty. One day, without asking permission, she took her mother's bonnet, wore it outside, and dropped it in the water.[17] Another time, she picked out all the pearls that were embedded in her mother's locket. When reprimanded, the child sometimes talked back. Mrs. Joslyn disapproved, but her father seemed almost proud that Matilda had a quick temper like his. Matilda's mother rewarded good behavior by making her daughter fancy cakes.[18]

Botany was a popular hobby then. Later Matilda recalled, "In the woods I spent many happy hours gathering flowers, or nuts, or spice bush, or young birch, or sassafras to eat or crinkle-root in the meadows and ground nuts, sequar berries and ground pine."[19]

Pressing and drying the plants she collected, she glued them into a scrapbook called an herbarium. Part of the fun involved identifying the plants and labeling them with their scientific names. Probably she used her father's books to do this, because doctors studied the medicinal use of plants.

Though Matilda attended public school, her parents also educated her at home. Mrs. Joslyn, who enjoyed historical research, taught her the joys and techniques of studying the past. Matilda especially liked learning about famous women.

Dr. Joslyn had his daughter write a letter each day for him to correct. By the time she was nine, she had read the entire Bible and had begun studying medical books from her father's library.[20] He wanted her to be a doctor, too, even though women were not allowed to practice medicine then. The Joslyns hoped that the rules would change by the time she was ready for medical school.

Matilda's grandfather died when she was ten and, later that year, her aunt and uncle moved to Ohio. Their departure marked the end of her childhood. Although she never saw these relatives again, the memory of their love and their accomplishments helped launch her into a new life.[21]

3 ✳ Think for Yourself 1837–1845

"My father taught me physiology in a practical way," Matilda said, "dissecting the eyes of animals, &c. I even helped him in minor, surgical operations, such as amputating a finger[,] bleeding, &c."[1]

Surgery took place in the doctor's home office or at the patient's house. Bleeding, or bloodletting, was a common treatment for many conditions. In those days doctors believed that a body had four humors: blood, phlegm, and black and yellow bile. Illness might be attributed to an imbalance of humors, which could be cured by draining blood, the dominant humor. The doctor opened a vein in the forearm or neck and let the patient bleed, sometimes to the point of faintness, before closing the incision. Matilda could have held a bowl to catch the flow.

Amputation was the only cure for serious infection at this time, and it was performed without anesthesia, though sometimes the patient was given alcohol to drink before the operation. A helper might have held a tourniquet tight, or, again, dealt with the flow of blood. Dr. Joslyn and Matilda would have needed extra help to hold a patient still while cutting off a finger.

Some sights and sounds that Matilda faced as a physician's assistant were hard to bear, even for an adult, but she liked the job. Someday, she felt sure, she would make a good doctor.

Matilda's father inspired her with his work and with his radical ideas about equality. Though she agreed with him, she worried about him, too, especially after learning that in some Northern cities, outspoken abolitionists had been attacked by proslavery mobs. Then she feared for

One of only a few photographs of the practice of bloodletting, c. 1860. *Stanley B. Burns, MD, and the Burns Archive*

her family's safety: what if their house were burned down?

But Dr. Joslyn taught her to consider violent resistance as a mark of progress for the rightful cause. Matilda knew that abolitionists campaigned by gathering signatures for petitions against slavery, so she decided to join them. After asking her father for antislavery petitions, she carried them throughout Cicero, knocking on doors, asking friends, neighbors, and even total strangers to sign.

Some people did. Others refused. Some told her that children should not get involved in such issues.[2] And others objected to a girl's speaking in public, on any subject.

Criticism only made her more determined to fight for equal rights for all. As she grew older, she worried increasingly about her future as a woman. The choices of even educated, wealthy women, she learned, were severely limited. Banned from colleges and universities, women were also excluded from most professions—even women who needed to work to earn a living. Women could not vote, speak in public, serve on juries, or testify in court, even against abusers or rapists. If a woman owned land, however, she had to pay taxes on it. But taxation without representation was wrong; Matilda had learned that from her grandfather.

Marriage was expected, but married women had to give up even the few rights their single sisters enjoyed. Wives could not own property or sign contracts. Anything they earned or inherited belonged to their husbands, who could beat them, starve them, rape them, have them locked up in jails or institutions known then as insane asylums, or throw them out of the home with nothing. If a marriage ended, the woman had no right to her children. If a husband died, his children went to the beneficiary named in his will.

Matilda heard stories of injustice like this one, printed in 1852 in an early feminist newspaper, the *Lily*.

When a woman dies leaving behind her a husband and children, no appraisers come into the desolated home to examine the effects; the father is the guardian of his offspring; the family relation is not invaded by law. But when a man dies, the case is entirely different; in the hour of the widow's desolation, strangers come into the house to take an inventory of the effects, strangers are appointed to be the guardians of her children, and she, their natural caretaker, thenceforth has no legal direction of their interests; strangers decide upon the propriety of the sale of the property—earned, perhaps, by her own and her husband's mutual efforts—and her interest in the estate is coolly designated as the "widow's incumbrance"!

In the extremity of her bereavement, there is piled upon her, not only the dread of separation from her children, but that of being sent homeless from the spot where every object has been consecrated by her tenderest affections.

Nor is the practical working of this law better than its theory; all over the country there are widows who have been made doubly desolate by its provisions—widows separated from their children, who, if they had had the disposal of their own and their husband's mutual property, might have retrieved their circumstances, and kept the household band together.[3]

"I have frequently been asked what first turned my thoughts towards woman's rights," Matilda wrote later. "I think I was born with a hatred of oppression, and, too, in my father's house, I was trained in the anti-slavery ranks."[4] In Matilda's youth, no organization existed to fight for the rights of women, but she came to realize that the reform strategies that worked for one group could work for others, too.

Meanwhile, she was shocked to learn that most churches considered

DEVOTED TO THE INTERESTS OF WOMAN.

VOL. VI.   MOUNT VERNON, OHIO, MAY 1, 1854.   NO. 9.

THE LILY,

PUBLISHED SEMI-MONTHLY, AT MOUNT VERNON, O.

Terms—Fifty Cents per annum in Advance, or Seven Copies for Three Dollars.

☞ All communications designed for the paper or on business, to be addressed to

Mrs. AMELIA BLOOMER, Editor & Proprietor.

Office—Over Sperry & Co.'s Store, Corner of Main & Gambier St.

For The Lily.

A LOVE MY SPIRIT BEARS.

BY WILLIE EDGAR PABOR.

I'll tell you of a spirit love
I've borne from earliest years;
Since I could speak with lisping weak
Her name in smiles and tears.

As rolling time, life's floating chime
In fuller volume threw,
My love increased and never ceased
To charm and bless me too.

Now as I stand upon the strand
That marks the verging shore,
When youth is lost on manhood's coast
This love flame burns the more.

This twenty years of hopes and fears
It never left my soul;
A nectar cup it filleth up
And from the sparkling bowl

My soul refreshed, moves its behest
And robes it for the strife;
It bolder grows as this love throws
A halo o'er my life.

It guides my feet from paths that meet
On sin's destructive plain;
It points the way where virtue's ray
Illumes the placid main.

Oh ! may this love for years yet move
My spirit's chancel through—
To robe hope's shroud and paint life's cloud
With tints of holy hue.

And dost thou claim the magic name
That doth my blessing prove ?
Ah ! minstrel rhyme bears " aidoune " chime
That speaks a mother's love.

And such is mine ; a love divine
In kindliness is given,
To light my way with sunny ray
And lead me up to heaven.

Harlem, N. Y. April 1854.

The late snow storms proved very destructive to the poor Birds who had ventured out previously to those storms. Large numbers perished in Worcester, Springfield and elsewhere; and, at the time, a gentleman from Columbia county informed us that many of the poor creatures perished from cold and starvation in his neighborhood.

☞ The admission to the Crystal Palace has been fixed at 25 cents.

MEMORIAL.

Of Mrs. Caroline M. Severance, of Cleveland, in behalf of Woman's Rights, in respect to Property and the Exercise of the Elective Franchise.—Presented and read to the Senate of Ohio—March 23, 1854.—Laid on the table and ordered to be printed.

We, your memorialists, respectfully represent to your Honorable Body, that by the common law of England, and the common law, constitution and statutes of the State of Ohio, which together constitute the law as at present administered, Woman is deprived of certain natural rights, which ought to be inseparable from her existence, and is subjected to certain legal disabilities, which circumscribe her sphere, and diminish her usefulness. Deprived of these rights, which were originally usurped by the husband; and subjected to these disabilities, which were afterwards by him enacted into laws, to insure his ill-gotten possessions, the *personal liberty, the property, and the children of* the wife, are legally, and by consequence, actually controlled by the husband. In the opinion of your memorialist, these usages, which are many and grievous, ought to be thoroughly and speedily redressed; and these disabilities, which are of a like character, ought to be as thoroughly and speedily removed. Therefore we earnestly pray you, in whom is vested the power of restoration, so to change the constitution and laws of this State, as:

1st. That marriage shall not destroy the legal individuality of woman.

By marriage the husband and wife are one person in law, that is, the very being or legal existence of the woman is suspended during the marriage, or incorporated and consolidated into that of the husband, and neither party by any conveyance at common law, can give an estate to the other, neither can they contract or covenant one with the other.. Black. 355, 356.

2d. That the husband shall not have power to control the personal liberty of his wife.

By this old law, the husband might give his wife correction in the same moderation that a man was allowed to correct his apprentices or children; but in the time of Blackstone the wife might have security of the peace against her husband, though the courts of law still permitted the husband to restrain his wife of her liberty. Black. 366. In the State of Ohio, the law and the practice of the courts are in every respect the same as in England, at the period above mentioned. The husband may compel his wife to remain at home when she would prefer to go abroad, to go to one church when she would prefer to go to another, to change her residence whenever it suits his convenience, and to do numerous other things of a similar character that need not here be enumerated.

3d. That the husband shall not have power to bind or apprentice his offspring without the consent of his wife.

By the law of England the mother has no legal power over her child at any age, and is only entitled to its reverence and respect, while the power of the father, which is almost absolute, extends to majority. Black. 373.

This power is also recognized in Ohio, the statutes of which provide, that any male person within the age of twenty-one years, or female person within the age of eighteen years, may be bound until they arrive at those ages respectively, or for a shorter period, to serve as clerk, apprentice, or servant, and that the indenture of service shall be signed and sealed by the father. Swan's Stat. 63.

4th. That the wife may sue and be sued independent of her husband or other person.

It is a rule of the common law, that every agreement of any nature, entered into by a married woman, without the express or implied consent of her husband, is absolutely void; and this rule prevails so strongly, that a woman may avail herself of her coverture to defeat a contract, though she may have been guilty of fraud. Black. 357.

In Ohio, where a married woman is a party, her husband may be joined with her, except when the action covers her separate property, she may sue without her husband, by her next friend. Where the action is between herself and her husband, she may be sued alone, but in every such action other than for divorce or alimony, she shall prosecute and defend by her next friend. Civil Code 61, 62.

5th. That the wife may maintain in her own name and right, an action for injury done her person, reputation, or property.

By the common law which prevails in Ohio, the wife could not bring or maintain an action for an injury done to her own person, but the husband could bring such action without the consent of his wife, the same as for an injury inflicted on his beast, and apply to his own use the damage thus obtained. He could also sustain an action for an injury done his wife's reputation, but the wife or daughter, being a minor, had not then, and have not now, any redress whatever but through the husband or the father. Female virtue is perfectly exposed to the slanders of malignity and falsehood; for any one may proclaim in convocation, that the finest maid, or the chastest matron, is the most meretricious and incontinent of women with impunity, or free from the animadversions of the temporal courts, and female honor, which is dearer to the sex than their lives, is left to be the sport of the abandoned calumniator. Black. 367.

6th. That all property accumulated during coverture shall be owned by husband and wife in common.

Woman's personal property by marriage, becomes absolutely her husband's, which at his death he may leave entirely away from her, and the husband is absolutely master of the profit of his wife's lands during coverture; and if he has had a living child, and survives the wife, he retains the whole of those lands, if they are estates of inheritance during his life, but the wife, if she survives, is only entitled to dower out of her husband's estates of inheritance. This is common law. Black. 367.

By marriage in Ohio, the husband so far becomes the owner of his wife's personal property, that if they unite in selling her real estate, and receive the money, it is his, and if the money is afterwards, and during the marriage, invested in lands and the title taken to himself, the lands are his, and decreed to his heirs. *Randall v. Craighill et al. O. R. 197.*

women inferior to men. Her parents, who attended a Baptist church, believed that opinions like this could be changed through discussion. They invited a group of clergymen to meet annually at their house.

Later a friend described the effect of these meetings upon Matilda: "Sitting up until midnight listening to the discussions of those reverend gentlemen upon baptism, original sin, predestination, and other doctrinal points, her thought was early turned to religious questions. . . . [She] became a church member at the early age of eleven, her parents, in accordance with their habits, not attempting to influence her mind for or against this step."[5]

Matilda chose the Disciples of Christ Church after reading a letter brought by a visiting abolitionist. The letter, from the Massachusetts General Association of Congregational Ministers to the Congregationalist churches under their administration, received national publicity. It was written in 1837, after women like Abby Kelly, Sarah and Angelina Grimké, and Lucretia Mott began to speak publicly to what were then called "promiscuous" groups, groups of both men and women, at antislavery conventions. The letter said, in part:

> We invite your attention to the dangers which at present seem to threaten the female character with wide-spread and permanent injury.
>
> The appropriate duties and influence of woman are clearly stated in the New Testament. . . . The power of a woman is her dependence, flowing from the consciousness of that weakness which God has given her for her protection.
>
> . . . When she assumes the place and tone of man as a public reformer, our care and protection of her seem unnecessary; we put ourselves in self-defence against her; she yields the power which God has given her for her protection and her character becomes unnatural. If the vine, whose strength and beauty is to lean upon the trellis-work, and half conceal its clusters, thinks to assume the independence and the overshadowing nature of the elm, it will not only cease to bear fruit, but fall in shame and dishonor into the dust.[6]

Matilda disagreed. She thought that women should be strong and independent, like her Aunt Perry.

Though the Disciples of Christ were more liberal than the Congre-

William Lloyd Garrison (center), attacked by a mob of anti-abolitionists, 1835.
New Hampshire Historical Society

gationalists, Matilda rejected many ideas that she heard at church. The story of Adam and Eve seemed particularly wrong to her.

"The Christian Church," she wrote later, "is based upon the fact of woman servitude; upon the theory that woman brought sin and death into the world, and that therefore she was punished by being placed in a condition of inferiority to man."[7] Matilda did not believe this concept, and she could not understand why anyone else would believe it either.

She began to read newspapers, discussing articles with her father and his friends. After William Lloyd Garrison, editor of the abolitionist newspaper the *Liberator*, was dragged through the streets of Boston and nearly killed by slavery supporters in October 1835, one journalist wrote, "Hereafter the leaders of the Abolitionists will be . . . treated as robbers and pirates, as the enemies of the human kind."[8]

Matilda wondered angrily how abolitionists could be considered evil. Surely the wicked were the people who owned slaves. She asked her father's friends how they had come to oppose slavery, and she argued with them about the best way to end it.[9] Should they try to convince slave owners that possessing other humans was morally wrong? Why did the Bible seem to support slavery? Why didn't churches protest against it? Could abolition be achieved without killing? Should they start a new political party to fight slavery? And what was the role of women in the abolitionist movement?

At age fifteen, Matilda publicly questioned the leaders of the Cicero Baptist Church—all of them, of course, men. The topic of her objection is unknown, but her father, who had gone to Geneva, New York, fifty miles away, to take some medical courses, sent his support in a letter to her mother. "That church are a rascally set," he wrote, "and they will hear from me when I get home."[10] What exactly he said to them, if anything, is unrecorded. When he returned, father and daughter resumed her studies in Greek and higher arithmetic. Matilda called him a stern teacher.[11]

When the Joslyns read in the *New-York Tribune* that three women had graduated from Oberlin College, becoming the first women in the United States to receive bachelor's degrees, they began to think about where Matilda might further her education. Dr. Joslyn did not want his daughter to attend a typical girls' finishing school, which taught art, music, needlework, and other skills considered necessary for marriage. She needed a rigorous, scholarly curriculum to prepare her for medical studies.

As they searched for a secondary school, Matilda suffered occasionally from health problems: Her heart would pound and then seem to stop. Sometimes she even fainted.[12] She must have recovered quickly from these episodes because she felt, and her parents agreed, that she was well enough to go away to school. Academically she was more than ready. Finally her father selected the Clinton Liberal Institute.

In January 1842, Matilda, not quite sixteen, boarded a public stagecoach for the forty-three-mile trip to Clinton, New York.[13] She would not be able to come home often—Clinton was too far away; travel was expensive. Luckily her father had relatives in the Clinton area who could look after her.

Unusual for the time, the Clinton Liberal Institute was coeducational. The school, started by the Universalist Church, had about two hundred boarding and local day students, ages thirteen to twenty-four.[14] Men and women studied the same subjects, with the same teachers, but in separate classrooms. Matilda took French, Greek, algebra, botany, painting, and "geography of the heavens," or astronomy.

"Algebra almost drives me mad," she wrote to her mother in her earliest surviving letter, from April 1842.

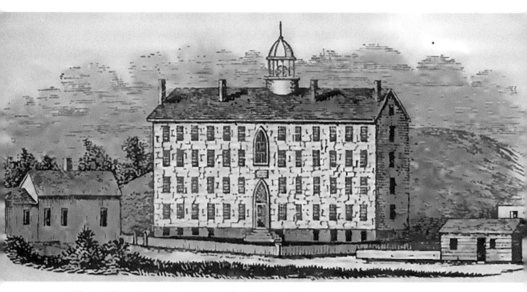

Clinton Liberal Institute, Clinton, New York, c. 1842.
Historical Collection of the State of New York, p. 362

"My Dear Mother," it began: "I received my things which I stood in great need of. Friday was a very warm day and I did not know but I should roast to death. I took off one of my skirts and corset."

Apparently her mother had sent some clothes. "My night caps I like very much indeed," Matilda wrote. "As soon as Elder Whitcher's wife saw them, she hollered right out where did you get that edging? I'm going right to the village to get some!"[15]

Then money grew tight in a slumping economy. Sometimes her father's patients could not pay him, and in Cicero the Joslyns took in a boarder to cover expenses.[16] Matilda offered to come home, but her parents insisted that she stay at school.

She watched her expenditures closely, reporting to her mother, "I paid my French teacher $6. . . . It only costs $1.77 for board and washing for three weeks."

Matilda had to "study like a beaver," she said, to master her lessons. Often she worked from five in the morning until nine at night, grateful for the opportunity.

She asked her mother to send her herbarium so that she could continue plant collecting. The girls had considerable freedom. They could walk to the village, but usually Matilda did not have time.

A classmate tried to get Matilda to go out with her and two young men. For Matilda's beau, the classmate had chosen a clerk in a local store. Though Matilda declined, her friend said she would invite the young men anyway.

"I guess if they do come," Matilda wrote to her mother, "they will find the door fastened for I have no idea of forming new acquaintances especially such as these. The loafing scoundrels."[17]

Her schooling lasted two terms until the end of 1843. In 1844, when Matilda was seventeen, she gave her first lecture, on astronomy, to a Cicero literary society. Some in the audience thought it unladylike for a young woman to speak in public to a promiscuous group. Others praised her knowledge and speaking ability.[18]

Now she was ready to begin studying medicine, but medical schools still banned women. Dr. Joslyn wrote letter after letter trying to get her admitted, even asking his former teacher for help, but the answer was always no.[19] Each response was devastating.

For years Matilda had planned and worked to become a doctor. She felt sure that medical schools would admit women someday—why shouldn't she be the first? And if she could not be a doctor, what would she do?

4 ✳ Defying the Law 1845–1850

Eventually Matilda realized that the battle was lost; she could not become a doctor. Even so, she vowed to help change the rules so that someday other women would be able to practice medicine. In the meantime she considered becoming a teacher, a job that was available to unmarried women.[1]

She knew the value of a good teacher. "I am indebted to my father for something better than a collegiate education," she said later. "He taught me to think for myself, and not to accept the word of any man, or society, or human being, but to fully examine for myself."[2] She was grateful to both parents, but at this point she did not realize that her mother's teachings about the study of history would lead her to a remarkable and new kind of career.

Matilda had grown up tall and slender with dark, shiny hair. She dressed well but simply, and she moved gracefully.[3] Men were attracted to her, and she returned the interest of those who seemed worthy. At age eighteen she enjoyed the company of Zebulon Weaver, a good-looking young lawyer. His practice was in Syracuse, but he owned land near Cicero, where he met Matilda. Like Matilda's father, he had put himself through school, but the resemblance stopped there. Zebulon Weaver was a conservative.

Somehow the two young people found common ground for a friendship, though Matilda's parents must have wondered how. One day Zebulon's horse threw him, breaking his hip. Bedridden for months, Zebulon hired Emma Gage, a childhood acquaintance of Matilda's, to care for him. At some point Weaver and his young nurse became engaged.[4]

Emma's brother, Henry Hill Gage, also called on Matilda. They were both from Cicero, so she had known him all her life, though he was eight years older. He lived in Syracuse, where he owned a store with his brother Ichabod.[5] Though Henry was quiet and not so handsome as Zebulon, he was good-natured, supportive, and reform-minded—and Matilda's parents liked him.

When Matilda was eighteen, she and Henry were married at the Joslyn house on January 6, 1845, by the minister from the Disciples of Christ Church. Matilda wore her mother's wedding beads and stockings but not her white crepe dress. Instead she chose a fashionable new gown of green-, yellow-, and gray-striped silk. For a wedding present, Mrs. Joslyn gave her daughter the Leslie family silverware.[6]

Matilda's father, Hezekiah Joslyn, date unknown. *Gage Foundation*

Matilda and Henry rented a small house in Syracuse near the brothers' store. Matilda enjoyed the bookstores and libraries in town. She found a congenial social life there and a larger reform community than in Cicero. Sometimes her father drove in to accompany her to meetings. Henry, too, escorted her at times, but he preferred to stay home in the evenings, reading or visiting with friends.[7]

Matilda and Henry were compatible in many ways. Decades later, when their son prepared to wed, Matilda wrote to him about his future. She could have been describing the first happy days with of her own marriage: "How nice it will be to sit at your own table, and have what you desire to eat, cooked for you by loving hands—to go to your rooms and find some one, with a smile, ready to greet you with loving words."[8]

Henry's store prospered, so Matilda had household help. She worked side by side with the hired girl, cooking three meals a day, baking, washing, ironing, cleaning, sewing, gardening, canning, and preserving. All domestic work had to be done at home, except for spinning and weaving. Fabric could be bought in stores, but ready-made clothing was not yet available. Sometimes Matilda hired a seamstress to sew with her.

After Matilda left home, her parents decided to move to Wisconsin. Her father, who suffered from a lung condition, thought the change might help his health. Their goodbye was heart-wrenching. Her father

Frederick Douglass, 1855.
My Bondage and My Freedom

seemed so frail that Matilda feared she would never see him again, but soon happy letters arrived from the West. Dr. Joslyn had found a new religion based on the teachings of a Swedish theologian, Emanuel Swedenborg. Matilda tried to read one of Swedenborg's books but found it hard to follow. Still, she appreciated the peace of mind that it gave to her father.[9]

For her own reading, she chose the autobiography of Frederick Douglass, a former slave who became a newspaper editor and abolitionist. Matilda heard him speak in Syracuse. His book told how he had learned to read as a child, though it was illegal for slaves to do so, and how he had stood up to a cruel "slavebreaker" and later escaped. Matilda found Douglass's views about religion particularly interesting.

"The slave auctioneer's bell," he wrote, "and the church-going bell chime in with each other, and the bitter cries of the heart-broken slave are drowned in the religious shouts of his pious master."[10]

Matilda read *Narrative of the Life of Frederick Douglass, An American Slave* while she was pregnant with her first child. She also read Margaret Fuller's book *Woman in the Nineteenth Century*.[11] Fuller denied the common belief that women were made to please men. Describing subtle ways in which females were made to feel inferior, she urged women to band together to obtain their rights. Matilda longed to respond to this call for action, but she had other responsibilities.

Ten months after her wedding, on November 3, 1845, nineteen-year-old Matilda gave birth to a baby girl, named for her mother, Helen Leslie. Even though Matilda had a nurse to help her for more than a month after the birth, she felt overwhelmed. Little experienced with babies, she was unprepared for the level of care that was needed for such a

Earliest known photo of Matilda, with her son Thomas Clarkson Gage
and his woolly dog, c.1849 or 1850. People looked serious in early
photographs; it was hard to hold a smile during the long exposure times.
Gage Foundation

tiny, helpless creature. She worried constantly that something might go wrong.[12]

Henry was often away from home at this time, fulfilling his duties as one of three elected public officers in Syracuse, the superintendents of the poor. They worried about Irish immigrants who were flocking to the United States, and to Syracuse, to escape a potato famine in their own country. Many of the newcomers contracted "ship fever" (probably cholera) while traveling.[13] Upon arrival they died in such numbers that the superintendents decided to build a small hospital for them. Henry took responsibility for the project.

Neighbors who feared catching the disease opposed the building's location, and before the hospital building could be finished, a mob tore it down. Henry rebuilt it, moving patients in while it was still under construction. This time the neighbors let them stay, but Henry had trouble finding caregivers. He nursed some patients himself, coming home from the store for dinner and then working late into the night at the hospital.

Matilda could not convince him to stay away from the dangerous task. Terrified that Henry might catch the disease and give it to the baby, Matilda kept little Helen away from him, on the other side of the house. Despite her precautions, Henry and Helen both fell dangerously ill. Their long recovery drained Matilda's physical and emotional strength, but somehow she pulled all three of them through.[14]

When father and baby daughter were well again, Matilda and Henry decided to move from Syracuse to Manlius, twelve miles to the southeast. Manlius was an attractive and prosperous village, with churches, factories, two cotton mills, and a new railroad passing through.

Henry sold his share of the Syracuse business to his brother and bought a store on the main street in Manlius. The Gages rented a house close by. At noon Henry and his store clerk walked home for a large lunch prepared by Matilda and Margaret, the Irish hired girl. All enjoyed two-year-old Helen, who was learning to talk, and by this time Matilda felt more confident as a mother.[15]

Having a baby daughter gave her a new reason to fight for women's rights. When the New York legislature proposed a change in state law to allow married women to keep or inherit property, she campaigned for the bill. Social reformers like Matilda and Henry formed an unusual partnership in this struggle, pairing with wealthy conservatives. "Solid, thrifty Dutch fathers," Matilda wrote later, "were daily confronted with the fact that the inheritance of their daughters, carefully accumulated, would at marriage pass into the hands of dissipated, impecunious husbands."[16] Matilda was six months pregnant with her second child in April 1848 when the legislature passed the Married Woman's Property Act.

On July 18 she gave birth to "a red and wrinkled faced baby."[17] She wanted to name him after her father, but Dr. Joslyn wrote asking her to call him Thomas Clarkson after a famous British abolitionist.[18] The baby was known by his middle name, Clarkson.

The day after his birth, July 19, 1848, marked the start of a famous women's rights convention. It took place in Seneca Falls, New York, just fifty miles west of Manlius. Though Matilda could not attend, she took a strong interest in the proceedings.

The convention was organized by Lucretia Mott, a Quaker activist from Philadelphia, and Elizabeth Cady Stanton, a young reform writer from Seneca Falls. The two had met in London in 1840 at the World's Anti-Slavery Convention. Although Matilda was only fourteen at that time, she had heard from her father's guests about events there. Mott, a well-known abolitionist, had gone to London as an elected delegate to the convention. Stanton, a young newlywed, accompanied her husband, who was a delegate, to the convention on their honeymoon.

In London both women were shocked to find that the male convention members refused to honor the credentials of woman delegates. Barred from speaking, the women had to sit in a separate section. Today this convention is remembered primarily for its discrimination against women. Lucretia Mott and Elizabeth Cady Stanton left London determined to found a women's rights movement in the United States.

It took them eight years, but in 1848 the Seneca Falls woman's rights convention (most people then used the singular form: *woman's rights*) attracted three hundred people, women and men. Although many people call this the first woman's rights convention, women's rights had been a cause of political activism in the United States since the Revolutionary War. This meeting, however, marked a new level of interest and organization. The participants met at the Wesleyan Chapel, where a hundred of them signed a "Declaration of Sentiments and Resolutions."

"We hold these truths to be self-evident:" it declared, "that all men and women are created equal."

Matilda followed the convention in newspaper articles.[19] The delegates, she learned, had voted unanimously for changes in law, education, and employment, but one idea seemed too radical to support: that women should obtain the right to vote. After all, nowhere, in any country in the world, could women vote. Opponents feared that this drastic idea would bring ridicule to the movement and detract from other reforms.

Elizabeth Cady Stanton, however, insisted that the right to choose rulers and make laws was the right by which all other rights could be secured.

Matilda agreed, and she was pleased to read that Frederick Douglass had spoken at the convention in favor of women's suffrage. With his support, the resolution passed: women would seek the vote.

"When I saw the reports," Matilda wrote later, "of the first convention in the New York *Tribune*, I knew my place."[20]

The uproar in 1848 over whether women should have rights equal to those of men is hard to imagine now. Preachers denounced the convention from their pulpits. Newspapers called the convention organizers Amazons, atheists, and hermaphrodites.[21] The Albany *Mechanic's Advocate* said:

The women who attend these meetings, no doubt at the expense of their more appropriate duties . . . affirm, as among their rights, that of unrestricted franchise, and assert that it is wrong to deprive them of the privilege to become legislators, lawyers, doctors, divines, etc., etc.; and they are holding Conventions and making an agitatory movement with the object in view of revolutionizing public opinion and the laws of the land, and changing their relative position in society in such as a way as to divide with the male sex the labors and responsibilities of active life in every branch of art, science, trades, and professions.

Now, it requires no argument to prove that this is all wrong. Every true hearted female will instantly feel that this is unwomanly. . . . Society would have to be radically remodeled in order to accommodate itself to so great a change . . . and the order of things established at the creation of mankind and continued *six thousand years*, would be completely broken up.

Elizabeth Cady Stanton and sons Daniel and Henry, 1848.
Library of Congress

. . . If *effected*, [this change] would set the world by the ears, make "confusion worse confounded," demoralize and degrade from their high sphere and noble destiny, women of all respectable and useful classes, and provide a monstrous injury to all mankind.[22]

Matilda was excited by reports of this convention and subsequent meetings and by the news that in 1849 Elizabeth Blackwell had become the first woman doctor in the United States. Matilda longed to participate in the women's movement, but family life and a new pregnancy kept her at home. In December 1849, she had a son named Charles Henry.

"The little boy born after Clarkson," she wrote later, "lived but a month and during the last ten or twelve days of his life was an intense sufferer—his moans even under anodynes wrung my heart. Nothing could be done for him, and I had suffered, oh so greatly, in giving him life and after, for days, myself being at the point of death."[23]

Reviving slowly, Matilda took comfort in her two living children. After some months she renewed her interest in newspapers, reading them and writing letters to their editors for publication. In September 1850 she read that the U.S. Congress had passed the Fugitive Slave Law to ensure that enslaved people who escaped to free states could be recaptured and returned to their so-called owners. Even in a free state like New York, a citizen who helped an escapee was subject to a $1,000 fine, six months' imprisonment, and civil damages for each former slave—each piece of "property"—lost.

Appalled abolitionists, like the Reverend J. W. Loguen, a former slave who had become the conductor of the Syracuse Underground Railroad, responded with petitions opposing the law. Signing such a document amounted to a public announcement that the signer intended to engage in criminal behavior. Matilda wrote later:

> One of the proudest acts of my life, one that I look back upon with most satisfaction is that when Rev. Lougen [sic] . . . went to the village of my residence to ascertain the names upon whom run-away slaves might depend for aid and comfort on the way to Canada, I was one of the two solitary persons who gave him their names. Myself, and one gentleman of Fayetteville, were the only two persons who dared thus publicly defy "the law" of the land, and for humanity's sake render ourselves liable to fine and imprisonment in the county jail, for the crime of feeding the hungry, giving shelter to the oppressed, and helping the black slave on to freedom.[24]

5 ✳ Bold and Daring 1851–1852

Matilda shared a joyful reunion with her parents when they moved back east. Her father opened a medical practice in Syracuse. The Joslyns were thrilled to meet little Helen and Clarkson, and on May 21, 1851, Matilda gave birth to a second daughter, Julia Louise.

Later Elizabeth Cady Stanton wrote about Matilda at this time: "Mrs. Gage was surrounded with a family of small children for years, yet she was always a student, an omnivorous reader and liberal thinker, and her pen was ever at work answering the attacks on the woman movement in the county and State journals. In the village of Manlius . . . she was the sole representative of this unpopular reform. When walking the street she would often hear some boy, shielded by a dry-goods box or a fence, cry out 'woman's rights.'"[1]

Matilda began clipping newspaper articles about women's issues, saving them for a scrapbook. Many papers at this time published stories about a fashion started by a New York woman, Elizabeth Smith Miller, who liked to garden.

"Working in my garden," Miller wrote later, "weeding and transplanting in bedraggled skirts that clung in fettered folds about my feet and ankles, I became desperate and resolved an immediate release."[2]

Stylish dresses of the time, worn over tightly laced corsets and six or seven petticoats, weighed up to fifteen pounds. Skirts dragged on the ground, making stairs, gardens, unpaved streets, and outhouses difficult to navigate. Miller developed a simpler ensemble that was worn without a corset: a loose dress ending four inches below the knee, worn over pantaloons. It resembled the clothing worn by some American

MISS ELIZABETH SMITH MILLER
FIRST WOMAN TO WEAR THE
BLOOMER COSTUME IN 1852 ·
PICTURE TAKEN SHOWING
VERGE ON HAREM SKIRT...

A 1906 newspaper clipping of Elizabeth Smith Miller, pictured in 1852. *Library of Congress*

Indian women in central New York—leggings under a loose-fitting tunic. The outfit proved so practical that Miller began to wear it all the time.

In 1851 she wore her new clothes to Seneca Falls where she visited her cousin, Elizabeth Cady Stanton. "To see my cousin," Stanton wrote, "with a lamp in one hand and a baby in the other, walk upstairs with ease and grace while, with flowing robes, I pulled myself up with difficulty, lamp and baby out of the question, readily convinced me that there was sore need of reform in women's dress."[3]

Stanton took up the style, as did her friend Amelia Bloomer, editor of the *Lily*, a Seneca Falls women's newspaper. Bloomer's illustrated articles about the new fashion created a furor. Other newspapers mocked the outfit, which they named after her: *bloomers*. The women who wore it, however, called it reform dress or short dress. Some who wore this new fashion bobbed their hair, too.

Although Matilda never adopted the style, she wrote about it in a short story. She had begun writing fiction in an effort to earn money on her own, like her Aunt Perry. Writing came easily to her, and it could be done at night, while the children slept.

She submitted her stories to newspapers in the hope that they would be serialized. Rejections followed, but these only made her more determined to succeed. Finally the *Democrat* of Skaneateles, a nearby town, published Matilda's story "The Heiress and her Cousin" in seven installments. After that, her stories were printed frequently in a variety of papers. Using popular plots, she often gave them a women's rights twist.[4]

In "The Fatal Mistake," a husband comes home at night and unexpectedly finds his wife sleeping with another. Seeing trousers, a shirt, and a big hat on a chair by the bed, he stabs both sleepers to death. Too late, he learns that the other was his wife's sister, whose bloomer costume he mistook for a man's clothing. His wife, thinking her husband would be away all night, had invited her sister to stay with her.[5]

Matilda got a chance to see reform dress at her first women's rights meeting. "When I read the notice of a convention to be held in Syracuse, in 1852," Matilda said, "I at once decided to publicly join the ranks of those who spoke against wrong."[6]

Wearing her best dress, in a gray brocaded silk, Matilda took her older daughter Helen, who was almost seven.[7] "I prepared my speech," she wrote later, "and going to the convention, sat near the front."[8] Two thousand people from eight states and Canada packed the Syracuse City Hall.

Matilda watched as the Reverend Samuel May, a liberal Unitarian pastor from Syracuse, gave the opening prayer. It was his first women's rights convention, though he had long been sympathetic to the cause. Matilda had read of his arrest in the famous Syracuse "Jerry Rescue" in 1851. At that time Samuel May and his colleague Gerrit Smith, Elizabeth Smith's father, helped a runaway slave called Jerry escape to Canada. Smith, a well-known abolitionist, gave his first women's rights speech at this convention, but most of the speakers were women.

Thirty-nine-year-old Lucy Stone, in short dress and bobbed hair, read the convention's "call," or statement of purpose. Stone said she hoped that everyone present, even if opposed to new demands by women, would take part in the debates and help to find truth.

Lucretia Mott was elected president of the convention. From the back of the room she rose, a slight woman, age fifty-nine, in plain Quaker clothing.

"Mrs. Mott . . . walked forward to the plat-

Amelia Bloomer, c. 1855. Trousers shocked; women were not supposed to show any part of a leg. Susan B. Anthony had a bloomer costume of pink dotted swiss. *Seneca Falls Historical Society*

Matilda as dressed for her first women's rights convention, 1852. *Gage Foundation*

form," Matilda wrote later, "her sweet face and placid manners at once winning the confidence of her audience."[9]

Like the rest of the crowd, Matilda knew that in the Society of Friends, or Quakers, women were equal with men, and had the right to speak in public. "[Mrs. Mott] was well fitted," Matilda said, "to guide the proceedings and encourage the expression of opinions from those to whom public speaking was an untried experiment."[10]

Susan B. Anthony, a Quaker and former school teacher from Rochester, New York, needed no particular encouragement. Like Matilda, she was attending her first women's rights convention. Formerly active in the temperance movement, she had switched causes after learning that women were not allowed to speak at temperance meetings. Age thirty-two, she was tall and thin, with sharp features and a contralto voice. Susan B. Anthony read a letter to the convention from her friend Elizabeth Cady Stanton, who could not travel to Syracuse because she was pregnant with her fifth child.

Matilda agreed with the proposals in Stanton's letter: that women who owned property should refuse to pay taxes until they could vote, that men and women should be educated together, and that the abuse of women in the name of religion should be investigated.

She listened to more speeches, waiting "with a palpitating heart," she said, "until I obtained courage to go upon the platform, probably to the interference of arrangements, for I knew nothing about the proper course for me to take."[11] Trembling in every limb and holding her daughter's hand, she made her way toward the stage, where Lucretia Mott welcomed her and invited her to speak.[12]

In a shaky voice, Matilda began:

This Convention has assembled to discuss the subject of Woman's Rights, and form some settled plan of action for the future. While so much is said of the inferior intellect of woman, it is by a strange absurdity conceded that very many eminent men owe their station in life to their mothers. Women are now in the situation of the mass of mankind a few years since, when science and learning were in the hands of the priests. . . . The Pope and the priests claimed to be not only the teachers, but the guides of the people; the laity were not permitted to examine for themselves; education was held to be unfit for the masses while the tenure of their feudal property was such as kept them in a continual state of dependence on their feudal lords.[13]

Previous speakers had focused on what women might accomplish if given the chance. Talking softly at first, Matilda celebrated "shining examples" of what women throughout history had already achieved. She praised Semiramis, an Assyrian queen; Sappho, a Greek poet; scientist Helena Lucretio Cornaro; astronomers Maria Cunitz and Caroline Herschel; and the seventeenth-century artist Anna Maria van Schurman (she spelled their names a bit differently). She described contemporary leaders, too: Queen Victoria of England, singer Jenny Lind, and author Harriet Beecher Stowe. As she spoke, her confidence grew.

Matilda's research, and her passion for her subject, amazed the audience. On several occasions they interrupted her with applause, surprising her in turn.

"Self-reliance," Matilda said, "is one of the first lessons to be taught our daughters; they should be educated with our sons, and equally with them, taught to look forward to some independent means of support."

"ONWARD!" she cried, at the end of her speech, "Let the Truth prevail!"

As the crowd applauded, Lucretia Mott again took the podium, obviously delighted with Matilda.

"The paper is so fine," she said, "I fear the young lady was not heard distinctly by the audience, and I move that it be published."[14]

The audience cheered approval.

"I was so sweetly welcomed by the sainted Lucretia Mott," Matilda wrote later, "who gave me a place, and when I had finished speaking, referred so pleasantly to what I had said, to her my heart turned always with truest affection."[15]

Matilda's speech established her as a scholar and challenged the commonly held idea that women needed to evolve and improve gradually in order to assume full roles in society. Why, her listeners wondered, had they not heard of the women she described? Her ideas made them question how they were taught history. Her message left them wanting to hear more of her ideas. Their response convinced her that she should get more involved in the movement.

As the convention proceeded, Susan B. Anthony, who the Syracuse *Journal* later noted had "a capital voice,"[16] moved that no woman should be allowed to speak whose voice could not fill the house.[17]

But the next speaker, Paulina Wright Davis, defeated Anthony's motion, telling the audience that many of her sisters (like Matilda) had come to the convention "with full hearts, but with weak untrained voices."[18]

The three-day convention made news across the country. The Syracuse *Daily Journal* said: "The galaxy of bold women—for they really were bold, indeed they are daring women—presented a spectacle the like of which we never before witnessed. A glance at the 'good old lady' [Lucretia Mott] who presided with so much dignity and propriety, and through the list to the youngest engaged in the cause [Matilda], was enough to impress the unprejudiced beholder with the idea that there must be *something* in the movement."[19]

Susan B. Anthony, c. 1856. *University of Rochester, River Campus Libraries*

But most papers condemned the event. Some called it "satanic." The Syracuse *Daily Star* said, "Perhaps we owe an apology for having given publicity to the mass of corruption, heresies, ridiculous nonsense, and reeking vulgarities which these bad women have vomited forth for the past three days."[20]

Soon ministers were attacking the convention from their pulpits. The Reverend Byron Sunderland, a Congregationalist, blasted reform dress by quoting Deuteronomy 22:5: "The woman shall not wear that which pertaineth unto a man, neither shall a man put on a woman's garment: for all that do are abomination unto the Lord thy God."

After his sermon was published in the Syracuse *Daily Star*, Matilda responded with another biblical passage, chastising him and other men for ignoring the law of Moses (Leviticus 21:5) "forbidding men to shave or 'mar the corner of their beards.'"[21] She signed her letter to the newspaper with the initial "M."

Sunderland responded, and eagerly she wrote back. Their *Daily Star* duel entertained readers for weeks, especially when "M," who was generally regarded as the winner, was revealed to be a woman.

Matilda's entry into the movement pleased her and interested others.

In late 1852, a notice appeared in the *New-York Tribune* announcing that Matilda Joslyn Gage would accept speaking engagements.[22]

"When I entered the woman suffrage work," Matilda said, "I was twenty-six, the youngest woman then in the cause, a brown-haired hopeful woman."[23]

6 ✳ A Woman of No Ordinary Talents 1853–1854

On March 28, 1853, four days after her twenty-seventh birthday, Matilda paid three dollars for a consultation with Orson Squire Fowler, the nation's leading phrenologist. These pseudoscientists believed that character was based on the shape of the cranium. They claimed to study moral and intellectual qualities by feeling the bumps on a person's skull, comparing their results to diagrams. The charts supposedly showed where different "organs" of the brain, like self-esteem or parental love, were located. Phrenologists taught that weak elements of character could be strengthened through practice. The notion of self-improvement based on self-knowledge pleased reformers, who liked the idea of a seemingly scientific way to understand human behavior. Matilda's father had his head read, too, as did Susan B. Anthony, Elizabeth Cady Stanton, and Lucretia Mott.

Fowler had Matilda sit in a chair while he stood behind her, measuring her skull. Then he felt her head, moving her scalp slightly with the tips of his fingers and dictating his comments to a secretary. Matilda received a nine-page handwritten analysis.

"You resemble your father," it began, "and he was a powerful man, and you are a woman of no ordinary talents. . . . Your aspiring organs are particularly developed, you are not satisfied with the state of your sex, but wish you were in a large sphere where you could do something more worthy or influential than woman now is permitted to do." Fowler advised Matilda to get more outdoor exercise, to wash daily in cold water, to seek congenial company, and to cultivate domestic feelings, especially a love of her husband.[1]

Matilda's Travels

Orson Squire Fowler's examining room in New York City, 1860.
New York Illustrated News

Matilda did love Henry, her understanding husband, who managed his store and their family, too, as she began to accept out-of-town speaking engagements. Even with a hired girl helping at home, Matilda's travel would have been impossible without his support.

Trips for women in those days proved difficult. It was considered improper for ladies to travel alone, but Matilda did anyway. Most restaurants did not admit women by themselves, and hotels refused to rent rooms to unescorted females. Matilda packed lunches and learned, like other women in the movement, how to find safe boarding houses that would accept respectable women in the cities where they met.

Her invitations to speak increased after her convention speech was published. Soon newspapers printed more of her short stories, along with articles, travel pieces, and letters she wrote to editors about women's issues. During this time she also got to know a congenial company of activists.

Phrenological report for Matilda. She likely did not know that phrenologists used head shapes to justify slavery, judging Africans to be weak and timid. *Gage Foundation*

No record exists of her first meeting with Elizabeth Cady Stanton, but the two women soon became friends. Stanton, a decade older, was short and plump, with blue eyes and curly dark hair. She, too, was making a name for herself as a writer. Like Matilda, she had children—five when they met (Matilda had three), and later two more. Both loved fashion; Stanton had her first bloomer costume made up in black satin.

"We had quite a magnetic circle of reformers in Central New York," Stanton wrote later in the book she coauthored with Matilda, the *History of Woman Suffrage*. She listed Frederick Douglass and Susan B. Anthony in Rochester, Amelia Bloomer in Seneca Falls, and Matilda Joslyn Gage. She wrote admiringly of Matilda in the early days of their friendship:

> On one occasion, at a large evening party at Mr. Van Schaick's, the host read aloud a poem called Rufus Chubb, a burlesque on "strong-minded" women, ridiculing careers and conventions, and the many claims being made for larger freedom. Mrs. Gage, then quite young, was surprised and embarrassed. Every eye was fixed upon her, as evidently the type of womanhood the author was portraying. As soon as the reader's voice died away, Mrs. Gage, with marked coolness and grace, approached him, and with an imaginary wreath crowned him the poet-laureate of the occasion, and introduced him to the company as "the immortal Rufus Chubb." The expressive gesture and the few brief words conferring the honor, turned the laugh on Mr. Van Schaick so completely, that he was the target for all the merriment of the evening.[2]

Elizabeth Cady Stanton with her sixth child (of seven), daughter Harriot, c. 1856.
Library of Congress

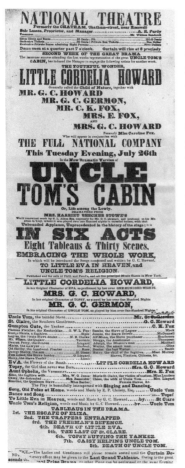

Advertisement for *Uncle Tom's Cabin* play. Harriet Beecher Stowe Center

In 1853 Matilda and her father attended several reform conventions in New York City. Activist groups often scheduled overlapping meetings so their members could attend more than one.

Matilda and her father went early to do some sightseeing, and they decided to take in a play, *Uncle Tom's Cabin*, based on the best-selling novel by Harriet Beecher Stowe. Stowe's depiction of the horrors of slavery had helped to strengthen the abolitionist movement, confirming Matilda's belief that fiction could bring about political change.

When they got to the theater, Matilda and Dr. Joslyn were shocked to find a sign posted that respectable colored people would be seated separately. They left in anger without seeing the play.[3]

Later Matilda wrote in the *History of Woman Suffrage*:

This week . . . was one of unusual excitement in the city of New York, as representatives of all the unpopular reforms were holding their several conventions. The fact that the Anti-Slavery Society held a meeting on Sunday morning, and Antoinette Brown [who, as a woman, could not be ordained] preached to five thousand people the same evening, called out the denunciations of the religious press, which intensified the mob spirit, culminating at last in the Woman's Rights Convention. That portion of the secular press which had shown the most bitter opposition to the anti-slavery cause, now manifested the same spirit toward the enfranchisement of woman.[4]

Several newspapers encouraged bad behavior. "The mob element held high carnival through that eventful week," Matilda wrote. "Starting in the anti-slavery and temperance meetings, they assembled at every session in the Woman's Rights Convention. Gentlemen and ladies alike who attempted to speak were interrupted by shouts, hisses, stamping, and cheers, rude remarks, and all manner of noisy demonstrations."[5]

More than two thousand people attended the women's convention, held at an influential Presbyterian church. Matilda was thrilled when William Lloyd Garrison, editor of the antislavery newspaper the *Liberator*, spoke for the first time at a women's rights convention. Her childhood hero was a slender, balding man who wore wire-rimmed spectacles.

"I have been derisively called a '*Woman's Rights Man*,'" Garrison said. "I know no such distinction. I claim to be a HUMAN RIGHTS MAN, and wherever there is a human being, I see God-given rights inherent in that being whatever may be the sex or complexion."[6]

Then Lucy Stone, wearing reform dress, described successful women: doctors, editors, a shoe merchant, a banker, and a would-be member of the clergy, Antoinette L. Brown. Ruffians in the audience hissed at the idea of a woman minister.

The evening session grew wilder still. When Horace Greeley, editor of the *Daily Tribune*, tried to quiet some demonstrators, they made so much noise that the program had to be stopped while police collared rowdies.

Matilda spoke on the second day, telling how some men tyrannized their wives. "A woman who was recently married," she said, "but obliged to quit her husband within two months after, for his abuse, took with her when she left her own clothing, and for the value of this the husband sued her friends and obliged them to pay, although it was the clothing her father purchased for her previous to her marriage."[7]

Matilda was followed on the platform by Sojourner Truth, a former slave and well-known abolitionist. She was about fifty-six at this time, tall and dignified, dressed in traditional Quaker garb.

"This was the signal for a fresh outburst from the mob," Matilda wrote later; "Sojourner combined in herself, as an individual, the two most hated elements of humanity. She was black, and she was a woman, and all the insults that could be cast upon color and sex were together hurled at her; but there she stood, calm and dignified, a grand, wise woman, who could neither read nor write, and yet with deep insight could penetrate the very soul of the universe about her."[8]

Matilda transcribed Sojourner Truth's speech in the *History of Woman Suffrage*. "Is it not good for me to come and draw forth a spirit," Truth asked, "to see what kind of spirit people are of? I see that some

Sojourner Truth, 1864. *New York Public Library*

of you have got the spirit of a goose, and some have got the spirit of a snake." Introducing herself as a citizen of New York, a former slave born in the state, she insisted on equal rights for women. "We'll have our rights," she said; "see if we don't; and you can't stop us from them; see if you can. You may hiss as much as you like, but it is comin'. Women don't get half as much rights as they ought to; we want more, and we will have it."[9]

The "mob convention" had one "redeeming feature," Matilda reported: admission cost each protestor twenty-five cents per session. "It paid all expenses," she wrote, "and left a surplus in the treasury."[10]

Roughnecks caused trouble outside the convention, too. At one point Susan B. Anthony and Lucy Stone, both wearing bloomers and short hair, walked out to mail a letter. A crowd of boys and men encircled them, yelling insults and trapping the women. Luckily an acquaintance ran for a policeman, and the women escaped "with only a little rough treatment at the last."[11]

Over time, antibloomer attacks increased, until many who wore short dress, like Elizabeth Cady Stanton, worried that their clothes were distracting from the movement. Eventually, women leaders gave up the style, though the name was retained as slang for women's underwear.

But Susan B. Anthony was still wearing bloomers at the New York state woman's rights convention in Rochester in late 1853. Matilda and another of her heroes, Frederick Douglass, sat with Anthony on the platform.

Matilda's speech there echoed her grandfather's Revolutionary War sentiments, protesting taxation without representation. She felt proud when she and Amelia Bloomer were elected as two of twelve convention vice presidents, the first office for either in a women's rights organization.

In May 1854, after a fire in Manlius burned down the cotton mill across from Henry's store, the Gage family moved three miles north, to Fayetteville. The village, eleven miles east of Syracuse, was thriving, thanks to a feeder canal that connected it to the Erie Canal. Fayetteville was a trading center for produce and products made in local factories—wooden farm implements, sawed lumber, leather, and paper.

The Gages moved to a small house that Matilda called "Sunset View," at 210 East Genesee Street, the town's main street. The half-acre lot had fruit trees, an apiary, a barn, a glass-covered hotbed for growing early

Looking west down Genesee Street in Fayetteville, New York, 1888.
Photo by L. Frank Baum. *Gage Foundation*

The west side of the Gage house after remodeling, 1888.
Photo by L. Frank Baum. *Gage Foundation*

seeds, a large vegetable garden, and an ice house. A round summer house with a marble floor and lattice work stood in the yard, covered with roses and grapevines. Matilda imagined serving summer dinners there.[12]

Renting the house with an option to buy, she and Henry soon began making improvements. Eventually they moved the original, small house back on the lot, adding a two-story front section with columns in the Greek Revival style, a bathroom, and what was said to be the first bay window in Fayetteville.[13] At some point they added a washhouse and a woodshed, too. Sunset View became Matilda's perfect refuge. She loved coming home from lecture tours to her family, her house, and her gardens.

Henry's new store, down the hill on Genesee Street, sold groceries, clothing, boots, crockery, and glassware. Henry, who became a stockholder in the local bank and newspaper, devoted much time to work, but he remained reform-minded. The Gages were pleased to find that Fayetteville had more liberal activists than Manlius had.

Matilda and Henry made their new home a stop on the Underground Railroad. A neighbor recalled a trap door in front of the fireplace that led to a tiny cellar where a person could hide.[14] Their daughter Helen said that one of her earliest memories was of a black man on his knees before her mother, thanking Matilda for a chance at life and liberty.[15]

In August 1854 Matilda traveled to Saratoga Springs, New York, perhaps to attend a convention. The beautiful resort town, with its famous racetrack, attracted wealthy tourists, including many southerners.

Two national conventions, one promoting temperance and the other abolition, were scheduled back-to-back in the same hall. Susan B. Anthony was there, too, preparing to host a third convention, on women's rights, in the same location. She was having a hard time. First, some-

Advertisement for Henry Gage's store, 1876. *Gage Foundation*

Lucretia Mott sits in front of her house, "Roadside" eight miles north of Philadelphia in 1860. Matilda visited Mott's previous home, a townhouse at 338 Arch Street (no image available), in 1854. *Old Road History*

one stole her purse with fifteen dollars, all the money she had brought. Then, one by one, her invited speakers—Elizabeth Cady Stanton, Lucy Stone, and others—sent word that they could not come.

"I didn't know what I was going to do," Anthony said later, "for at that time I was no speaker, and thought I didn't know how to address an audience. At the last moment, I happened to run across Mrs. Gage on the street, and I told her my predicament, and begged her to speak. She said she had not a thing there, no material whatever for a speech. So I asked her if she could not telegraph home for a speech, and she did."[16]

Anthony spoke, too, and with the help of Sarah Pellet, a third colleague from the New York state women's movement, the three women put on a successful convention.

The *Daily Saratogian* reported: "Mrs. Matilda Joslyn Gage, a medium-sized, lady-like looking woman, dressed in a tasty plum-colored silk with two flounces, made the first address upon some of the defects in the marriage laws."[17]

"The husband is the baron, king, or despot," Matilda said, "and the wife the dependent, the serf, or slave. . . . If the husband choose, he has his wife as firmly in his grasp and dominion, as the *hawk* has the *dove* upon whom he has pounced."[18]

"That speech helped me out greatly," Anthony said later, "our hall was crowded . . . and all those Southern women came to hear a woman speak in public, which was something unheard of at that time."[19] Profits from the twenty-five-cent admission charge enabled her to pay expenses, buy a ticket home, and give Matilda and Sarah Pellet each a speaker's fee of ten dollars.

In October 1854 Matilda spoke proudly of female achievements at the fifth national woman's rights convention in Philadelphia. Before traveling, she wrote to Lucretia Mott, who lived in Philadelphia, asking help in finding a suitable boarding house. Mott wrote back, signing her letter "Thy friend" in the Quaker style.[20] When Matilda arrived at the convention, Mott invited her to dinner at her home.[21] The young protégée had become a respected colleague.

Matilda, age thirty-five, in a "spoon" bonnet, the height of fashion during the Civil War, 1861. *Gage Foundation*

7 ※ Liberty for All 1855–1865

Sometimes Matilda's political life intruded at home. Helen, her oldest child, could not understand why schoolmates said bad things about her mother. Assuring Helen that the children did not understand what they were saying, Matilda kept her daughter close as she worked in the house and garden. Henry, who was sometimes called names like "hen-pecked husband," did not mind when he himself was teased. He consoled Helen by taking her on trips to Syracuse and by bringing her small gifts from the store.[1]

Matilda always said that Clarkson, her second child, was her most beautiful. When the hired girl took him out in his willow baby carrier, passersby stopped to admire his blond curls.[2] Fond of attention, he resented his baby sister Julia, who was born when he was almost three. To distract him, Matilda got him a goat for a pet. When the animal chased the screaming boy to a neighbor's house, Matilda banished it to the country to live with Clarkson's cousins. Watching the goat ride away on the top of a stagecoach pleased her son. After that, he waited regularly for the stagecoach to pass, so he could ask the driver how his goat was doing.[3]

By the time Julia was four, her favorite word was *no*. Matilda wrote her a poem called "Julia's Lessons," in which a bird, a bee, a flower, and the wind all offered advice. The wind told her:

Little Julia you may play
Run about as shadows do,
What your mama says you may
That is right that you should do.

Julia often requested "my poem," sitting on Matilda's lap to listen. It ended:

Little Julia shut her eyes
Murm'ring as to sleep she went
"Little girls should never cry
When upon an errand sent."[4]

When the children were ill, Matilda canceled her speaking engagements to stay home with them. While in Fayetteville, Matilda continued working for causes she supported. She collected signatures on petitions for women's rights and women's suffrage, the two issues kept separate because the idea of voting rights for women was still a divisive issue, even to people who otherwise supported increased rights for them. She held parties to raise money for free-staters in the territory of Kansas, where voters would soon decide whether Kansas would enter the Union as a free or a slave state. Henry joined a new political organization, the Republican Party, which opposed slavery.[5]

Matilda and Henry needed money for themselves, too. Remodeling the house while opening a new store had stretched their budget. Though she still had part-time help, Matilda had to let the hired girl go for a time, and she took in two boarders.[6] Part of the Gages' problem was that Henry had allowed too many customers to buy on credit. By the time he admitted his financial dilemma to Matilda, he was $8,000 in debt.[7] In March 1857 she accompanied Henry to New York. While he settled bills, she used the trip to follow her own interests.

"My Dear Mother," Matilda wrote later, "While I was in New York, I took a fancy to examine the Heraldic works in Astor Library in regard to your ancestry. I took Grandpa's seal with me and compared. The Griffin is described as an imaginary animal, the upper half, that of an eagle, and the lower half that of a lion."[8] She still had the Leslie family silverware, the spoons decorated with griffins.

By 1858 the Gages' financial situation had improved. In October they signed papers to buy their house for $1,325, putting a quarter down and taking a mortgage on the rest.[9]

The next summer they converted the back room of the original house into a space for Matilda's parents. Matilda thought that her mother, age sixty-seven, needed assistance. Her father continued to practice medicine, though his health was poor.[10] Matilda was glad to help them and write to me,

Newport R.I. Sunday Aug 7

My darling Boy,

How are the doves? and is my little white chicken well?

Pa says you are up early to drive the cow. I hope she has not run away again.

Do you and Eddy keep store any more? Are there any more chicks hatched?

[~1858]

[2]
I send you a paper It has the picture of Mons Blondin crossing Niagara on a rope, dressed as a monkey.

I want you to be in the house before dark, and in bed by eight; and Helen by nine. I want the Bay window blind, kept shut through

[3]
the day to keep out the sun and rain.

There are a great many children who take baths with their parents or servants.

The sea roars and the big waves chase me when I am in the water, and lift me off from my feet.

Sharks have

A letter from Matilda to her son, Clarkson, 1858.
Harvard University, Schlesinger Library

happy to have her father close for political discussions, but two additional people in the house made more work for her. By August she had fallen ill. Her doctor, diagnosing exhaustion, prescribed a rest before canning season.[11] She went by herself to the resort town of Newport, Rhode Island, where she carefully printed a letter to Clarkson:

My darling Boy,

How are the doves? and is my little white chicken well?

Pa says you are up early to drive the cow. I hope she has not run away again.

Do you and Eddy keep store any more?

Are there any more chicks hatched?

I send you a paper.

It has the picture of Mons[.] Blondin [Charles Blondin, a French tightrope walker] crossing Niagara on a rope, dressed as a monkey.

I want you to be in the house before dark, and in bed by eight; and Helen by nine. I want the Bay window blinds kept shut through the day to keep out the sun and rain.

There are great many children who take baths with their parents or servants.

The sea roars and the big waves chase me when I am in the water and lift me off from my feet.

Sharks have been caught lately in Boston and Providence.

I have sea fish every morning for breakfast, and as many huckleberries as I can eat in milk.

The clock is striking twelve and I must stop writing for I am tired. Good Bye, dear boy. Your loving Mother.[12]

When Matilda returned, Clarkson had a new pet, a baby crow. Asked to name the bird, Matilda chose "Uncle Tom," after the hero in Harriet Beecher Stowe's novel. The bird fit right in with the family. Often he knocked at the door with his beak, and when someone opened it, he walked into the house like an honored guest. When Matilda worked in her garden, he stayed so close that sometimes she hit him with her hoe. Then he gave a little squawk and flew onto her shoulder or perched on the top of her head. If she sat down, he jumped into her lap and snuggled close like a kitten.[13]

Family life provided Matilda and Henry with a welcome distraction from the mounting uproar over slavery. In October 1859 the radical abolitionist John Brown and his followers raided a federal armory in Harpers Ferry, Virginia (now West Virginia). Brown planned to use the guns stored there to arm enslaved people, starting a war to win freedom. Instead he was captured, tried, and condemned to death.

In Fayetteville on the day of Brown's hanging, Henry draped his store in mourning, and Matilda decorated their house in the same way.[14] John Brown's death revitalized the weary abolitionist movement, as did the election in 1860 of Abraham Lincoln as the first Republican president. Lincoln offered to support a new constitutional amendment, guaranteeing the right to slavery where it already legally existed, but Southern leaders believed that under Republican leadership, emancipation was inevitable. Before Lincoln had even been inaugurated, South Carolina, Mississippi, Florida, Alabama, Georgia, Louisiana, and Texas seceded from the United States to form the Confederate States of America. Equipping and training soldiers, the Southern states seized federal forts and arsenals within their jurisdictions.

President Lincoln called their actions illegal. When he took office on March 4, 1861, he refused to remove federal troops from Fort Sumter, which stood at the entrance to the harbor in Charleston, South Carolina. Union soldiers stationed there prepared for battle, but they were ill equipped.

Reading the newspapers, Matilda dreaded war, but she thought it inevitable. Despite this worry, she was celebrating. On March 27, 1861, three days after her thirty-fifth birthday, she gave birth to a baby girl, Maud. Helen, age fifteen, was old enough to help with the baby. Clarkson was twelve and Julia nine when their little sister was born. Uncle Tom, the crow, soon liked Maud better than anyone else in the family.[15]

Two weeks after Maud's birth, Confederate troops fired on Fort Sumter. Soon, lacking arms, ammunition, and, eventually, food, the Union soldiers inside surrendered. Though no lives were lost, hostilities increased. Lincoln called for seventy-five thousand volunteers to save the Union. Four more Southern states, Virginia, Arkansas, North Carolina, and Tennessee, seceded. The Civil War had begun. Nine million people lived in the Confederacy, including four million slaves. Twenty-one million people lived in the twenty-three Northern and border states.

Clarkson Gage in a Union uniform (costume), 1861. *Gage Foundation*

Battles made news, followed by reports of staggering losses. In all, 530 men served for the North from the town of Manlius, which included the villages of Fayetteville and Manlius. Of these, 105 never returned.[16] When survivors trickled back, they were often missing arms and legs, since amputation was the only way to stop infection. No family was untouched, but the war's effect on Matilda's and Henry's many relatives is unknown.

The women's movement suspended meetings during the war, diverting their efforts to war work. Matilda prepared hospital supplies for soldiers and held teas at her house to raise money for the North. She made small American flags for each of her children and hung a large flag over the house on Genesee Street. She sent gifts, such as tea, to soldiers she knew and saved the letters they wrote to thank her.[17]

In 1862 the women of Fayetteville chose Matilda to present an elegant

Matilda made this flag for Clarkson at the outbreak of the
Civil War, c. 1861. *Gage Foundation*

silk ceremonial flag to a group of soldiers who were going off to fight.
Waving it enthusiastically before a large audience, Matilda became one
of the first American political leaders to challenge President Lincoln's
ideas in public. At this time he believed that if the North won the war, it
could reconcile with the South, preserving the Union and slavery with
it, but Matilda disagreed.[18]

"There can be no permanent peace," she told the soldiers, "until the
cause of the war is destroyed. And what caused the war? Slavery![19] . . .
Until liberty is attained—the broadest, the deepest, the highest liberty
for all—not for one set alone, one clique alone, but for man and woman,
black and white, Irish, Germans, Americans and negroes, there can be
no permanent peace."[20]

Eventually President Lincoln, too, decided that the only way to win
the war and preserve the Union was to end slavery. In the autumn of
1862, he announced an executive order to be signed January 1. The
Emancipation Proclamation freed slaves in the rebel states. Henry decorated his store with red, white, and blue flags and bunting in celebration.[21] But the proclamation did not free slaves in loyal border states,
and it did not end slavery—a constitutional amendment would be required for that.

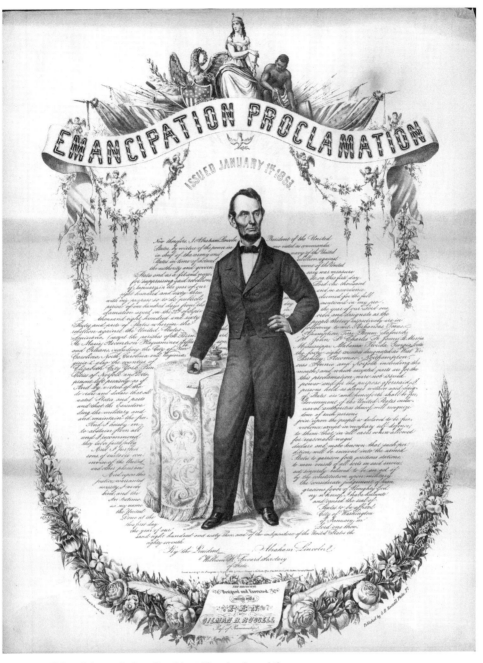

Matilda celebrated when President Lincoln signed the
Emancipation Proclamation, 1863. *Library of Congress*

Matilda's pleasure at the Emancipation Proclamation was tempered by sadness. Her mother, whose health had been failing steadily, died from a stomach tumor on November 24, 1863. "I cried so as to get all in the house up in the night," Matilda recalled later.[22] But she kept working, collecting signatures on petitions urging Congress to pass a constitutional amendment freeing all slaves.

On January 1, 1865, Congress passed the Thirteenth Amendment to the Constitution, abolishing slavery. The Civil War ended on April 7, 1865, when General Robert E. Lee, commander of the Confederate forces, surrendered. It was the deadliest American war ever—before or since—killing more than 750,000 people. More died from infection and disease than from bullet and bayonet wounds.

On April 14 President Lincoln was shot; he died the next morning. Even though she had criticized him, Matilda felt distraught over his death. Again she draped her house in mourning.[23]

There was one more loss to bear: her beloved father died on October 30, 1865. Matilda had his tombstone inscribed as he had requested: "an early abolitionist."

When the Thirteenth Amendment was ratified on December 6, 1865, Matilda and other activists rejoiced. They had worked for decades to end slavery, at the end putting aside other causes to focus on abolition. Their success could have inspired the same groups to work together toward new goals, like universal suffrage. Instead the reform movement split in two.

8 ✳ The Negro's Hour? 1866–1869

Matilda disagreed with a new slogan, "This is the Negro's hour," which she heard all too often in 1866. After the war, many abolitionists, Republicans, and temperance workers who had formerly supported the women's movement decided that votes for black men took priority over the fight for women's suffrage. To Matilda, the hour had come for equal rights for all.

Of course she was appalled that racial prejudice continued unabated. Newspapers published horrific reports about the suffering of blacks in the South, where the newly formed Ku Klux Klan terrorized and killed powerless people. Southern states passed laws to deny rights to former slaves. In 1866 Congress passed a Fourteenth Amendment to the Constitution, which declared that all persons born or naturalized in the United States were citizens of the country and of the state where they resided and that states could not abridge or deny their privileges without due process, meaning all citizens would be treated fairly under the law. This first section of the amendment pleased Matilda, as it seemed to include women as citizens.

But a later part of the amendment also prescribed penalties to states that denied voting privileges to male citizens aged twenty-one or older. Once the amendment was ratified, the word *male* would be used in the Constitution to describe voters for the first time. To Matilda, this part of the amendment wrongly pitted the rights of black men against those of all women, black and white.

In protest she joined the American Equal Rights Association, founded in 1866 by Elizabeth Cady Stanton and Susan B. Anthony. Matilda's

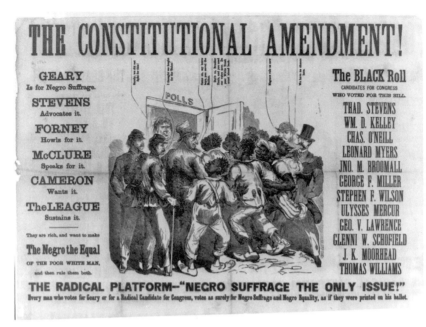

THE CONSTITUTIONAL AMENDMENT!

GEARY
Is for Negro Suffrage.

STEVENS
Advocates it.

FORNEY
Howls for it.

McCLURE
Speaks for it.

CAMERON
Wants it.

TheLEAGUE
Sustains it.

They are rich, and want to make

The Negro the Equal
OF THE POOR WHITE MAN,
and then rule them both.

POLLS

The BLACK Roll
CANDIDATES FOR CONGRESS
WHO VOTED FOR THIS BILL.

THAD. STEVENS
WM. D. KELLEY
CHAS. O'NEILL
LEONARD MYERS
JNO. M. BROOMALL
GEORGE F. MILLER
STEPHEN F. WILSON
ULYSSES MERCUR
GEO. V. LAWRENCE
GLENNI W. SCHOFIELD
J. K. MOORHEAD
THOMAS WILLIAMS

THE RADICAL PLATFORM—"NEGRO SUFFRAGE THE ONLY ISSUE!"
Every man who votes for Geary or for a Radical Candidate for Congress, votes as surely for Negro Suffrage and Negro Equality, as if they were printed on his ballot.

A white supremacist cartoon portraying Republicans as seeking to grant suffrage to black men in order to create a voting bloc for themselves, 1866.
Library of Congress

beloved Lucretia Mott was president. Matilda agreed with the organization's position that women could not "work in two separate movements to get the ballot for the two disfranchised classes—the negro and women—since to do so must be at double cost of time, energy, and money."[1] She liked the association's "one grand, distinctive, national idea—universal suffrage."[2]

Undoubtedly Matilda worked toward this goal in Fayetteville, but her actions from 1866 and 1867 are little known. She returned to national attention in 1868, when Susan B. Anthony, joined by Elizabeth Cady Stanton, started a feminist newspaper called the *Revolution* in New York City. Parker Pillsbury, an abolitionist who supported universal suffrage over male suffrage, was coeditor with Stanton; Anthony was the proprietor and business manager.

Lively and controversial, the *Revolution* published female authors who could not get jobs in mainstream journalism, and it covered the women's movement as no other publication did. It printed accounts of meetings, editorials, financial news, reports from other countries, and

The Revolution.

PRINCIPLE, NOT POLICY: JUSTICE, NOT FAVORS.

VOL. I.—NO. 1.   NEW YORK, WEDNESDAY, JANUARY 8, 1868. $2.00 A YEAR.

The Revolution;

THE ORGAN OF THE

NATIONAL PARTY OF NEW AMERICA.

PRINCIPLE, NOT POLICY—INDIVIDUAL RIGHTS AND RESPONSIBILITIES.

THE REVOLUTION WILL ADVOCATE:

1. IN POLITICS—Educated Suffrage, Irrespective of Sex or Color; Equal Pay to Women for Equal Work; Eight Hours Labor; Abolition of Standing Armies and Party Despotism. Down with Politicians—Up with the People!

2. IN RELIGION—Deeper Thought; Broader Idea; Science not Superstition; Personal Purity; Love to Man as well as God.

3. IN SOCIAL LIFE—Morality and Reform; Practical Education, not Theoretical; Facts not Fiction; Virtue not Vice; Cold Water not Alcoholic Drinks or Medicines. It will indulge in no Gross Personalities and insert no Quack or Immoral Advertisements, so common even in Religious Newspapers.

KANSAS.

THE question of the enfranchisement of woman has already passed the court of moral discussion, and is now fairly ushered into the arena of politics, where it must remain a fixed element of debate, until party necessity shall compel its success.

With 9,000 votes in Kansas, one-third the entire vote, every politician must see that the friends of "woman's suffrage" hold the balance of power in that State to-day. And those 9,000 votes represent a principle deep in the hearts of the people, for this triumph was secured without money, without a press, without a party. With these instrumentalities now fast coming to us on all sides, the victory in Kansas is but the herald of greater victories in every State of the Union. Kansas already leads the world in her legislation for woman on questions of property, education, wages, marriage and divorce. Her best universities are open alike to boys and girls. In fact woman has a voice in the legislation of that State. She votes on all school questions and is eligible to the office of trustee. She has a voice in temperance too; no license is granted without the consent of a majority of the adult citizens, male and female, black and white. The consequence is, stone school houses are voted up in every part of the State, and rum voted down. Many of

ence outside as well as inside the State, all combined might have made our vote comparatively a small one, had not George Francis Train gone into the State two weeks before the election and securing 9,000 votes for woman's suffrage. Some claim that we are indebted to the Republicans for this vote; but the fact that the most radical republican district, Douglass County, gave the largest vote against woman's suffrage, while Leavenworth, the Democratic district, gave the largest vote for it, fully settles that question.

In saying that Mr. Train helped to swell our vote takes nothing from the credit due all those who labored faithfully for months in that State. All praise to Olympia Brown, Lucy Stone, Susan B. Anthony, Henry B. Blackwell, and Judge Wood, who welcomed, for an idea, the hardships of travelling in a new State, fording streams, scaling rocky brinks, sleeping on the ground and eating hard tack, with the fatigue of constant speaking, in school-houses, barns, mills, depots and the open air; and especially, all praise to the glorious Hutchinson family—John, his son Henry and daughter, Viola—who, with their own horses and carriage, made the entire circuit of the state, singing Woman's Suffrage into souls that logic could never penetrate. Having shared with them the hardships, with them I rejoice in our success.

E. C. S.

The first issue of the *Revolution*, 1868. *Lewis and Clark Digital Collections*

articles about abortion, jobs, education, churches, and women's clothing, including advertisements for some of the new, ready-made women's clothes. The newspaper was controversial, too, because one of its financial supporters was George Francis Train, an eccentric and flamboyant entrepreneur. Train supported women's rights but opposed suffrage for African Americans. Even though Anthony and Stanton did not entirely agree with him, they needed his money to finance the publication. Lucy Stone and William Lloyd Garrison, among others, criticized Anthony and Stanton for accepting his support.

Matilda became a principal contributor to the *Revolution*, offering strong opinions on many topics. "Nowhere has the marital union of the sexes been one in which woman has had control over her own body," she argued in 1868. "Enforced motherhood is a crime against the body of the mother and the soul of the child."[3]

In a six-part series, "Woman as Inventor," she told how women had invented silk, underwater telescopes, straw bonnets, obstetrical instruments, lace, wood engraving, a superior kind of horseshoe, new tunneling techniques, and the cotton gin. She sent the paper notices of her upcoming lectures and mailed reports from the field as she resumed touring and lecturing.

The *Revolution* took a stand against the Fourteenth Amendment for not including women, but in July 1868 the amendment was ratified. By this time a Fifteenth Amendment had been proposed that would prohibit the United States or any state from denying citizens the right to vote based on "race, color, or previous condition of servitude."

To Matilda, the word "sex" should have been added to the list. Now she realized that a separate amendment would be required to include women as voters and full citizens in the United States.

Matilda did not attend the first national Woman's Suffrage Convention held in Washington in January 1869, but she sent an equal suffrage petition signed by 234 people. She had gone door-to-door with her middle daughter, Julia, collecting signatures.

"On the petition you will find the names of all my family but little Maud," she wrote to the *Revolution*. "My children grow up imbued with the spirit of this great reform."[4]

Clarkson, now a student at Cornell University in Ithaca, New York, wrote to his mother in March 1869, shortly before Matilda's forty-third birthday and Maud's eighth:

> This letter you must call your birth-day letter. It is my wish that you might live to see as many years (but with more happiness) as you have seen already.
>
> Grandfather Joslyn advocated the anti-slavery cause and lived to see slavery done away with.
>
> You advocate woman's suffrage. May God grant that you may live to see that cause granted.
>
> From your son.
>
> T. Clarkson Gage.
>
> PS. Give Maudy 8 birthday kisses for me.[5]

The whole family doted on Maud. In the spring of 1869, Matilda went to a convention, leaving Henry to care for their youngest child. "Next Sunday Maudy and I are going to the woods," he wrote to Clarkson, "and we are intending to take for our dinner Boiled Eggs, Salt, leaks [sic], pie, Cold Beans, Lemons, and Maple Sugar."[6]

While they picnicked, Matilda attended a meeting of the American Equal Rights Association at Steinway Hall, one of the largest assembly rooms in New York. From her seat on the platform, she had a good view of the audience of 2,500, mostly women.

In the absence of President Lucretia Mott, First Vice President Elizabeth Cady Stanton chaired the convention. Calling for a Sixteenth Amendment to secure women's right to vote, she said, "this fundamental principle of our government—the equality of all the citizens of the republic—should be incorporated in the Federal Constitution, there to remain forever."[7]

However, unlike Matilda, Stanton did not believe in the equality of all citizens. In the *Revolution*, Stanton complained about "lower orders, natives and foreigners, Dutch, Irish, Chinese and African," making laws for educated women. She said that senators who voted against women's suffrage "degrade their own mothers, wives and daughters, in their political status, below unwashed and un-lettered boot-blacks, hostlers, butchers, and barbers."[8]

"Think of Patrick and Sambo and Hans and Yung Tung," Stanton urged, using names considered derogatory even at that time, "who do not know the difference between a Monarchy and a Republic, who never read the Declaration of Independence or Webster's spelling-book, making laws for . . . Lucretia Mott."[9]

"Think . . . of the daughters of Adams, Jefferson, and Patrick Henry," she said, "in whose veins flows the blood of two Revolutions." These women, she asserted, would not be content with rights less than those granted to men whom she considered inferior.[10]

Frederick Douglass, who spoke at the convention after Stanton, criticized her attitude. "There is no name greater than that of Elizabeth Cady Stanton," Douglass began, "in the matter of woman's rights and equal rights, but my sentiments are tinged a little against the *Revolution*. There was [in the *Revolution*] . . . the employment of certain names, such as 'Sambo,' . . . and the daughters of Jefferson and Washington. . . . I have asked what the difference is between the daughters of Jefferson and Washington and other daughters."[11]

His question drew laughter, but his next comments, coming from a man who had supported the women's movement from its start, surprised many. "I must say," he continued:

that I do not see how anyone can pretend that there is the same urgency in giving the ballot to woman as to the negro. With us, the matter is a question of life and death, at least, in fifteen States of the Union. When women, because they are women, are hunted down through the cities of New York and New Orleans; when they are dragged from their houses and hung upon lamp-posts; when their children are torn from their arms, and their brains dashed out upon the pavement; when they are objects of insult and outrage at every turn; when they are in danger of having their homes burnt down over their heads; when their children are not allowed to enter schools; then they will have an urgency to obtain the ballot equal to our own.[12]

Lucy Stone responded:

I want to remind the audience that when he says what the Ku-Kluxes did all over the South, the Ku-Kluxes here in the North in the shape of men, take away the children from the mother, and separate them as completely as if done on the block of the auctioneer. Over in New Jersey they have a law which says that *any* father—he might be the most brutal man that ever existed—*any* father, it says, whether he be under age or not, may by his last will and testament dispose of the custody of his child, born or to be born . . . and that the mother may not recover her child; and that law modified in form exists over every State in the Union except Kansas.[13]

Then, in a striking reversal, she added, "But I thank God for that Fifteenth Amendment, and hope that it will be adopted in every State. I will be thankful in my soul if *any* body can get out of the terrible pit."[14]

For three days, the delegates wrangled over suffrage priorities, never resolving the conflict between abolitionists and feminists. Longtime advocates of women's rights, as well as new Midwestern converts to the cause who had been recruited by Elizabeth Cady Stanton and Susan B. Anthony on recent lecture tours, were dismayed. Margaret Longley of Ohio reported that they had "supposed that they were going to a women's rights meeting . . . and that equal rights meant the equal rights of women with men."[15]

"This is the Negro's hour," came the refrain, again and again. By the

Lucy Stone, c. 1850. When she married in 1855, she did not take her husband's last name. Other women who followed suit were known as "Lucy Stones." *Library of Congress*

convention's close the choice seemed clear: a line had been drawn; women could wait.

But women like Matilda and the hopeful Midwesterners would not wait. At the close of the convention, Elizabeth Cady Stanton and Susan B. Anthony invited some specially chosen delegates to stay on in New York for another meeting.

Currier and Ives cartoon, "The Age of Iron: Man as He Expects to Be," 1869.
Library of Congress

9 ❈ The National Woman Suffrage Association
1869

O n May 15, 1869, Matilda made her way to a four-story brownstone at 49 East Twenty-Third Street in New York.[1] The evening air was cooling after a warm day. As Matilda approached the stylish neighborhood near Fifth Avenue, she saw other women arriving, some on foot, others by horse-drawn cab or omnibus. They wore dresses of silk, pongee, velour, or piqué in black or dark colors. Skirts were full, flattened in front, with drapery and bows behind. Matilda's hem probably swept the ground (she dressed well but conservatively), and Quaker dresses hung full-length, but some skirts daringly showed ankle boots or pantaloons. These were walking dresses: not bloomer costumes but stylish frocks, tightly fitted over corsets and puffed out by layers of petticoats.[2]

Hairstyles were elaborate, too. Matilda, prematurely gray in her early forties, had curly hair, which she sometimes supplemented with extra ringlets. Other women wore hairpieces called chignons, switches, puffs, braids, or waterfalls, or dressed their hair over frames. Hats, which had grown smaller, were worn perched atop these elaborate hairdos. Quaker women wore their traditional bonnets.[3]

As the twilight deepened, gas lights came on inside the row of townhouses. One of them, called the Woman's Bureau, was a meeting place for women activists. The first floor housed the rented offices of the *Revolution*, which had just moved into the building. This may have been Matilda's first chance to see the offices of the paper for which she wrote. The rooms were handsomely furnished with Brussels carpets on the floors and engravings on the walls, along with portraits of Lucretia Mott and Mary Wollstonecraft, a British author whom Matilda admired. Wollstonecraft's most famous book, *A Vindication of the Rights of Women* (1792), advocated equality of the sexes and called for equal education for women and men.

Climbing to the second floor, Matilda found spacious parlors filling with more than a hundred women from nineteen states. Big skirts crowded the stairways and elegant rooms as the crowd chatted and viewed an art exhibition.

Soon the reception became a meeting. Standing behind a table, Elizabeth Cady Stanton took charge as the group decided to form a new organization, the National Woman Suffrage Association. Its primary goal, the women agreed, would be to lobby for the passage of a Sixteenth Amendment guaranteeing votes for women. But the National would work for other women's causes, too, like equal pay and fairer marriage laws.

The group elected a president, Elizabeth Cady Stanton, who proposed that membership should be limited to women. After some discussion, the women decided to admit men as members, but not as officers. They adopted a constitution making the National a grassroots organization: anyone who paid the one-dollar dues could attend conventions and vote as a full-fledged member.[4] They planned a national meeting for the following spring; in the meantime they would build state organizations.

That night Matilda left the Woman's Bureau as one of the National's first hundred charter members and as an officer, an advisory counsel.[5] In her mind, she was already planning the first New York state convention.

Not everyone was pleased with the new organization. Lucy Stone, who had not been invited to the reception, complained publicly about the secretive way in which the National had been formed. She sent letters to a different group of women's rights supporters, inviting them to organize a "'*Truly*' 'National Woman's Suffrage Association.'"[6]

Lucy Stone's new organization, co-led by the writer Julia Ward Howe, chose the name the American Woman Suffrage Association. The American, which condemned the National as too radical, chose to permit men in leadership roles. The American would campaign for equal suffrage at the state level. Its conventions would be open only to delegates from approved state organizations. Allied closely with abolitionist, temperance, Republican, and conservative women's groups, the American Woman

Suffrage Association announced that its first goal would be suffrage for black men.

The old American Equal Rights Association no longer existed. The women's movement had split into two organizations with opposing viewpoints. As usual, Matilda felt energized by opposition.

"The longer I work," she wrote, "the more I see that woman's cause is the world's cause. No other reform ever equalled this in its magnitude and its prospective results. Not one class, nor one race, but the half of all humanity is, through it, to be raised from the despotism of the past into the full liberty of christian [sic] responsibility and opportunity."[7]

10 ✳ Strong-Minded Women 1869–1871

I
n July 1869, eight hundred "strong-minded women," "with back bows and loops a-flying," according to a newspaper report, converged on the New York resort town of Saratoga Springs. "Strong-minded" was a belittling term in those days, used to ridicule women's rights activists, but it was kinder, and more accurate, than other insults they received. "Those horrid women whose names were in the newspapers," the article continued, in a surprised vein, "were not so dreadful after all. They neither wore beards nor pantaloons. On the contrary they seemed to be decidedly appreciative of 'good clothes.'"[1]

Arriving by train from all parts of the state, the ladies traveled by horse-drawn omnibus from the depot to the Congress Hall Hotel. Some greeted friends on the elegant front piazza, where people gathered to see and be seen. Fashionable vacationers watched the women flocking in with interest, and some leisure visitors even attended the meetings to organize the New York State Woman Suffrage Association.

Skirts swished and heels clicked as the women gathered on July 13 on the first floor of the grand hotel. When Matilda called the convention to order, the crowd filled four adjoining parlors. She presided as the group passed a constitution and elected officers, including herself as secretary.

The group adopted a plan of organization which Matilda had designed.[2] It asked convention-goers to create lists of their friends, organized alphabetically by name and county, and to form support groups at home. Town groups would report to county organizations, which would report to the new state association. To help people organize local events, the National Woman Suffrage Association would supply speakers and tracts.[3] If this proposal worked in New York, as Matilda felt sure it would, it would then be adopted in other states.

As soon as the convention ended, Matilda began organizing county conventions. "Friends, *this is work*," Matilda wrote as her plan was published in the *Revolution*. "Do not wait for the choosing of a Vice-President for your county," she wrote. "Call conventions . . . and elect your own Vice-President. CHOOSE A WORKER. Put none in office on account of their social position. . . . Too much has been lost by striving to make the *names* of persons work for them. One active, energetic worker, never yet heard of outside a radius of five miles from her home, will, at this stage of our movement, accomplish more and do more to advance the reform, than will a dozen high-named non-workers."[4]

By December she had workers in more than fifty of New York's sixty counties.[5]

In January 1870 Matilda broke new ground for women as she and her colleagues addressed the United States Congressional Committee on the District of Columbia during a formal hearing. The *Revolution* described "the cool light of a winter morning, the bare walls of a committee room, the plain costumes of everyday use," contrasting the simple scene with the historic significance of the event: it was the first time women had spoken on behalf of their countrywomen at the Capitol.[6]

Congress Hall, the largest hotel in Saratoga Springs. *New York Public Library*

Congress Hall parlor, 1870. *New York Public Library*

Matilda, age forty-five, 1871.
Gage Foundation

Matilda had proposed the National's committee,[7] which included herself, Elizabeth Cady Stanton, Susan B. Anthony, Phoebe Couzins, a law student from Saint Louis,[8] and seven other women. The hearing attracted many spectators in addition to the two committees.

"The gentlemen took their seats around a long table in the middle of the room," the *Revolution* reported later. "Mrs. Stanton stood at one end, serene and dignified. Behind her sat a large semi-circle of ladies, and close about her a group of her companions, who would have been remarkable anywhere for the intellectual refinement and elevated expression of their earnest faces. Opposite, at the other end of the table, sat Charles Sumner, looking fatigued and worn, but listening with alert attention. So these two veterans in the cause of freedom were fitly and suggestively brought face to face."[9] Sumner, a Republican senator from Massachusetts, believed that the "consent of the governed" was essential to a democracy.

One by one, the National's leaders asked the legislators to grant voting rights to the women of the District of Columbia, and eventually to all women in the United States.

"We ask but justice," Matilda told the senators and representatives, "and we say to you that the stability of any government depends upon its doing justice to the most humble individual under it."[10]

In the question-and-answer session following the formal speeches, one man asked how the women could be sure that large numbers of American women desired the ballot.

"Mrs. Stanton and Miss Anthony," the *Republic* explained later, "recounted their experience at conventions, the numerous signatures to petitions, the many demonstrations here and in England in favor of

Woman Suffrage, but reminded the gentleman that no such separate expression is required from the unwashed, unkempt immigrants upon whom the government makes haste to confer unqualified suffrage, nor from the southern negroes, who are provided for by the Fifteenth Amendment."[11]

Although Matilda disagreed with her friends about their depiction of immigrants, she felt proud to be part of the historic meeting. At the end, the participants shook hands cordially and chatted.

"Senator Sumner said he had been in Congress for twenty years," Matilda wrote to Clarkson, "in all the exciting times . . . but in all this time he had never seen as many Senators and Representatives present, or as many spectators; or had never heard speeches of as much *interest and power* as those made by the ladies this morning."[12]

Although the congressmen did not follow the National's recommendations, their attention showed that the association's goals were gaining respect. Publicity for the issue increased.

"Let the friends everywhere rejoice and take a new faith," Matilda wrote in the *Revolution*, "for we are now before the world a recognized moral power, and *the end is sure.*"[13]

As word of the movement spread, some people were confused by the fact two organizations existed to champion women's rights. On several occasions representatives of the National, based in New York, and the American, based in Boston, met to discuss a union. But negotiations failed, and the groups continued on separate paths.

In May 1870 Matilda traveled south to organize the Virginia State Woman Suffrage Association.[14] In July she put on another New York convention in Saratoga Springs.[15]

Around this time, rising debts forced Susan B. Anthony to sell the *Revolution*, which continued for two years with a new editor.[16] After selling the paper, Anthony and Elizabeth Cady Stanton began to travel extensively on speaking tours, but Matilda stayed closer to home, serving as president or secretary of the New York State Woman Suffrage Association while also holding office in the National. She organized conventions for both groups.

The work tired her. "I feel quite discouraged," Matilda wrote a friend, "not only as to conventions, but also in the matter of our state organization. So many, many people refuse to take responsible, working po-

Victoria Woodhull addressing the House Judiciary Committee, *Frank Leslie's Weekly*, 1871. Elizabeth Cady Stanton sits behind Woodhull; Woodhull's sister Victoria Claflin is at bottom right. *Library of Congress*

sitions in it. . . . 'God help you, go ahead', [they say] 'I am with you in everything I can do', and do nothing; neither work themselves, or pay the paltry membership fee, that others may work."[17]

Matilda wanted to find more time for her writing. The New York State Woman Suffrage Association had published "Woman as Inventor" as a thirty-two-page booklet. Advertised in the *Revolution*, it sold for ten cents a copy.[18]

In December 1870 the *Revolution* and many other newspapers carried stories about Victoria Claflin Woodhull, "the most controversial suffragist of them all."[19] Woodhull and her sister Tennessee Claflin were well known—clairvoyants and former medicine show stars who had become the first female brokers on Wall Street. The sisters were notorious for their support of "free love," the right of a woman to marry, divorce, and bear children as she pleased without government interference, and for their personal lives, which reflected their beliefs.

Woodhull had gone to the Washington women's suffrage conference in January 1869, which Matilda had not attended, but Woodhull had not made contact with the leaders. Unhappy with Elizabeth Cady Stanton's racist and elitist pronouncements there, Woodhull struck out on her own for equal rights, announcing that she would run for president.[20] She and her sister founded a newspaper, *Woodhull and Claflin's Weekly*, to support her candidacy.

In December 1870 Woodhull submitted a "Memorial" address to both houses of Congress, claiming that as a citizen of the United States, she had the right to vote under the Fourteenth and Fifteenth Amendments. She pointed out that the Constitution made no distinction between citizens on account of sex and she asked Congress to make such laws "necessary and proper for carrying into execution the right vested by the Constitution in the citizens of the United States to vote, without regard to sex."[21]

Both the Senate and House referred Woodhull's address to their respective judiciary committees.

The *Revolution* praised "Mrs. Woodhull's brilliant and unanswerable argument."[22] Press coverage of her campaign continued in January 1871 as National members gathered in Washington for a convention. Matilda did not attend, but she certainly followed the proceedings closely.

By coincidence, on the first morning of the Washington convention—which, again, Matilda did not attend—Woodhull was scheduled to address the House Judiciary Committee. Chairman Isabella Beecher Hooker postponed the convention's opening session so that she, Susan B. Anthony, and other National members could attend the committee hearing. There they, too, spoke in support of Woodhull's plan.[23] Another Woodhull supporter, a lawyer and former member of Congress, A. G. Riddle, suggested a "new departure" theory: that the fastest method of changing the law would be for women to register and vote.[24]

Woodhull so inspired the National's leaders that they invited her to return with them to their convention, to read her address there. And although Congress took no action on Woodhull's idea, the National did. After the conference, Susan B. Anthony left for a speaking tour with a lecture called "The New Situation," based on the "Woodhull Memorial."[25]

Matilda bolstered Woodhull's theory by writing a "Woman's Rights Catechism," published in the Fayetteville *Weekly Recorder* on June 27, 1871, and soon reissued as a separate booklet which was sold in the *Revolution*. It began:

A respectable woman with heavy burdens shunning Victoria Woodhull, "Get thee behind me (Mrs.) Satan" cartoon by Thomas Nast for *Harper's Weekly*, February 17, 1872. *Library of Congress*

Question: From whence do governments derive their just powers?

Answer: Governments derive their just powers from the consent of the governed. *Declaration of Independence.*

Q: Are rights granted people by governments or through constitutions?

A: No, rights existed before governments were founded or constitutions created.

Q: Of what use then are governments and constitutions?

A: To protect people in the exercise and enjoyment of their natural and fundamental rights, which existed before governments or constitutions were made. *Declaration of Independence* and *Constitution.* . . .

Q: Are those persons who, under color of law, forbid woman the ballot, law-keepers or law-breakers?

A: They are law-breakers, acting in defiance to both National and State law, in thus refusing to women citizens the exercise of a right secured to them by the Constitution of the United States; and they render themselves liable to prosecution thereby.[26]

Matilda still felt that the federal government should protect women citizens' right to vote with a constitutional amendment. Meanwhile she and other suffragists believed that unjust laws, like the defunct Fugitive Slave Act, should not be obeyed.

Using Matilda's catechism as a guide, the National launched a campaign of nonviolent civil disobedience.[27] The organization urged women citizens to register to vote and to file lawsuits if they were denied.

In July 1871 Matilda tried to vote in Fayetteville. "The fun of the thing," she wrote later to her friend Lillie Devereux Blake, "was that I had *nine* women with me in the sitting room of the hotel. I went down first and offered my vote. They voted in the bar room but had their box on the door into hall where I stood. I was refused on the ground that I was a married woman."

Matilda was not discouraged. "Then I took down two single women," she said, "who supported themselves and owned their own home. . . . Their votes were refused also."

She had planned the progression carefully. "Then I took down . . . war widows, whose husbands had left their bones to bleach on the field of battle, in defense of their country, and they, too, were refused, and so on through the whole nine."

The vote, supposedly, was for taxpayers only. Matilda pointed out that in Fayetteville, it was a woman who paid the most taxes, and a woman who paid the least.

"With each one," she continued proudly, "I made appropriate arguments, and had a big and attentive crowd to hear me. . . . It created a great stir."[28]

11 ✳ The United States on Trial 1871–1873

"Oh, wise men," Matilda asked in the Syracuse *Journal*, "can you tell why he means she, when taxes are to be assessed, and does not mean she, when taxes are to be voted upon?"[1] Like Matilda, hundreds of women across the country, including Victoria Woodhull and her sister Tennessee Claflin, tried to vote, and when they were barred, some sued their local voter registration boards. The lawsuits brought publicity but no success. In 1871 and 1872, Congress, courts, and various state legislatures all issued the same disappointing ruling: citizens did not necessarily have the right to vote.[2]

During this time, some National leaders grew closer to Woodhull. It is not clear when Matilda or Elizabeth Cady Stanton actually met her, but they supported her ideas and her presence in the organization. Other National members remained wary of the beautiful celebrity. Susan B. Anthony worried that Woodhull's ideas on free love would distract from the National's mission or that Woodhull might try to take over the organization, but the others convinced Anthony that Woodhull was important to their effort.

Matilda saved several articles about the National's January 1872 convention, which she attended in Washington. Lincoln Hall was "crowded to overflowing"[3] with a huge, boisterous audience. In one clipping Matilda underlined the phrase, "The last of the great sensational meetings of the Woman's convention."[4] Another article describes the speakers as they took the stage:

Victoria Woodhull and her sister Tennessee Claflin attempting to vote, c. 1870. *New York Public Library*

MRS. ELIZABETH CADY STANTON,
in a heavy black silk trimmed with taste, and cut after an approved modern pattern. She has a handsome face, and is of portly proportions. Then followed

MISS SUSAN B. ANTHONY,
a woman evidently well over the forties, of angular features, and wiry, active frame. Not endowed with a handsome face, but full of vim and logic. She was dressed in a wine-colored silk, with two narrow flounces of the same material. Her white collar was relieved with a blue tie.

MRS. WOODHULL
came next, and was greeted with applause. She wore a black silk, plainly trimmed, and a short, double-breasted coat made of purple beaver. She is quick of movement, and of well-developed form; has a pleasing face. Her hair is cut short, and given to a slight curl.

appears to be about forty-five years of age, and of firm and decisive character; not comely, nor yet bad looking. She has an eye of magic attraction and a lily-white complexion. She attired herself for the occasion in a brown poplin, with a saque of the same material, in a jockey hat and feather, and kept her neck enclosed in a boa of mink.[5]

Matilda, who had organized the convention, suffered heart problems while it was underway. Luckily she recovered sufficiently to give a rousing speech against taxation without representation and against unfair jury trials for women, who could not be judged by their peers.[6] Susan B. Anthony called it "a splendid argument." While in Washington Matilda also testified before the Senate Judiciary Committee, called upon the new attorney general, attended several receptions, did research at the U.S. patent office, gave a talk on "Women in Ancient Egypt," visited the government greenhouses, and toured the Smithsonian Institute, where she saw the cast of a gorilla's head.

At this time there were no gorillas in U.S. zoos. "It is simply frightful," Matilda wrote to her son of the head. "I should infinitely prefer to meet a lion."[7]

Matilda volunteered to chair the National Woman Suffrage Association's spring convention in New York. Susan B. Anthony was on a western speaking tour when she read the convention call in *Woodhull and Claflin's Weekly*, which invited readers to meet to form a new political party and to nominate candidates for president and vice president. It was signed, "Elizabeth Cady Stanton, Susan B. Anthony, Isabella B. Hooker, and Matilda Joslyn Gage."[8]

Anthony vehemently opposed the idea of a new political party, a fact well known to her colleagues. She

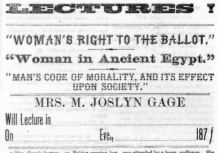

Promotional flyer for Matilda's lectures. "Egyptomania" was a nineteenth-century fad. *Gage Foundation*

felt sure that Woodhull had put the others up to this new plan. After telegraphing to have her name removed from the call, she rushed to New York, arriving three days before the convention.[9]

As a single woman, Anthony often signed contracts for the National (married women could not sign contracts in most states), and she had rented Steinway Hall, the site of the convention, in her name. The contract specified that the hall was to be used solely for a woman suffrage convention. Citing this clause, Anthony blocked the National's president, Elizabeth Cady Stanton, from seeking nominations for third-party political candidates.

Later, when Victoria Woodhull took the stage, uninvited, Anthony declared that Woodhull was not a member of the organization. She asked Stanton to rule Woodhull out of order. Stanton declined, leaving Anthony and Woodhull to shout it out. In the uproar that followed, Anthony asked the janitor to turn out the gas lights, and the meeting ended.[10]

Woodhull eventually formed a third party to support her candidacy for president. During her campaign, she waged a battle against hypocrisy in high places, publishing a "scandal issue" of her newspaper with two shocking stories. One detailed the adulterous affair of the Reverend Henry Ward Beecher, a famous minister (and the brother of Isabella Beecher Hooker, then a leader in the National); another described a stockbroker, Luther Challis, who abused young girls. When the issue was distributed, Woodhull and her coeditor sister were arrested for sending obscene materials through the mail. They spent weeks, including the day of the presidential election, in jail, but later the charges against them were dropped.[11]

The National gave up on Woodhull as a leader within the organization but not on her idea that women should try to vote. In 1872 Matilda and Susan B. Anthony decided to support President Ulysses S. Grant, a Republican, for reelection, as the Democrats and other parties opposed women's suffrage.

For the first time in American history, a political platform took note of women's suffrage: "The Republican party is mindful of its obligations to the loyal women of America for their noble devotion to the cause of freedom; their admission to wider fields of usefulness is received with satisfaction; and the honest demands of any class of citizens for equal rights should be treated with respectful consideration."[12]

Matilda's children, c. 1872. Clockwise from bottom left: Helen, Julia, Clarkson, and Maud. *Gage Foundation*

Dissatisfied with this weak statement, Matilda and Susan B. Anthony consulted often on National strategy. Elizabeth Cady Stanton did not support the strategy of civil disobedience and women's voting to the extent that Matilda and Anthony did, so the two of them grew closer. During the presidential campaign, Anthony stayed at the Gage home so frequently that Matilda's children named an upstairs bedroom "the Susan B. Anthony Room," and Anthony carved her name in its window pane with a diamond ring.[13]

Following their plan, on November 1, 1872, Susan B. Anthony took her sister and a woman friend to register to vote in a barber shop in their hometown of Rochester, New York. When the registrars hesitated, Anthony read them the Fourteenth Amendment and the New York State Constitution, which did not mention gender as a qualification for voting.[14] Finally the men relented. On November 5 Anthony voted for Grant, joined in this illegal act by fourteen other women in her ward. Her accomplishment made headlines across the country.

Two weeks later a United States deputy marshal came to Anthony's home to arrest her under the federal Enforcement Act of 1870, which said: "Any person . . . who shall vote without having a legal right to vote . . . shall be deemed guilty of a crime."[15]

The marshal told Anthony she could go the district attorney's office on her own.

"Oh, dear, no," Anthony said, "I much prefer to be taken, handcuffed, if possible."[16]

The other women voters were rounded up, too, and questioned, as Matilda wrote later, "in the same small dingy office where, in the days of slavery, fugitives escaping to Canada had been examined and re-manded to bondage. This historic little room is a double disgrace to the American Republic, as within its walls the rights of color and of sex have been equally trampled upon."[17]

Anthony asked to have her trial postponed so as not to lose any speaking dates, and her request was granted. Soon she was giving a new speech on the lecture circuit: "Is it a Crime for a Citizen of the United States to Vote?"

When Anthony attended the National's January 1873 convention in Washington, people were thrilled to see her. Some had thought that she was in prison. Matilda emerged from this convention as Anthony's strongest supporter.

Anthony's trial was postponed until June 1873. Twenty-two days be-fore it started, the trial was moved to Ontario County. Anthony had blan-keted Monroe County, where she was arrested, with so many speeches that the district attorney thought it would be impossible to provide a fair selection of jurors from that area.[18]

Anthony called on Matilda to help her gain public support in On-tario County. In the days before the trial, Anthony made twenty-one speeches there and Matilda gave another sixteen. Matilda's speech, "The United States on Trial, Not Susan B. Anthony," ended with a plea to potential jurors.

"To you, men of Ontario county," Matilda said, "has come an important hour. . . . You, of all the men in this great land, have the responsibility of this trial. . . . Your decision will not be for Susan B. Anthony alone; it will be for yourselves and for your children's children to the latest generations."[19]

The trial opened on June 18. "The lovely village of Canandaigua," Matilda wrote later, "with its placid lake reflecting the soft summer sky, gave no evidence of the great event that was to make the day and the place memorable in history."[20] Matilda, the only National leader who had come to Anthony's aid, sat with Anthony and the other women who had voted with her. The second-floor courtroom was packed; one spectator was a former president, Millard Fillmore, who lived in Buffalo.[21] The defendant wore a black dress and a new bonnet lined with blue silk, draped with a dotted veil.[22]

Susan B. Anthony in top hat and spurs in the most famous cartoon of the women's movement, "The Woman Who Dared," by Thomas Wust, 1873. *Library of Congress.*

"On the bench sat Judge Hunt," Matilda wrote later, "a small-brained, pale-faced, prim-looking man, enveloped in a faultless suit of black broadcloth, and a snowy white neck-tie."[23]

Judge Ward Hunt, a Supreme Court justice recently appointed by President Grant, ruled Anthony incompetent to testify. Following long speeches by her lawyer and the district attorney, Judge Hunt took out a piece of paper and began to read from it.

"This was the first criminal case he had been called on to try since his appointment," Matilda wrote later, "and with remarkable forethought, he had penned his decision before hearing it."[24]

"Gentlemen of the Jury:" the judge read, "Miss Anthony knew that she was a woman, and that the Constitution of this State prohibits her from voting. She intended to violate that provision—intended to test it, perhaps, but certainly intended to violate it. . . . She voluntarily gave a vote which was illegal, and thus is subject to the penalty of the law."[25]

Without allowing the jurors to deliberate, he directed them to find her guilty and instructed the court clerk to enter the verdict. Then he dismissed the jury.

"No juror spoke a word during the trial," Matilda said, "from the time when they were empaneled to the time of their discharge."[26]

The judge fined Anthony one hundred dollars, plus court costs.

"May it please your honor," Anthony said, "I shall never pay a dollar of your unjust penalty." And she never did.[27]

Susan B. Anthony, c. 1870.
Library of Congress

Later the Albany *Law Journal* published a review of the case. Matilda commented on the review in a newspaper article: "The Albany *Law Journal*," she said, "once advised Miss Anthony and ourself if we were not pleased with 'our laws,' that is, laws made by men, to leave the country, to exile ourselves. This legal journal does not even recognize woman's right of protest, but if for any reason, women are not pleased with '*our laws!*' they are bidden to leave the country. Under such a monstrous perversion of justice, . . . cannot all women say We are Without a Country?"[28]

12 ❋ To Us and Our Daughters Forever
1873–1876

"What is to be done with women?" Matilda asked.

> They will persist in being born. . . . The old heathen fashion was to bury the unwelcome female infants alive; throw them to the crocodiles, or expose them to die of cold and starvation. I am not quite sure but we had [better] return to these customs. It is quite certain they cannot all marry, and many who do marry are not only compelled to support themselves, but also a husband and children. We do not want to pay them good wages—we do not want them to govern themselves—in fact, we don't need them—so many of them, in the world, anyway. . . . There has been a mistake made somewhere, and I am quite sure it is in women's being born at all.[1]

Matilda's lifelong focus on working women set her apart from others in the movement, which was largely middle class and often elitist. She wanted justice for all. When a letter from Mr. M.S. Taylor appeared in the *Revolution*, opposing the vote for "negro wenches" (a racist slur), she replied, "Being on an equality with negro women now, in our equal deprivation with them of suffrage, we have hopes we could survive an equality with them in the ballot."[2]

Though Matilda, Elizabeth Cady Stanton, and Susan B. Anthony did not always agree, their common interests outweighed their differences. In the 1870s they exchanged roles as officers of the National Woman Suffrage Association.

"We had a good meeting," Anthony wrote to Isabella Beecher Hooker after an 1873 convention, "Mrs Stanton splendid—dear Mrs Mott—sweeter than ever—Mrs Gage excellent—the resolutions are hers mainly."[3]

Matilda's speech had included these words, which became her motto: "There is a word sweeter than mother, home, or heaven—that word is 'liberty.'"[4]

Later that year, on the centennial of the Boston Tea Party, Matilda announced a new plan of civil disobedience: tax resistance for women.[5] Across the country, women withheld tax payments in protest. Some even let the tax collectors sell their houses at public auction rather than pay what they considered an unfair tax.

In 1873 Matilda also published a brochure, "Who Planned the Tennessee Campaign of 1862," about Anna Ella Carroll. Carroll advised the North on a winning strategy during the Civil War. Matilda's booklet described Carroll's actions, explaining that President Lincoln and others in the federal government did not want people to know that a civilian, especially a woman civilian, had played a major role in winning the war.

Matilda's writing from this time also focused on another lifelong interest: the culture of American Indians who lived near her. The extent of her direct contact with them is unknown, but she attended their public events, such as fairs, and read books about their culture. Local newspapers, which Matilda always read, routinely covered American Indian events, including council proceedings and spiritual ceremonies.

In 1875 and 1876 Matilda wrote a series of articles for the New York *Evening Post* about the Haudenosaunees. This confederacy of six nations—Mohawk, Oneida, Onondaga, Cayuga, Seneca, and Tuscarora—also known by its French name, Iroquois, was based in upstate New York. Before the Revolutionary War, the Six Nations had controlled a large part what would become the northeastern United States. In Matilda's lifetime, the U.S. government tried to make the Haudenosaunees give up their land and customs. Some moved to Canada. Others moved to reservations further west, but many stayed in New York.

Matilda admired their form of government, the world's oldest participatory democracy. Like many historians, Matilda believed that the Haudenosaunee system had influenced the United States' founding fathers as they established a constitution and laws for a new nation. But the Haudenosaunees granted rights to women that the United States did not.

"The division of power between the sexes in this Indian republic was nearly equal," Matilda wrote. "Its women exercised controlling power in peace and war. . . . No sale of lands was valid without consent" of the women, while "the family relation among the Iroquois demonstrated woman's superiority in power . . . in the home, the wife was absolute. . . . If the Iroquois husband and wife separated, the wife took with her all the property she had brought. . . . The children also accompanied the mother, whose right to them was recognized as supreme. . . . Never was justice more perfect, never civilization higher."[6]

On May 12, 1875, Matilda was elected president of the National Woman Suffrage Association. During her yearlong term, the United States made plans to celebrate its hundredth birthday. A national ceremony would be held in Philadelphia, to coincide with a huge, six-month Centennial Exposition designed to attract millions of visitors to the city.

Belva Lockwood, c. 1870.
Library of Congress

National members planned for the centennial, too, during their January 1876 convention in Washington. Matilda shared the platform with lawyers Belva Lockwood and Phoebe Couzins; the Reverend Olympia Brown; Sara Andrews Spencer, co-owner of a business school in Washington; and Lillie Devereux Blake. Susan B. Anthony and Elizabeth Cady Stanton did not attend.

The convention received considerable newspaper coverage. On the second evening, police arrived to shut it down.

"Mrs. Gage . . . arose," reported the Washington *National Republican,* "and took her audience by surprise by saying that probably she would remain as a resident of the District of Columbia for some time. She understood that she was to be arrested for having dared to hold a convention without paying a license. The preamble of the Constitution granted free speech and the right of redress, but she was to be arrested for holding a woman's convention. The amount they wanted, she believed, was $5. She would not pay five cents."

"I shall remain in your District of Columbia jail," Matilda said, "where you can all come and see me. . . . I have a lawyer, one of my own sex, Squire Belva Lockwood, who will take the case in hand."[7]

"In adjourning the convention," the newspaper reported, "Mrs. Gage said that it would be adjourned until next January, unless she was held here in jail, in which case she would hold a convention constantly."[8]

The audience cheered. "We will be there!" someone yelled.[9]

The police gave up and left.

From Washington, Matilda went to Philadelphia to look for a headquarters for the National to rent for the summer. She tried, and failed, to get rooms in the Woman's Building at the Centennial Exposition. She asked to rent the hall where the first Continental Congress had met. Wherever she went, the answer was no.

Through winter mud and slush, Matilda kept looking. "The most abominable prices are asked for rooms," she wrote to Clarkson, "$100 a month for one *unfurnished* parlor. All the Philadelphia people expect to get rich and retire after this year."[10] Finally, deciding to try again later, she went home.

The National held its May 1876 convention in New York, electing Elizabeth Cady Stanton as president to succeed Matilda. As soon as the convention ended, Matilda, now chairman of the executive committee, and in charge of centennial activities,[11] went directly to Philadelphia to resume her hunt for rooms.

Finding a suitable place on Arch Street, she drew up a lease with the woman who owned it. But married women could not sign leases in Pennsylvania; the landlady's husband, who opposed women's rights, tore it up.[12]

When Matilda finally found a good apartment, she sent for Susan B. Anthony to come to Philadelphia, as she needed an unmarried woman to sign the contract for the National. While waiting, Matilda spent several days at the Centennial Exposition, writing to Clarkson of the wonders she had seen: models of Arizona cliff houses, a forty-foot wooden figure from Puget Sound, India rubber, a rhododendron annex, Japanese woodcarvings, British paintings, stuffed birds, and exquisite Bohemian glass, "delicate as a dream," from Austria and Hungary.[13]

Enjoyable though the exposition was, Matilda found it lacking in recognition of women's achievements. She sent letters to the editors of several newspapers, complaining that women had been overlooked in the

Centennial Exhibition opening, Philadelphia, May 10, 1876. *New York Public Library*

exhibition. She attached lists of women's inventions, including many on display that were mistakenly credited to men.[14]

Susan B. Anthony took her time in coming. As days passed, Matilda worried that she was outstaying her welcome at a friend's home. She was also running short on money. "I was compelled to stay in N.Y. much longer than was best," she wrote to Clarkson, "and now here, owing to Susan Anthony's *stupid* method of doing business."[15]

Finally Anthony arrived and signed the rental agreement, making herself financially responsible for the rooms. But Matilda, Anthony, and Elizabeth Cady Stanton had developed a plan to fund their headquarters: they would write a history of woman suffrage. When this pamphlet of several hundred pages was published, they would send a free copy to anyone who donated five dollars to help with centennial expenses. Fifty-two women responded quickly to this offer, enabling them to rent the apartment that Matilda had found.[16]

On May 25, 1876, Matilda and Anthony took charge of the large, first-floor rooms at 1431 Chestnut Street in Philadelphia's fashionable West End. The suite included sleeping rooms where the officers could stay. The ladies stocked their public parlors with books, speeches, posters, cartoons, photographs of famous women, and a centennial autograph book for supporters to sign. They posted mottos on the walls: "Rebellion is the justice of slaves" from Matilda and "Call no man master" from Lucretia Mott.[17] When the headquarters opened on June 1, a flag floated from the window, a white banner with a blue border and blue letters spelling out "National Woman Suffrage Association."[18] Visitors flocked in.

By then Matilda was involved in a new issue involving another of her favorite causes, the separation of church and state. Liberals like her campaigned to have the Centennial Exposition open on Sundays so that working people could attend on their only day off from work. Opponents wanted a legislated day of rest, with Sunday meetings restricted to religious events. Matilda's side won the battle, but when the first Sunday opening was announced, protests grew so extreme that some liberals feared mob violence.

"I want you to bring my revolver and cartridges," Matilda wrote to Clarkson, who was planning to visit her; "have them serviced first. . . . We might be attacked. . . . This question of opening the Exposition on Sunday, is part of the great religious questions of the age."[19]

Whether he brought the gun is unknown, but Clarkson arrived in Philadelphia just as Matilda finished writing the National's address to the Republican National Convention. Mother and son set off for the exposition, and while they were gone, Susan B. Anthony sent copies of the address to the press, signing her own name to it.

When Matilda found out, she was furious. "Have you seen the N.Y. papers?" she wrote later to Clarkson. "Not only is *her* name attached, but *hers alone*. Just think how I am cheated out of my reputation, and this summer's chances."[20] Matilda's income came largely from lecturing. She needed to keep her name before the public.

"This address to the Rep party is mine entirely, every phrase, word, etc.,"[21] she assured Clarkson, reminding him of an earlier occasion when her name had been omitted from a published address that was then credited to Anthony. "It is very queer," Matilda complained, "when

CENTENNIAL HEADQUARTERS

National Woman Suffrage Association,

1431 CHESTNUT STREET.

Pres., ELIZABETH CADY STANTON, N. J.
First Vice-Pres., LUCRETIA MOTT, Pa.
Chair. Ex. Com., MATILDA JOSLYN GAGE, N. Y.
Cor. Sec'y, SUSAN B. ANTHONY, N. Y.

Philadelphia, Pa., *June 12th* 1876

Mr Boyles
    Dear Cousin

        The bearer — Mr
Clarkson Gage — is the
son of my friend Mrs
Matilda Joslyn Gage — and
is seeking employment
in the West — His father
is a merchant — & Mr Gage
has been reared in that
business — is an upright

Susan B. Anthony's request that her cousin help Clarkson Gage
find employment in the West, 1876. *Rochester Public Library*

Susan Anthony *writes nothing*, that she has the credit of writing everything and that as speaker or writer, I get no credit. What is the reason?"[22]

Later she wrote to her son: "I wish I could forget this incalculable injury to me, but it haunts my every night and disturbs my sleep. I try in vain to banish it but it is *too dreadful*. . . . Mrs Stanton says I have not enough *self-assertion* [to confront Anthony]."[23]

Stanton arrived in Philadelphia on June 16. She and Matilda, the National's two primary authors, were writing the "Woman's Declaration of Rights and Articles of Impeachment Against the Government of the United States." Each wrote a separate draft, then they combined the two versions.[24] But one part of the document remained entirely Matilda's: her "Five Principles of Just Governments," taken from the speech she had given before Susan B. Anthony's trial:

> *First.* The natural right of each individual to self-government.
> *Second.* The exact equality of these rights.
> *Third.* That these rights when not delegated by the individual, are retained by the individual.
> *Fourth.* That no person can exercise these rights of others without delegated authority.
> *Fifth.* That the non-use of these rights does not destroy them.[25]

The declaration ended with words written jointly by Matilda Joslyn Gage and Elizabeth Cady Stanton: "We ask of our rulers, at this hour, no special favors, no special privileges, no special legislation. We ask justice, we ask equality, we ask that all the civil and political rights that belong to citizens of the United States, be guaranteed to us and our daughters forever."[26]

The declaration was signed by all the National's senior leaders, including Matilda, and by hundreds of other women, including ninety-four African American women from the District of Columbia. Sara Andrews Spencer "handsomely engrossed" a copy onto a three-foot wide piece of parchment. Rolled and tied with colorful ribbons, this was the document that Matilda and her friends would deliver to the centennial ceremony on behalf of all American women.

13 ✳ A Hundred Years Hence JULY 1876

After presenting their scroll at Independence Hall, Matilda and her colleagues walked seven hot blocks to Philadelphia's First Unitarian Church. The building, which they had rented for the afternoon, was packed. A large, mostly female, audience saluted their entrance and their achievement with applause.

Matilda collapsed. "The heat and the exciting scenes in which I participated," she wrote later to Clarkson, "gave me an attack of prostration at the meeting in the church. I was treated with wine, raw egg, cold water on my head, &c &c."[1] She revived quickly.

Lucretia Mott, age eighty-four, opened the centennial meeting of the National Woman Suffrage Association. As she climbed the long winding staircase into the old-fashioned, octagonal pulpit, she told the crowd, "I climb this pulpit, not because I am of lofty mind, but because I am short of stature that you might see me." As her face appeared in the pulpit, the Hutchinsons, a well-known family singing group, sang the hymn "Nearer, My God, to Thee," and the audience stood and spontaneously joined in.[2]

Mott was followed by Elizabeth Cady Stanton, whose voice choked with emotion as she read the "Woman's Declaration of Rights" that she and Matilda had written.

Belva Lockwood said that the old fathers of 1776 had declared that all persons were made free and equal. She asked whether women were not persons.

Matilda's topic was habeas corpus, a right of United States citizens. The term, Latin for "that you have the body," refers to the requirement

Hutchinson Family Singers, c. 1881.
Library of Congress

that a prisoner must be brought before a court to determine if there is a reason for the prisoner to be detained. This right, guaranteed by the Constitution, was often suspended in the case of married women, whose husbands could imprison them or have them admitted to "insane asylums" at will.

Lucretia Mott reviewed the history of the movement. After Mott, Lillie Devereux Blake protested the idea that women could not fulfill the duties of citizenship, and Susan B. Anthony described her arrest, trial, and conviction for voting.

"Pretty Phoebe W. Cozzens [*sic*]," as one newspaper described her, "made a sparkling speech," asking the audience to contribute money to the cause of her sister-suffragists. "The little lady raised $150 on the spot," said the paper, "and paid it into the treasury. What a campaigner she would make!"[3]

Judge Esther Morris of Wyoming told how that territory had granted women the right to vote.

The Hutchinsons closed with a song, "A Hundred Years Hence." It began:

Mrs. W. S. Sonnesberger of Sheridan, Wyoming, who voted legally in Wyoming, c. 1870. *Wyoming State Archives*

One hundred years hence, what a change will be made,
In politics, morals, religion and trade,
In statesmen who wrangle or ride on the fence,
These things will be altered a hundred years hence.

The fourth verse addressed the women's movement:

Then woman, man's partner, man's equal will stand,
While beauty and harmony govern the land;
To think for one's self will be no offense,
The world will be thinking a hundred years hence.[4]

"My darling son," Matilda wrote to Clarkson on July 6, "We had the most enthusiastic, grandest meeting of all these years, holding nearly five consecutive hours. Mrs Parker, an English liberal from Manchester said ours was the historic meeting of the day and the historians of a hundred years hence would seek every incident connected with it and the portraits of the women on that platform would be sought for the next hundredth celebration."

"But my greatest shock came last night," Matilda told Clarkson, "when Maud failed to come at the hour she and your father had telegraphed she would be here."[5]

Matilda's older daughters had already arrived in Philadelphia on July 5 when Maud went missing. Helen, age thirty, was a school principal, and Julia, twenty-five, was a teacher. Maud, a fifteen-year-old high school student, was to join them in Philadelphia, traveling alone by train. When she did not come as expected, Matilda, Helen, and Julia split up to look for her, each going to a different railroad station.

"I nearly died on the spot," Matilda wrote to Clarkson. She knew that young girls were sometimes kidnapped and forced into prostitution.

"I got up to the depot with great difficulty," she said, "I was unable to move . . . thought she had been carried off, or enticed away, when she came in . . . with a conductor. My heart was relieved but the terrible physical prostration still continued, and I had to take wine again, lie down &c &c."[6]

Regaining her strength, Matilda stayed in Philadelphia long enough to enjoy her daughters' visits and to read about the results of her work.

"Tea, with speeches, was a daily function," said one newspaper report of the headquarters, "and a crowd of strangers, many from Europe, came every afternoon to meet and to listen to the women who had made the militant demonstration of July 4th."[7]

Reactions to the protest varied. The editor of the New York *Semi-Weekly Tribune* called the episode "ominous,"[8] stating: "The demand of Miss Anthony and Mrs. Gage to be allowed to take part in a commemoration which they and their associates discouraged and denounced, would have been a cool proceeding had it been made in advance. [It had been.] Made as it was, by a very discourteous interruption, it prefigures new forms of violence and disregard of order which may accompany the participation of women in active partisan politics."[9]

Another newspaper said, "It is good to be zealously affected in a good cause, but this piece of ill-mannered sensationalism was only calculated to excite disgust."[10]

The *New York Times* summarized the declaration, quoting Matilda's five principles. Of the church meeting, the *Times* said, "The building

was thronged by a large audience, composed almost entirely of women; and the enthusiasm of the audience was certainly a striking indication of the heartiness of the endorsement of the reform."[11]

Matilda saved another article, which she labeled "Times." It said: "We notice a disposition among the men to waive discussion and await the progress of events. And if events march on in the same direction for another hundred years, the Woman's Declaration of Independence which shall be handed up to the presiding officer at the bi-centennial celebration will be read by her to the assembled stateswomen and ratified without a call for the nays."[12]

Elizabeth Cady Stanton, c. 1875.
Cornell University Library

14 ✴ The *History of Woman Suffrage* 1876–1878

Susan B. Anthony does not write, you know," Matilda wrote to a friend, "She says so, again and again, and it is true. Her forte is letters—nothing otherwise, but she is a good suggestor, critic, etc., looks over letters, reads proof, attends to the publishers, etc., is general factotum while Mrs. Stanton and myself do the writing."[1]

Although Matilda was still angry that Anthony had taken credit for her work, she decided to move forward with their next joint project. For years Matilda, Anthony, and Elizabeth Cady Stanton had been saving documents and letters, intending to write an account of their struggle. With the centennial behind them, they began compiling the *History of Woman Suffrage.*

"Mrs Gage has a wonderful file of facts and data," Anthony wrote to a friend after staying with Matilda in Fayetteville, "which she can produce in right time and place—invalid, though she has been, so much of the time—her accumulations of everything pertaining to our movement are wonderful."[2]

Matilda kept her files at home, but Anthony shipped trunks and boxes of records to Stanton, who now lived in Tenafly, New Jersey. Although they all needed money from lecturing, Anthony asked Stanton to decline speaking engagements for the fall of 1876 to clear time for them to work on the book.[3]

Tenafly, on "the blue hills of Jersey," was a wealthy suburb of New York.[4] Matilda and Anthony met there at Stanton's stately white two-story house in a large sunny room with an immense bay window, hardwood floor, and open fire.[5]

On November 15, having completed six chapters, they signed a contract: "Elizabeth Cady Stanton and the said Matilda Joslyn Gage shall write, collect, select and arrange the material for said History, and the said Susan B Anthony shall as her part of the work, and as an equivalent for the work done [by Stanton and Gage would] secure the publication of said work by and through some competent publishing house. . . . Profits of the History, if there shall be any, shall be equally divided between the said parties, share and share alike."[6]

Matilda wanted the book to include firsthand accounts from women in the movement. Anthony, as business manager, began contacting some who might prove helpful. Lucy Stone refused to provide information about the American or even about herself ("Your 'wing' surely are not competent to write the history of 'our wing,'" she wrote), but others responded enthusiastically.[7] Soon each day's mail brought new information, which they used to create a new kind of history.

"Many who study the past with interest," Matilda and Stanton wrote, "and see the importance of seeming trifles in helping forward great events, often fail to understand some of the best pages of history made under their own eyes. Hence the woman suffrage movement has not yet been accepted as the legitimate outgrowth of American ideas—a component part of the history of our republic—but is falsely considered the willful outburst of a few unbalanced minds, whose ideas can never be realized under any form of government."[8]

While the other two wrote, Anthony fact-checked and made handwritten copies of the manuscript. She collected photographs, too, so that the book could include pictures of the movement's pioneers, though steel engravings needed to print the portraits, were costly—$126 each.[9]

As they worked on the *History*, the women also sent out thousands of appeals for a Sixteenth Amendment that would give women the right to vote. Ten thousand people in twenty-six states signed petitions supporting the idea and mailed them to Washington, where Sara Andrews Spencer organized them.[10]

The National's January 1877 Washington convention attracted more than 1,500 people, including senators and representatives. Matilda gave a speech there called "Republican Outrages against Women."[11]

After this convention, Matilda summoned her confidence to confront Susan B. Anthony, either for publishing Matilda's work under her name or for some more recent problem. As the women closed their offices in

Washington, preparing to go home, Anthony tried to kiss Matilda good-bye, as usual.

"Mrs Gage did not return my kiss," Anthony wrote in her diary, "but turned her cheek."[12]

Two months later Anthony noted in her diary that she had written a long letter to Matilda, "trying to soothe her suspicions that I have not always been *just* to her in bringing her to the front—or trying to—She is a dear, good woman—but desperately misanthropic—distrusts everybody's loyalty to her and the truth."[13]

By 1877 the Supreme Court had ruled that states could deny or grant voting rights. Matilda thought that voting rights should be under federal control and that, in many cases, they already were. She learned that through the Amnesty Act of 1872 and individual acts of Congress, the federal government had restored voting rights to almost five thousand Southern men who had formerly been considered traitors to the Union. Matilda's research revealed that another group, 2,500 criminals convicted of breaking civil laws, had also petitioned Congress in the past five years, successfully regaining the right to vote.[14]

Why, Matilda asked, if the government could refranchise traitors and criminals, could it not also give loyal women the vote? At her request, her congressman introduced "an act to relieve the political disabilities of Matilda Joslyn Gage."[15]

The National Woman Suffrage Association adopted Matilda's strategy, distributing printed forms to women across the country. In an effort that brought good press coverage, hundreds of women petitioned to be granted the same rights as former criminals and traitors. No one on either side of the argument seemed to doubt that Congress had the right to grant the requests, but the bills, including Matilda's, always failed.[16]

In January 1878 Matilda returned to Washington for another convention of the National Woman Suffrage Association. Dr. Clemence S. Lozier, the National's president and a woman gynecologist from New York, presided as delegates discussed an international exhibition being planned for Paris. The United States intended to send only male representatives, but Belva Lockwood asked Lozier to appoint a committee of intelligent women to be commissioners to the exposition. Lozier chose five, including Lockwood and Matilda, to correct the situation.

As Matilda wrote later, the committee "at once repaired to the white-house, where they were pleasantly received by President [Rutherford B.]

President Rutherford B. Hayes, c. 1875. Matilda met with him three times at the White House. *Library of Congress*

Hayes."[17] They suggested to the president that he nominate women commissioners, saying that women might be more suitable to report on industries like laces and embroideries.

"But, ladies, you are too late," he said, according to a report Matilda wrote for a newspaper. "You should have petitioned Congress a year ago; these appointments have been settled a long time."[18]

But later, Matilda wrote in the *History of Woman Suffrage*, "after learning the object of their visit, the president looked up the different classes of industries for which no commissioners had been appointed, asked the ladies to nominate their candidates, and assured them he would favor a representation by women."[19] It is possible that President Hayes did both things.

On January 10, 1878, Senator A. A. Sargent of California introduced, for the first time ever, a joint resolution in Congress to pass a Sixteenth Amendment that said, "The right of citizens of the United States to vote shall not be denied or abridged by the United States or by any State on account of sex." The National tried to get Congress to allow a few of its members to "plead for their own freedom," but neither the Senate nor the House of Representatives would permit the women to speak.[20]

The Washington *Union* wrote: "To allow the advocates of woman suffrage to plead their cause on the floor of the Senate . . . would be a decided innovation upon the established usages of parliamentary bodies. If the privilege were granted in this case it would next be claimed by the friends and the enemies of the silver bill, by the supporters and opponents of resumption, by hard money men and soft money men, by protectionists and free-traders, by labor-reformers, prohibitionists and the Lord knows whom besides."[21] In fact, two women who opposed the amendment had already been allowed to address the Senate, and soon after denying the National's request, the House allowed Charles Stew-

Elizabeth Cady Stanton addressing the Senate Committee on Privileges and Elections, January 16, 1878. Matilda (not shown) also testified.
Library of Congress

art Parnell to take the floor, "that he might plead the case of oppressed Ireland."[22]

The resolution was referred to the Senate Committee on Privileges and Elections, which did allow the National's representatives to comment. Matilda, with eleven other women, spoke at the committee hearing.

"Our demands are often met by the most intolerable tyranny," she said, noting that she had once been advised to leave the country if she did not like the laws. She continued:

It is our country, and we shall stay here and change the laws. We shall secure their amendment, so that under them there shall be the exact and permanent political equality between men and women. Change is not only a law of life; it is an essential proof of the existence of life. This country has attained its greatness by ever enlarging the bounds of freedom.

In our hearts we feel that there is a word sweeter than mother, home, or heaven. That word is LIBERTY. We ask it of you now. We say to you, secure us this liberty—the same liberty you have yourselves. In doing this you will not render yourselves poor, but will make us rich indeed.[23]

Although the committee recommended that the amendment be postponed, the idea was catching on. The Washington *Evening Star* said, "The woman suffrage question will be a great political issue some-day. . . . It cannot fail in time to be weighed as a matter of policy. . . . This question is of a nature to become a living political issue after it has been sufficiently ridiculed."[24]

15 ❋ The *National Citizen and Ballot Box*
1878–1880

I n April 1878 Matilda bought an Ohio women's suffrage newspaper, the *Ballot Box*. After moving it to Syracuse, she renamed it the *National Citizen and Ballot Box*.

As editor and publisher, Matilda did most of the writing, but Elizabeth Cady Stanton and Susan B. Anthony, as corresponding editors, wrote many letters to the paper, which soon became the official newspaper of the National Woman Suffrage Association. For some time, Sara Andrews Spencer contributed a column from Washington.

The monthly publication, "the cheapest paper in the country, $1 a year," offered three and a half pages of news and a half page of advertisements. Matilda inherited two thousand subscribers.[1]

The National Citizen published letters and firsthand accounts of women's experiences. Editorials offered a feminist perspective on marriage customs, rape, labor laws, taxes, the status of women in foreign countries, and the church. Matilda wrote a column, "Women, Past and Present," and covered conventions extensively, knowing that many of her readers could not afford to attend. She printed selections from the *History of Woman Suffrage* as they were completed, asking readers to send in corrections.

Suffering often from poor health, Matilda kept working on the *History* and wrote for other publications, too, including a newspaper in San Francisco. When six young girls were arrested for streetwalking in Fayetteville, she protested to the local newspaper. Two of the girls were just fifteen; the men who had hired them were "village respectables"

A page from *The National Citizen and Ballot Box.*

who were not named in court or charged. As usual, Matilda's opinion was more liberal than that of her colleagues. She viewed prostitution as an economic rather than a moral issue, the product of unjust labor laws and the lack of education for women.[2]

"Women of every class, condition, rank and name, will find this paper their friend, it matters not how wretched, degraded, fallen they may be," she said on the front page of each issue of the *National Citizen and Ballot Box.*

In her paper she described a mother of ten who was jailed for stealing food for her children and a man who got a shorter sentence for beating his wife than he would have received for beating a horse (six months for a wife, two years for a horse).[3] She reported on women living collectively and starting cooperative businesses, and she advocated for boarding houses for working women. Leaders of the women's movement who fought to open universities and professions to women took less interest than Matilda in the rights of female factory workers, but the *National Citizen* fought for these women, too.

The paper was not completely serious. One article told of a Russian sect that required husbands to confess sins to wives once a week.

"Would not that require the whole week?" Matilda asked.[4]

Matilda, like other feminists, was often called a man-hater. The Vineland *Times*, a New Jersey paper, criticized the *National Citizen*: "It is too aggressive, and too bitter against men."

"As to 'aggressiveness,'" Matilda responded, "bless your soul, that is the way to carry on a warfare."[5]

The paper gave Matilda a new forum in which to promote the American Indian society she admired. In May 1878 the United States was trying to force citizenship on native people, who were fighting it.

"Our Indians are in reality foreign powers," Matilda wrote, "though living among us. With them our country not only has treaty obligations, but pays them, or professes to, annual sums in consideration of such treaties. . . . Compelling them to become citizens would be like the forcible annexation of Cuba, Mexico, or Canada to our government, and as unjust."[6]

In July Matilda traveled to Rochester, New York, for the thirtieth anniversary celebration of the Seneca Falls convention. The convention call said that the meeting would be "largely devoted to reminiscences." Rochester, known as "The Flower City," provided beautiful floral decorations for the meeting in the Unitarian church on Fitzhugh Street.[7] Some blossoms drooped in record high temperatures as old friends greeted each other happily, with damp hugs. Fans fluttered and cooling liquids were offered as people gathered under

Matilda, 1880. *Gage Foundation*

"twining wreaths, running through the low, wire lattice, about the platform, and in hanging clusters of vines from the chandeliers."[8]

Elizabeth Cady Stanton spoke of progress made in the women's movement and goals still to be achieved. Letters and telegrams from across the country and from Europe, were read aloud. William Lloyd Garrison, who had broken with the National over women's suffrage after the Civil War, now sent warm congratulations "on the cheering progress which the movement has made."[9] Even Lucy Stone sent her best wishes. Lucretia Mott expressed joy at the number of young women sitting on the platform for the first time.

"Though in her eighty-sixth year," the *History of Woman Suffrage* later described Mott, "her enthusiasm for the cause for which she had so long labored seemed still unabated, and her eye sparkled with humor as of yore while giving some amusing reminiscences of encounters with opponents in the early days."[10]

Mott yielded the podium to Matilda, watching eagerly as her former

protégée proposed a series of resolutions. Three of these, written by Matilda herself, became particularly controversial:

> *Resolved*, That as the duty of every individual is self-development, the lessons self-sacrifice and obedience taught women by the Christian church have been fatal, not only to her own highest interests, but through her have also dwarfed and degraded the race.
>
> *Resolved*, That the fundamental principle of the Protestant reformation, the right of individual conscience and judgment in the interpretation of scripture, heretofore conceded to and exercised by man alone, should now be claimed by woman, and in her most vital interests she should no longer trust authority, but be guided by her own reason.
>
> *Resolved*, That it is through the perversion of the religious element in woman, cultivating the emotions at the expense of her reason, playing upon her hopes and fears of the future, holding this life with all its high duties forever in abeyance to that which is to come, that she, and the children she has trained, have been so completely subjugated by priestcraft and superstition.[11]

Then Matilda, along with everyone in the hot, crowded church, listened sadly as Lucretia Mott gave what all knew would be her last speech. Her family had tried to stop her from attending the convention, worried that the trip from Philadelphia in such extreme heat would prove too much for her. But she had insisted on coming, traveling with a friend, and staying in Rochester with her husband's nephew, a doctor.

The doctor, fearing that she would be exhausted, called for her to stop before she had finished her closing remarks. Climbing down from the platform, Mott continued speaking as she walked down the aisle, swinging her bonnet by one string, as she often did,[12] and shaking hands on either side. The audience rose simultaneously, out of respect for her.

"Good-by, dear Lucretia!" Frederick Douglass called, speaking for all of them.[13]

After the convention, Matilda's resolutions created a second heat wave in newspapers and pulpits around the country.

"There was never a clearer illustration," said the *New York World*, "of the evil tendencies of the Woman's Rights movement than in the resolutions adopted at the Rochester convention."[14]

"Too hazardous," proclaimed the Reverend A. H. Strong, president of the Baptist Theological Seminary in Rochester. "Bad women would vote."

"Well, what of it?" Matilda responded, in a *National Citizen and Ballot Box* editorial, "Have they not equal right with bad men to self-government?"[15]

Members of both women's suffrage organizations, the National and the American, complained about the antireligious nature of Matilda's ideas. Matilda saw the vote as a tool that could be used to remove other injustices to women. Worried that by increasingly focusing on suffrage and only suffrage, women's rights organizations had "ceased to be progressive,"[16] she turned to a group that she and her husband Henry admired, the Freethinkers. Freethinkers believed that truth should be based on knowledge and wisdom and prided themselves on forming opinions based on fact, scientific inquiry, and logic. This secular movement reached its height in the United States between 1860 and 1900, when new scientific discoveries contradicted traditional religious beliefs.

On August 24, 1878, Matilda spoke at a Freethought Convention in Watkins (later Watkins Glen), New York, eighty-five miles southwest of Fayetteville. The group met in a large tent in a beautiful park. Earlier on the day Matilda spoke, a woman had been arrested at the convention for selling a pamphlet called "Cupid's Yokes."[17] This free love document said that marriage was nothing more than a social contract that made a woman "a prostitute for life."[18]

"Ladies and Gentlemen," Matilda began her speech:

> You have seen a great deal of excitement here this afternoon, especially intensified by the fact that a woman was arrested and taken to a town jail because she dared to sell certain literature. Do you know that every woman here who chances to be a married woman has the same danger of arrest if she dare to claim her child for her own? It is a fact. But lately, in a Western State, a mother was imprisoned in the county jail because she dared to take her own child into her possession. Now if any one thing is more evident than another, it is that the mother has a natural right to her own child—the child to which she has given birth. It is a fact that God has given that child directly into the mother's care; has made it dependent upon her after its birth for nourishment for months. Yet what is the condition of this State, and almost all the States in the Union? A mother has no right to her own children except under the direction of the father.[19]

Matilda blamed the Christian church for this inequity, "based upon the fact of woman servitude; upon the theory that woman brought sin and death into the world, and that therefore she was punished by being placed in a condition of inferiority to man—a condition of subjection, of subordination. This is the foundation to-day of the Christian Church."[20]

The New York *Herald* wrote of Matilda at this convention: "She looks anything but a reformer . . . more like a loving grandmother with a room full of grandchildren. She was dressed in black velvet, with passamenterie lace and silk trimming. Her plentiful white hair was combed into a great bunch at the back of her head. She constantly played with a fan during her speech."[21]

January 1879 found Matilda in Washington, D.C., at a National convention. Afterwards President Rutherford B. Hayes received a committee from the convention at the White House. As chair, Matilda read aloud their formal request for Hayes to mention "disfranchised millions of wives, mothers, and daughters of this republic" in his next national address.[22]

"The president invited the ladies into the library," reported the *History of Woman Suffrage*, "that they might be secure from interruption, and gave them throughout a most respectful and courteous hearing." Though Hayes promised sincere consideration of the request, nothing came of it.[23]

That same year Congress passed the Lockwood Bill, allowing women lawyers to practice before the U.S. Supreme Court. When Belva Lockwood was formally admitted, the National sent large baskets of flowers to the three senators who had championed the bill.[24]

In 1879 Matilda celebrated the Fourth of July by decorating the outside of her house in red, white, and blue. Over this she draped black bunting, signifying mourning, and posted a sign: "GOVERNMENTS DERIVE THEIR JUST POWERS FROM THE CONSENT OF THE GOVERNED. THE BALLOT IS THE METHOD OF CONSENT. WOMAN HAS NOT CONSENTED."

Neighbors stopped to look. "All right," said some who knew her, and "Glad to see you thus presenting your principles." Children and strangers asked her what she meant.[25]

In December 1879 President Hayes met with the National's presidential committee. Matilda was the committee chairman. They were received, she said, "with infinite courtesy and 'chivalry'—the courtesy and 'chivalry' that Americans pride themselves upon showing to women. They were invited to an audience in the President's private apartment—were attentively listened to—Mrs. Hayes sent for and introduced; they received all that little, meaningless attention which, giving women, men think they have given them their due—and that was all."

For this behavior, she wrote in the *National Citizen and Ballot Box*, "We arraign President Hayes before the bar of eternal justice and a jury of his country-women pronounced him guilty."[26]

In the summer of 1880 Matilda traveled west to present the National's views on woman suffrage to the nominating committees of three political conventions—Republican, Democratic, and Greenback (a farmer-labor third party)—who were all meeting in Chicago.

The July edition of the *National Citizen and Ballot Box* summarized the positions of the major candidates. James A. Garfield, the Republican, was "not convinced" of the need for woman suffrage.

"We are 'not convinced,'" Matilda editorialized, "that he is fit for president."

James B. Weaver, the Greenback candidate, was said to be a woman suffragist, but he did not mention the fact in his platform. For the Democrats, General Winfield Scott Hancock was supposedly writing a letter stating his position.

"Gen. Hancock, lacking either time or brains will not have his letter ready in a fortnight yet," Matilda wrote, "but being a species of political prophet, we need not wait to see it."[27]

16 ✴ Fayetteville's First Woman Voter 1880–1881

"When men begin to *fear* the power of women," Matilda said in the *National Citizen and Ballot Box*, "their voice and their influence, then we shall secure justice, but not before. When we demonstrate our ability to kill off, or seriously injure a candidate, or hurt a party, then we shall receive 'respectful consideration.' . . . We must be recognized as *aggressive*."[1]

In the same way that she swapped offices with Elizabeth Cady Stanton and Susan B. Anthony in the National Woman Suffrage Association, Matilda traded roles in the New York State Woman Suffrage Association with her friend Lillie Devereux Blake. Each served as association president during a four-year campaign to unseat the incumbent governor of New York.

In 1876 the New York State Legislature had passed a bill allowing women to run for school boards. When Governor Lucius Robinson refused to sign it, believing that "the God of Nature did not intend women for public life," Matilda and Blake vowed to retire him from public life.[2]

"Thousands and tens of thousands of the Woman's Protests were circulated," Matilda wrote, "sent to every newspaper in the state . . . widely distributed at political meetings . . . handed to passengers over the ferries most traversed, placed in manufactories and workshops where many hands were employed, in woman's clubs, in religious and temperance meetings, while privately the work was unceasing."[3]

Their effort paid off. The newly elected governor, Alonzo B. Cornell, asked the legislature to pass a bill allowing women to serve on school boards and also permitting women property owners to vote in school board elections. He signed the bill on February 12, 1880.[4]

Matilda sent articles about the law to newspapers throughout New York. She gave sample answers for women to use if questioned by voting inspectors, and she organized meetings to educate women voters. To honor her, Matilda's friends and neighbors asked her to be Fayetteville's first woman voter.

On election day, nine carriages assigned to different parts of the village took women to the polls.[5] "The Inspectors were at first disposed to be very curt and cranky," Matilda wrote later, "challenging frequently, and refusing woman a place at their table."[6] Matilda insisted on sitting with the inspectors, and three other ladies stood by to help if needed. Their strategy worked; of the 102 women who came to the polls, none was turned away. For four school board positions, three women candidates prevailed, including Matilda's oldest daughter, Helen.

Lillie Devereux Blake, Matilda's closest friend, as seen in the *History of Woman Suffrage*, vol. 3, 1886. *Library of Congress*

"To myself," Matilda wrote later, "it was in many respects the most gratifying day of my life."[7]

Her joy was moderated by the sad news that Lucretia Mott had died at the age of eighty-eight. That same year, Elizabeth Cady Stanton, age sixty-five, retired from her strenuous schedule as a touring lecturer, though she continued to speak at selected conventions. Susan B. Anthony, then sixty, and Matilda Joslyn Gage, fifty-four, became the movement's senior leaders.

On November 18, 1880, Anthony sent Matilda a printed call for an upcoming convention, enclosed in a letter:

My Dear Mrs. Gage

I beg a thousand pardons of you for not thinking to ask you to sign the enclosed Call, indeed I have found it very difficult to *think* of *those* I *most ought to*—But do attend the Convention—the object you see is practical—I am very, very sorry I did not write you sooner....

Your[s] full of hope in the great
Cause—it thrives gloriously—
Susan B. Anthony[8]

Matilda must have accepted the apology because they were soon back in Tenafly, working on the *History of Woman Suffrage*. Elizabeth Cady Stanton later wrote:

The arrival of Miss Anthony and Mrs. Gage, on November 20, banished all family matters from my mind. What planning now, for volumes, chapters, footnotes, margins, appendices, paper, and type; of engravings, title, preface, and introduction! I had never thought that the publication of a book required the consideration of such endless details. We stood appalled before the mass of material, growing higher and higher with every mail, and the thought of all the reading involved made us feel as if our lifework lay before us. Six weeks of steady labor all day, and often until midnight, made no visible decrease in the pile of documents. However, before the end of the month we had our arrangements all made with publishers and engravers, and six chapters in print.[9]

But in Tenafly, Matilda again felt overlooked when she found out that Stanton and Anthony had omitted to give her credit for their current project. A reporter had come to interview the authors of a *History of Woman Suffrage*, she learned. The reporter, she wrote to a friend in December, "called over before I went down [to Tenafly], and they [Stanton and Anthony] coolly appropriated the entire history to themselves, never hinting towards me. Consequently only Mrs. Stanton and Miss Anthony were put in as its editors, and from the Herald it was copied and went to France in a paper—with myself left out. I feel such things and they wrong me."

Nevertheless she continued to work on the book. "In my bay window," she wrote from Fayetteville, "stands a table from my library and a stand and two chairs, all covered with books and papers. I say nothing of books, papers and boxes . . . on the floor. It is confusion, but out of it grows a history chapter."[10]

Matilda kept her displeasure with Susan B. Anthony and Elizabeth Cady Stanton private; the three women remained supportive of each other in public. They praised one another in the *National Citizen and Ballot Box*, but still the newspaper caused problems for Matilda. Even though its number of subscribers had more than doubled, to 4,300, it did not earn a profit.[11] She supplemented it when she could, paying for extra pages from her own pocket.

Usually each issue contained an editorial by Matilda, but not in April 1881—she was too busy to write one. In its place, a letter from Susan B. Anthony offered wedding greetings to Matilda's eldest daughter.

On April 21, school board member Helen Leslie Gage, age thirty-five, married Charles Henry Gage, called Charly, a distant cousin, at the Gage home in Fayetteville. Fashionable weddings usually took place in the evening, an inconvenient time for guests who needed to catch trains home. So for the afternoon ceremony, the windows were covered and the inside of the house was lit to make it seem like night.[12]

Matilda and Henry liked Charly, a businessman, though they were somewhat concerned about his advanced age—he was six years older than Matilda. Matilda felt close to tears as the couple departed—until Charly called out "Good bye, Mother!" giving everyone a good laugh.[13]

In May Matilda went on a speaking tour of New England with Susan B. Anthony and other National representatives. The *Hartford Courant* said, "The number of thoughtful, cultured young women appearing in these conventions, is one of the hopeful features for the success of the movement."[14]

The increasing number of young women resulted from a plan by Matilda, Stanton, and Anthony to involve a new generation in their organization. Stanton, they decided, would retain the ceremonial office of president. Matilda and Anthony remained vice presidents at large, but Matilda retired as chair of the executive committee. That office and the position of corresponding secretary were filled by "Susan's nieces," the nickname for young women in the movement who were particularly loyal to Anthony. The relationship between Matilda and Anthony deteriorated as Anthony increasingly favored her young associates.

At this same time, Anthony grew closer to a friend she had met five years earlier, Frances E. Willard, president of the Woman's Christian Temperance Union (WCTU). Anthony, who had begun her activism in the temperance movement, still believed in the cause. The WCTU, along with other conservative organizations, wanted Congress to declare Christianity the United States' official faith. They advocated for religious instruction in public schools. Matilda and Stanton opposed these goals and thus the organization, but Anthony wanted allies, even imperfect ones, to join them in their struggle for women's suffrage.

Despite their differences, the three women respected each other, especially as the first volume of the *History of Woman Suffrage* was published in May 1881. The 878-page book, covering the period from 1848 to 1861, sold for five dollars apiece. The preface thanked those who responded to requests for information to be included in the book.

"A few have replied," the preface said. "'It is too early to write the history of this movement; wait until our object is attained; the actors themselves can not write an impartial history; they have had their discords, divisions, personal hostilities, that unfit them for the work.' Viewing the enfranchisement of woman as the most important demand of the century, we have felt no temptation to linger over individual differences. These occur in all associations, and may be regarded in this case as an evidence of the growing self-assertion and individualism in woman."[15]

The introduction began with these words: "The prolonged slavery of woman is the darkest page in human history."[16] In the first chapter, "Preceding Causes," Matilda summarized women's accomplishments throughout history, describing ninety-three women, from powerful rulers like Queen Elizabeth I of England, to Bridget Graffort, who in 1700 donated land for the first public school in the United States, only to find that girls were denied admission.

Matilda also wrote a chapter on "Woman in Newspapers," and her chapter on "Woman, Church, and State" closed the book with a scathing analysis of how the church, supported by the state, oppressed women. Matilda argued that women had more power in pre-Christian civilizations and that the Christian church removed these rights, justifying its actions with the argument that woman had introduced sin into the world.

She described Christian customs like the one known as Marquette, which, in the Middle Ages, sentenced newly married European serf women to a kind of sexual slavery. "They were regarded as the rightful prey of the Feudal Lord," Matilda wrote, "from one to three days after their marriage, and from this custom, the oldest son of the serf was held as the son of the lord, 'as perchance it was he who begat him.'"[17]

Laws like this, she said, caused women to meet at night and to mock the church, leading to charges of witchcraft. "Catholic and Protestant countries alike," Matilda wrote, "agreed in holding woman as the chief accessory of the devil."[18]

Matilda was one of the first historians to describe how "witch" trials, conducted by the church and later by the state, resulted in the slaughter of innocent women. She gave a history of persecutions, from European burnings to American dunking stools.

"Friends were encouraged," Matilda wrote, "to cast accusations upon friends, and rewards were offered for conviction. From the pulpit people were exhorted to bring the witch to justice. Husbands who had ceased to care for their wives, or in any way found them a burden, or who for any reason wished to dissolve the marriage tie, now found an easy method. They had but to accuse them of witchcraft, and the marriage was dissolved by the death of the wife at the stake."[19]

Susan B. Anthony had opposed the inclusion of this chapter on religion, which all three partners knew would upset conservative women and the clergy, but Matilda and Elizabeth Cady Stanton overruled her.

Many reviews of the book liked its portraits, which included pictures of Susan B. Anthony, Elizabeth Cady Stanton, and Matilda Joslyn Gage.

But Matilda did not like her picture. "Miss Anthony," she wrote to Lillie Devereux Blake, "does as she pleases. She did not even consult me as to which of my likenesses I wanted engraved. . . . It was not in my knowledge *at all* what my engraving was to be until it was done and sent me. I *hate it!*"[20]

The *New York Times* said: "Mrs. Matilda Joslyn Gage . . . has a face as bright and thoughtful as the chapter on 'Woman, Church and State,' which she contributes to this volume. It is a terrible indictment and it must be confessed that the Catholic and Protestant churches suffer grievously at her hands."[21]

Reviews were generally favorable. The *New-York Tribune* said, "Some one may hereafter make a more compact and symmetrical history of this period, but it can hardly be more interesting."[22]

Five months after the *History* came out, the *National Citizen and Ballot Box* ceased publication. When paid advertisements decreased, for a time Matilda subsidized it with her own money. But business was bad in central New York; her husband's store was losing money. Finally she gave it up.

Her last editorial was called "The End Not Yet": "To those who fancy we are near the end of the battle, or that the reformer's path is strewn with roses, we say them nay. The thick of the fight has just begun; the hottest part of the warfare is yet to come, and those who enter it must be willing to give up father, mother, and comforts for its sake. Neither shall we who carry on the fight, reap the great reward. We are battling for the good of those who shall come after us; they, not ourselves, shall enter into the harvest."[23]

17 ☀ Intolerable Anxiety 1881–1883

"None of "the ads have amounted to anything more than a few letters," Matilda wrote to Clarkson in October 1881. She was trying to sell the family store. "No one has been here even to look," she said.[1] The business was failing rapidly, as was her husband's health.

"I have advised your father to get out large Posters of '*Closing Out Sale*,'" Matilda wrote, "and to have small card signs painted or printed, such as *Very Cheap, Below Cost* &c. &c. fastened to certain goods. I don't think he is hardly fitted for it, but if he will stay at the house and let me manage, I will do it."[2]

Ten years before, the store had been valued at $60,000. Its profits had provided for the children's education. Now Matilda needed to find a new way to support herself and Henry and to keep Maud at Cornell, where she was a sophomore in the second class to accept women students.

Julia, the middle daughter, still lived at home. She helped Matilda in the store, but she, too, had serious health problems. "She is obliged to see a doctor twice a week," Matilda told Clarkson, "at $2. each time. I paid $3. for her for the first examination, but I can't help her in that way any more."[3]

Clarkson, after graduating from Cornell, had worked with his father in Fayetteville for a time. Then he had moved to Aberdeen, in Dakota Territory. "Western fever" called many people to this new, fast-growing town where three railroad lines crossed. Settlers, even single women and immigrants, could homestead nearby on 160-acre lots owned by the federal government (after the government had forced American In-

New York to Dakota Territory

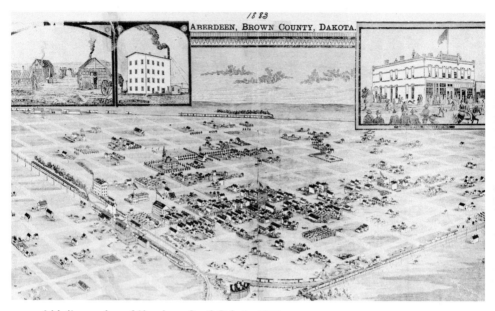

A bird's eye view of Aberdeen, South Dakota, 1883.
South Dakota State Historical Society

dians off the land). If a farmer "proved up" by building a home on the property, and grew crops there for five years, that lot became his or hers with the payment of a small registration fee.

When Clark moved to Aberdeen, business was booming. He opened a general store with two brothers, Frank and Charles Beard, family friends from Fayetteville. In time he bought a homestead lot and built a small cabin there.

Matilda, too, considered buying property in Aberdeen or Syracuse. Hoping that Clarkson might invest with her, she wrote him almost daily, asking whether a business lot or a residence lot or perhaps a farm would yield the best profit.

"I have again, again, and again asked if you were coming home this winter," she wrote. "I get no reply. It will make some difference as to my investments."[4]

Sometime later she wrote, "My dear son, Your letter of Nov 18th is just at hand. From its tenor I fear I have hurt your feelings; but if so I must beg you to overlook it and attribute it to my *intolerable anxiety* on money affairs."[5]

Eventually she bought investment property in East Syracuse for

$2,350: one bare lot and another with a new building, not yet completed. She hoped to resell these at a profit in the future. *"If I live* and *have my health,"* she told Clarkson, "I shall pull through all right, but *it is a mighty* hard pull, for a woman who never did business until she was over fifty."[6]

"I take a sort of general oversight of the store," she told him. "After so hard a Day's work Thursday that I had to lie down twice, I went to the store in the evening and engineered the clothing stock, staying until after ten, helping your father up the hill, bathing his back after we reached home, putting away clean clothes and getting to bed after eleven. . . . My coauthors are pressing me on the history,—I am still in fall house-cleaning. . . . Have moved the Leslie card table down for my work table, but have thought I should be obliged to move my writing to the store."[7]

Though her letters to Clarkson are the ones that survive from this time, Matilda remained closely involved with all four children. "Helen is now married," she wrote to Clarkson, "but the commercial reporter does not rate [her husband Charly] as high nor his credit as good as your father; as long as he remains well, they will probably get along but he is an old man and I fear her future is not very bright."[8]

Julia was engaged to one of her former students. "A poor man," Matilda called him, referring to finances. "Her wedding will nearly kill me," Matilda said, "she expects as large a wedding as Helen had *if not larger*, and how I am to get through with it is more than I see, especially if you do not come home."[9]

When Maud was home for the holidays, Matilda wrote to a friend, "things buzz. A dress-maker clicking the sewing machine in one room— the door bell continually ringing for calls, fancy work going on—i.e. finishing up Christmas things—My sitting room is trimmed with cedar on wires running from each corner and fastening on a hook in the center of the room, with picture frame ends and wires covered with cedar."[10]

Maud's roommate, Josie Baum, who lived in Syracuse, invited her to a New Year's Day open house where Maud met Josie's twenty-five-year-old cousin. Lyman Frank Baum, called Frank, had come home for New Year's to the Syracuse suburb of Mattydale. The son of a wealthy family, he had just opened a theater his father built for him in Richburg, New York.[11]

Their meeting became a family legend: when Frank arrived at the

L. Frank Baum, c. 1880.
Alexander Mitchell Library

party, his Aunt Josephine took Maud's arm and led her to him.

"This is my nephew, Frank," Aunt Josephine said. "Frank, I want you to know Maud Gage. I'm sure you will love her."

"Consider yourself loved, Miss Gage," said Frank.[12]

Soon after the party, Frank borrowed a black buggy and a bay mare from his father and drove to visit Maud in Fayetteville, arriving on baking day.[13] He was tall and handsome, with a full mustache and a good singing voice.

Maud's beau did not impress Matilda. Even though Frank was writing a musical play and planning to star in it himself, show business seemed to her unlikely to be a stable career. Matilda wanted Maud to finish college, so she was relieved when her daughter went back to Cornell and Frank returned to Richburg.

On February 9, 1882, Matilda's middle daughter Julia, age thirty, married James D. "Frank" Carpenter, her former student, who was twenty-two, before seventy or eighty guests at the Gage home. She wore a white organdy dress and her grandmother's silk wedding hose and necklace. Matilda gave the couple an autographed copy of the *History of Woman Suffrage.*

Although they lived in Syracuse, Matilda's eldest daughter, Helen, and her husband, Charly, were unable to attend the wedding because Helen had given birth the day before to a daughter, Leslie, Matilda's first grandchild.

The new bride and groom, Julia and Frank Carpenter, moved to a homestead claim in Dakota Territory, about seventy miles north of Aberdeen, near Edgeley. There they lived a hard life; Frank Carpenter took up farming while Julia kept house in a one-room shanty.

Meanwhile Baum's Opera House in Richburg burned down on March 8, 1882. Recovering quickly, Frank Baum opened his musical *The Maid of Arran* in Syracuse on May 15, 1882, his twenty-sixth birth-

Julia Gage and James D. "Frank" Carpenter, 1882.
University of North Dakota

day. He had written the play, the song lyrics, and the music, and, as Louis F. Baum, he also played the lead. The show was so successful that he took it on tour in the area and to Kansas, Canada, and New York City.[14]

That summer Frank Baum proposed to Maud in her parents' front parlor, and she accepted. Years later their eldest son described what happened next, likely inventing the dialogue himself, based on a well-known family story.

Closing the sliding pocket doors between the front and back parlors, Maud went alone to break their news to Matilda. But Frank could still hear them talking. According to his son, Frank said, "I heard Mrs. Gage say: 'I won't have my daughter be a darned fool and marry an actor.' Maud snapped back: 'All right mother, if you feel that way about it, good bye.'"

"What do you mean, good bye?" Matilda demanded.

"Well," Maud said, "you just told me I would be a darned fool to marry an actor and you wouldn't have a daughter of yours do that. I'm going

The Gages' front parlor, where all three girls were married, 1888.
Photo by L. Frank Baum. *Gage Foundation*

to marry Frank, so, naturally, you don't want a darned fool around the house."

"All right, Maud," Matilda said, laughing. "If you are in love with him and really determined to marry him, you can have your wedding right here at home."[15]

Frank adored Maud, whom he called "Dimple Siren." He tried to please Matilda, too.

"Frank addresses me as mother," she wrote to Clarkson, "and tells me that I am not to lose a daughter, but to gain a son."[16]

In the autumn, volume 2 of the *History of Woman Suffrage* was published, covering the years 1861–1876. Matilda, as agreed upon with Elizabeth Cady Stanton and Susan B. Anthony, had written the chapter on women's attempts to vote under the Fourteenth Amendment. When she saw the printed version, she was outraged. The text she submitted documented many women's efforts to vote, including her own, with other women in Fayetteville. But the published chapter, revised by both Anthony and Stanton, omitted many stories, including Matilda's. Instead it added considerable material about Anthony's trial, making that event the chapter's main focus.[17]

"I have been up [in my] garret and everywhere looking for the documents on my voting," Matilda wrote later to Lillie Devereux Blake. She wanted to find the original version of her chapter in order to demonstrate that Anthony had changed her account of history.

"I prepared all the ms [manuscript of the chapter] and sent it on with the rest," Matilda told Blake, "but Susan B. did not put it in or rather left it out. A long time afterwards Susan sent that and other material that was *agreed upon* . . . back to me, but I have mislaid it. . . . I felt so disgusted and disappointed at the way matters were run that I have put this *rejected ms* where I cannot now lay my hand on it."[18]

Presumably Matilda was happier with another chapter she wrote for volume 2. In "Woman's Patriotism in the War," she described women strategists, fundraisers, politicians, nurses, and even soldiers who had fought in the Civil War, dressed as men.

As the second volume appeared, the Gage family suffered two fires, one in Aberdeen and the other in Fayetteville. On September 29 Matilda was up at three o'clock in the morning, too excited to sleep, writing to Clarkson. "Dear Son[,] Your letter received yesterday. How fortunate that you were not in your cabin when the prairie fire took it. I don't care for your house as long as you are safe. But we, that is the store is all burned out[.] The cry of fire and a violent ringing of the door bell came about half past twelve, and men shouting that our store was all on fire. It took in the front part . . . and what with fire and smoke and water, everything is ruined."[19]

Insurance covered part, but not all, of the damage at the store. Henry's health never fully recovered from the shock of this loss.[20] The fires came at a particularly bad time, as the national economy worsened. But despite their hardships and health problems for both, Matilda and Henry managed to put on a third wedding in just seventeen months.

On November 9, 1882, Maud, wearing white brocaded silk, married Frank Baum in the room where he had proposed. This time all the Gage children attended. Clarkson and Julia came from Dakota, and Helen brought her baby daughter Leslie. Once married, the honeymooners began traveling with Frank's touring show, *The Maid of Arran*.

After the wedding, Matilda's financial worries resurfaced. She had

Maud and Frank Baum, wedding photos, 1882. *Gage Foundation and Gita Dorothy Morena*

counted on earnings from the *History of Woman Suffrage*, but sales were poor, and the three partners argued over money. They sent free copies of the first volume, as promised, to people who had donated to the National's centennial headquarters, losing money on each one.

Matilda and Elizabeth Cady Stanton worried that Susan B. Anthony was charging convention expenses to the book. Anthony, who had agreed in their contract to provide monthly financial statements about the *History*, produced only one in a nine-year period.[21]

In 1882 Stanton and Anthony went to England to visit Stanton's daughter who lived there. Meanwhile Matilda updated her "Woman as Inventor" for publication in the *North American Review*, the United States' longest running magazine and one of its most progressive.

Women inventors, she observed, faced special hardships due to laws prohibiting married women from owning property or signing contracts.

"Should such a [married] woman be successful in obtaining a patent," Matilda asked, "what then? Would she be free to do as she pleased with it? Not at all. She would hold no right, title, or power over this work of her own brain. She would possess no legal right to contract, or to license anyone to use her invention. Neither, would her right be infringed, could she sue the offender. Her husband could take out the patent in his own name, sell her invention for his own sole benefit, give it away if he so chose, or refrain from using it, and for all this she would have no remedy."[22]

Matilda earned fifty dollars for the article. She used the money to buy clothes, her financial woes having affected her usual elegant style of dress. "I am determined not to go so beggarly any more," she wrote to Clarkson.[23]

She was trying to finish another manuscript, *Ancient Libraries*, two hundred pages long. "Don't know as anybody will print it," she told Clarkson, as she neared the end, "yet I shall at least have it *off my mind.*"[24]

On February 14, 1883, Matilda and Henry went to Syracuse to see their new son-in-law's play, *The Maid of Arran.*

"Like 'The Maid' very much," Matilda wrote to Clarkson. "The ship scene is especially beautiful. [The company goes] from here to Troy, Albany and the New England states. Frank B. has just made an arrangement with Oliver Ditson, the great song publisher, to have his songs printed. . . . His acting and singing his songs in the play will be a great advertisement for them. *Now* people ask for them at places he has played. Of over 600 [theatrical] companies going out [on tour] this winter 460 have failed. Speaks well for Frank."[25]

Henry enjoyed the play, too, despite feeling poorly. Matilda wrote to Clarkson that on the way home from the show, "Charly [Helen's husband] and Frank supported him from the corner, home[.] His walking was like a little child's between two older persons."[26]

18 ✳ Broken Up 1883–1884

In March 1883 Henry Gage, while walking alone outside, fell on the street. "Boys would not help him up," Matilda wrote to Clarkson, "but laughed and jeered at him as if he were drunk. A little girl picked him up and he asked her to keep hold of him as he still felt [ill]. But she, poor thing, did not have the strength . . . and he fell again, when a man assisted him up. . . . This morning he went to sweep off the kitchen hall steps and fell headlong there."[1]

By this time Matilda and Henry had leased what was left of the store. They planned to mortgage their house and move to Aberdeen. "We shall certainly *not* stay here another winter," Matilda wrote to her son. "I many times think your father will never live to go to Dakota."[2] Nevertheless she discussed the move with Henry, just to cheer him up.

Frank Baum stayed with *The Maid of Arran* until it failed on the road. By then Maud was pregnant. The young couple moved to Syracuse where Frank opened a store that sold wholesale oil products. After it went under, he worked with his brother and uncle manufacturing and selling a lubricant called Baum's Castorine.[3]

In Dakota Territory, Clarkson, still part-owner of the Beard, Gage, and Beard General Merchandise Store, had opened a branch store fifty miles north in the town of Ellendale.[4] He was doing well, but Matilda worried about her daughter Julia, who was homesteading under difficult conditions with her husband near Edgeley, about seventy miles north of Aberdeen.

Matilda longed to see her two middle children in the western country where they lived. By summer 1883 Henry's health seemed stable enough for her to leave him for a time. Helen and Maud urged her to go, promising to care for their father in Syracuse while she was away.

Matilda had a women's rights mission in Dakota, too. The southern part of the territory was preparing to hold a constitutional convention leading to statehood. Both Susan B. Anthony and the National's vice president for Dakota, Marietta Bones, asked Matilda to help get women's suffrage into the new state constitution.[5]

Matilda took the train west. The Dakota prairie, flat, treeless, and grassy, bore no resemblance to the tall forests, blue lakes, and green hills of central New York. Wheat and corn fields surrounded Aberdeen, a flourishing town to which the railroad brought settlers and delivered lumber and other supplies.

Matilda's husband, Henry Hill Gage, c. 1880. *Gage Foundation*

"I stop with Clarkson," Matilda wrote to her friend Lillie Devereux Blake, "rooming over the store in an unfurnished apartment where I can see the rafters over my head, and my blanket door shuts off the gaze of passers by. A drygoods box is my wash-stand but I have a nice spring bed."[6]

Aberdeen pleased her. "This is a lively frontier town of about 2,000 inhabitants," she told Blake. "I like the style, but not the intolerable heat of the last few days—98° in the shade. Wheat looks good but rain is needed. The present is poor corn weather."[7]

On July 15, 1883, Matilda's daughter Julia wrote in her diary: "About 3 o'c in the P.M. a carriage drove up [to the claim shanty where she lived with her husband], and who should be in it but Mother and T.C. [Clarkson]."[8] She was expecting them but did not know exactly when they would arrive.

"Seems they had written a second letter," she wrote, "for us to meet them in Ellendale which we had not received. The livery costs $10.00. Mother stood the long ride 30 miles wonderfully well for her—yet was *very, very,* tired. A cup of tea revived her."[9]

Matilda and Clarkson brought presents: beefsteak, canned fruits, oranges, lemons, sardines, canned mackerel, and candy. That same day Clarkson helped Julia's husband Frank Carpenter and a friend finish the Carpenters' sitting room, doubling the size of their house. Then they cleared the floor of shavings, wood, and nails.

"T.C. and Frank with King's help scrubbed the room," Julia wrote, "spread the carpet, hung pictures, &c. &c. while the box of bedding was unpacked and I made the bed. Poor Mother, it was a poor reception for her." Matilda and Julia slept in the new room while the men slept in the kitchen.[10]

After visiting Julia, Matilda traveled throughout the territory, giving lectures about women's rights. She taught her audiences about current and proposed laws and about the value of women's suffrage. Wide distances between towns made travel and campaigning difficult. Then, too, many settlers were foreign immigrants who did not speak English.[11]

Matilda published a letter: "*To the Women of Dakota*: A convention of men will assemble at Sioux Falls, September 4," she wrote, "for the purpose of framing a constitution and pressing upon congress the formation of a State of the southern half of the territory. This is the moment for women to act: it is the decisive moment."

Her letter explained inequities of the Homestead Act: "The code of Dakota, under the head of 'Personal Relations,' says: 'The husband is the head of the family. He may choose any reasonable place, or mode of living, and the wife must conform thereto.' Under this class legislation, which was framed by man entirely in his own interests, the husband may, and in many cases does, file a preëmptive claim, build a shanty, and place his wife on the ground as 'a reasonable place and mode of living,' while he remains in town in pursuit of business or pleasure."

If the wife left the claim, Matilda said, the husband could say that she had left his bed and board, even though he was not living with her. Although the wife was recognized as a joint owner in the homestead, the husband, as "head of the family" could sell it or give it away, Matilda said, and the wife had no redress.

"Every woman in Dakota should be immediately at work," Matilda wrote, urging them to keep the word "male" out of the new state constitution. "Make known your wishes on this point. . . . You have not been permitted to help make these laws which rob you of property, and many other things more valuable. Many women are settling in Dakota.

Unmarried women and widows in large numbers are taking up claims here, and their property is taxed to help support the government and the men who make these iniquitous laws."

Matilda urged the women to write letters to convention delegates and to go to Sioux Falls during the meeting to exercise their only power, the power of protest. "Above all," she ended, "remember that *now* is the decisive hour."[12]

To the male convention delegates, she wrote: "We simply ask you to make your state a true republic, in which all your citizens may stand equal before the law. While foreign men of every nation are welcomed to your magnificent prairies as equals, it is humiliating to the women of the territory, who are helping you to develop its resources, who have endured with you all the hardships of pioneer life, to be treated as inferiors."[13]

Thanks in part to Matilda's efforts, Marietta Bones was invited to address the constitutional convention. By that time Matilda had returned to New York. She was saddened but not surprised to learn later that women had failed to win the vote in Dakota.

Matilda and Henry spent the winter in Fayetteville, celebrating the birth of their first grandson, Maud's son, Frank Joslyn Baum, on December 4, 1883. His father sang him "Bye, Baby Bunting" so often that the baby was nicknamed Bunny or Bunting.[14]

As spring came Henry's health worsened. Sometimes he was too ill to turn himself in bed. Then Matilda fell on the kitchen steps, spraining her wrist.

"I have grown old very fast within a year or two," she wrote to Clarkson, "and especially since last summer. My hair is entirely white and very thin."

"Miss Anthony . . . and Mrs Stanton are at work on Vol. 3 [of the *History of Woman Suffrage*]," she told him, "to which I also, must give some attention. Had the garden plowed Monday and planted today. . . . Frank B's business is constantly on the increase."[15]

Frank Baum's job as a traveling salesman kept him away from home much of the time. Since Maud and Matilda both wanted company, the Baums, their baby son, and a nursemaid moved to the Gage home for the summer. Matilda, who had a hired girl to help with housework, took care of Henry and also painted, papered, gardened, canned cherries, and made currant jelly.[16]

Matilda, 1881.
Gage Foundation

When Clarkson came to Fayetteville that summer, Henry rallied at the sight of his son. "I am so glad you had a chance to visit with him when he was so well,"[17] Matilda wrote to Clarkson later. By August her husband suffered from dizzy spells, fainting, and perhaps a stroke. The doctor diagnosed diabetes. Henry could barely walk.

On September 4, he suffered an attack that left him unable to speak. Helen came from Syracuse to help care for her father. Maud, still in Fayetteville, did what she could, but her baby boy was ill, too. Coping with an incontinent patient who could not move on his own was difficult for the women. Neighbor men came often to help change Henry's clothes and rubber blankets and to move him back and forth from a bed to a cot. Sometimes Julia's in-laws, the Carpenters, came twice a day.

Though the weather was hot, Henry alternated between chills and a high fever. While he could not speak, he could still press Matilda's hand in response to questions. From this she knew that his right leg hurt him terribly, despite medication.

"It pains me to see him suffer," she told Clarkson.[18] Exhaustion and sadness overwhelmed her.

Helen spent hours digging earth to put in the privy. Mother and daughter struggled constantly to keep things clean and free from infection. Eventually Matilda hired a man to help care for Henry and found a washerwoman to help with the bedding. They used carbolic acid to destroy odors.

On the doctor's advice, Maud and her family, the baby still ill, left the Gage house, and Julia was summoned home from Dakota.

Henry could speak occasionally. On September 14, 1884, Maud and Frank Baum came to see him, and he told them both goodbye. He died two days later.

Clarkson returned to Fayetteville for the funeral. Matilda wrote to Lillie Devereux Blake, "Your letter came to me while Mr Gage lay dead in the house. He died Tuesday and was buried yesterday. It will be impossible for me to do anything in regard to a meeting in Syracuse. Business affairs must be settled and I must decide where to live. My children from Dakota are here but they must return soon. The two living in Syracuse can stay but a short time. . . . I am all broken up at present."[19]

19 ⁂ A Courageous, Fateful Woman
1884–1886

"Do not see how I can stay here this winter," Matilda wrote to Lillie Devereux Blake after Henry's death, "do not see how I can go elsewhere. I am now left entirely alone, in this big house, which I do not know as I can sell or rent . . . yet the taxes, insurance and repairs must be kept up."[1]

Matilda spent the winter with Maud, Frank, and baby Bunting in their rented home in Syracuse, moving back to Fayetteville in the spring of 1885. Then her oldest daughter Helen, with husband Charly and their daughter Leslie, age three, came for a long stay.

In Aberdeen Clarkson married a young woman named Sophia Jewell, called Sophie. Matilda did not attend the wedding, but she wrote to her son, "You know somewhat my views upon the marriage relation, and the rights of the wife in it. . . . I doubt not that you will find in Sophia a wise counsellor and friend. Her judgment will be of more service to you than that of any outside party."[2]

On June 8 Matilda wrote to Clarkson, "On the evening of your marriage we had a little pleasant time of our own[.] As long as we could not be with you, we had 'a wedding' at home, and I fear that dear little Leslie [her granddaughter] is somewhat mystified as to what a wedding really is."

Matilda had created a festive scene. "Chandeliers in both parlors lighted," she wrote, "bright wood fire in the grate, table set for refreshments in the back parlor; Leslie and her papa dancing in the front parlor, Helen trying her hand at the piano."

They tried to eat at the same time as the guests at the wedding in

Dakota. "Our refreshments were cake of two kinds," Matilda wrote, "ice cream of two kinds . . . and wine, only Charly and Helen took the latter."[3]

Matilda savored that summer. Charly took over her vegetable garden, which thrived as never before. They grew red raspberries, currants, and several kinds of pears, which Matilda preserved or baked into pies.

In July she wrote to Clarkson's wife Sophie, "We are engaged upon the completion of Vol. 3. Wom. Suff. Hist. and all must bend to the completion of the great task, now nine years since its inception. Today is Sunday, scarcely dark, I sit by my table, writing; Leslie is in bed, Charly and Helen on the front piazza, where I hear them chatting. We look for Maud, Frank and dear little Bunting Friday to spend the Fourth. I believe Frank is to come armed with fire crackers[,] torpedoes and other similar methods of enjoyment."[4]

Maud and Bunting, who spent the rest of July in Fayetteville, were there to welcome Susan B. Anthony when she came to work with Matilda on the *History*. The third volume should have been the easiest, as they

Bunting (baby boys wore dresses) and Maud on Matilda's front porch, 1888. Photo by L. Frank Baum. *Gage Foundation*

were relying on state leaders to supply most of the writing, but involving more people created delays. Most of the submissions were far too long. Their old friend Amelia Bloomer fought even the smallest changes in her piece.[5] For Volume 3, which covered the years 1876–1885, Matilda wrote the preface, the national section, and the parts about New York.

In October Julia came to Fayetteville for a long visit. She was expecting her first child and wanted to give birth with her mother there, at her childhood home. In Syracuse Maud was pregnant, too, with her second child, and in Aberdeen, Sophie was also expecting.

Matilda loved planning treats for her grandchildren. In 1885 Maud and Frank had a Christmas tree for two-year-old Bunting. His cousin

Leslie, sick in bed, was too ill to go see it, so Matilda got her granddaughter a tree of her own, trimmed with golden nuts, strings of popped corn, and lighted candles. She could not give Leslie the baby brother she had requested, but Matilda did get her a boy doll dressed in maroon velvet knickerbockers.

The New York family mailed three boxes of gifts to Dakota and received numerous presents in return. Matilda unwrapped polished buffalo horns, a holder for hat pins, a cut glass vase, a book of synonyms, bed slippers with blue satin ribbons and lemon-colored wool soles, an onyx pin set with pearls, a photograph, and doilies.

Holiday dinners were festive. The New Year's menu in Fayetteville included tomato soup, chicken pie, raw oysters, mashed potatoes, mashed turnips, pickled pears, cucumber pickles, quince jelly, pumpkin pie, lemon jelly, almonds, raisins, and chocolate.

"Dinners are matters of small moment to me," Matilda wrote to Clarkson and Sophie, soon after this impressive meal. "I have eaten no meat since March, and care very little for *winter* foods, am very fond of fruit in season."[6]

On January 17, 1886, Julia gave birth at Matilda's house to a son, Harry Carpenter. She recovered quickly, but the baby was sickly for some time.

Two weeks after Harry's birth, Maud had her second son, Robert Stanton Baum. The baby, nicknamed "Robin," was plump and healthy, but Maud was dangerously ill for six months after his birth. Bunting, her older son, spent much of this time in Fayetteville, and Matilda cared for Leslie then, too, as Helen was ill.

After putting her grandchildren to bed at night, Matilda pursued new interests like palmistry, spiritualism, and especially Theosophy, a newly popular system of belief. The name, based on the Greek word *theosophia* (*theo* means *god, gods,* or *divine*; *sophia* means *wisdom*), can be translated as "divine wisdom." The term had been used in various spiritual movements for centuries, and in the late nineteenth century it was revitalized as "modern Theosophy," with a capital T.[7]

The Theosophical Society, created in New York in 1875 by psychic Helena Petrovna Blavatsky and lawyers Henry Steel Olcott and William Quan Judge, attracted many members. Madame Blavatsky's books, especially *The Secret Doctrine*, popularized the movement.[8] Matilda, who always sought new ways to comprehend life, may have been drawn to the philosophy because its cofounder was a woman.

Theosophy sought to understand divinity, humanity, and the world. Theosophists promoted a universal brotherhood of humanity, with no distinctions of race, creed, sex, caste, or color. Matilda read many books about Theosophy, which was also known as esoteric Buddhism. She shared these with family members and discussed them with Clarkson in letters.

Theosophists believed in reincarnation, the concept that after life ends, the soul or spirit begins a new life in a new body. Matilda liked this idea, which held that each life was a state of being.

"Theosophy is *not* a religion," she wrote to Clarkson. "It is a science. . . . It seems much more reasonable that the soul should perfect itself through a variety of experiences—than that one short term of fifteen, fifty or even one hundred years should decide its fate everlastingly. . . . To me, it is more wise, more reasonable, to think of 'states of being' than of creation. Perhaps my biological studies of the past year or so help me in this thought. Water is found as ice, steam, vapor—all *states of being* of one and the same thing."[9]

Clarkson was a kindred spirit, but she had to be careful not to upset her new daughter-in-law. In a private note to her son, Matilda wrote, "Sophie does not know me and even now, is quite likely to misjudge me. She is [a] member of a conservative church [Episcopal], and even this talk of Theosophy must shock her pre-conceived training so keep to yourself the fact that I am investigating astrology."[10] Her astrological investigations, she told Clarkson, showed that Helen's husband, Charly, would soon die and that "dangerous influences" were affecting her granddaughter Leslie.

On April 22, 1886, Clarkson and Sophie had a daughter in Aberdeen, naming her Matilda Jewell Gage. The older Matilda was happy to learn that they called the baby by her full name instead of by the nicknames *Mattie* or *Millie*, which she judged less dignified.

"You spoke of my name as old-fashioned," she wrote to Clarkson. "It is a name of renown in old German and Scotch history. Its meaning is 'a heroine'—a courageous, fateful woman—one who dares to do what seems right in face of all opposition. Such an [sic] one I hope my dear little granddaughter will grow up to be."[11]

20 ✳ Protesting Lady Liberty 1886

"This place has no more surf than Oneida Lake," Matilda complained in a letter to her oldest daughter Helen on August 18, 1886. "It was a complete swindle for that woman to get me here. It is a small land-locked bay . . . *20 miles* from the ocean proper. But perhaps this milder air will be much better for Leslie as it is sea-air and salt water."[1]

She was staying with her granddaughter in a small hotel in Onset Bay Grove, on Cape Cod, Massachusetts. Leslie, then four, had developed "a gathering on her ear" which caused a discharge and obstructed her hearing. Doctors prescribed a seaside stay for the little girl, whose father was also ill. While Helen cared for her elderly husband in Syracuse, Matilda took Leslie to the beach.

"Am sorry that Charly is so poorly;" Matilda wrote to Helen, "but a bad condition for him was prophesized me last fall, so I am not sur-prized [*sic*]."[2]

Onset was a summer camp for spiritualists. Charming cottages accommodated people from East Coast cities who claimed to communicate with the dead. Matilda was interested, of course, but Leslie occupied her time. Matilda had to clear the little girl's ear with a syringe. "L. hates that puffer," she wrote to Helen.[3] To distract the child, Matilda told her stories. She also had her examined by a clairvoyant, who diagnosed a weak spine, poor circulation, and "waves of bad feeling over her," prescribing a syrup made of mullein and plantain leaves.

"No narcotics," Matilda assured Helen.[4]

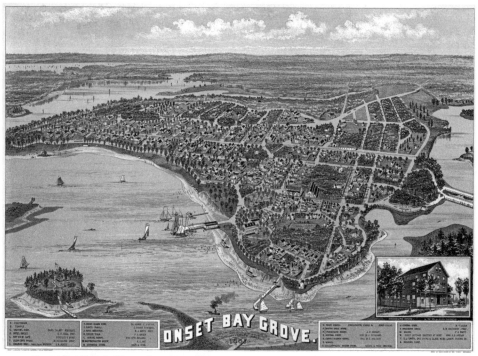

Onset Bay Grove, Massachusetts, 1885.
Library of Congress

By the time they went home, a month later, Leslie felt better. Matilda was always glad to help her relatives, and she had time to do so in 1886, when the *History of Woman Suffrage* was finally finished.

"The three volumes now completed," Matilda and Elizabeth Cady Stanton wrote in the preface, "we leave as a precious heritage to coming generations."[5] With these volumes, Matilda, Elizabeth Cady Stanton, and Susan B. Anthony had created a new field of study.

"Stanton, Anthony and Gage," historian Lisa Tetrault wrote later, "were the architects of social history, well before that field existed. They insisted that the deeds of women, not just military generals and statesmen, were critical places of national life. They argued that women, even obscure, ordinary women, could and did change the course of history. . . . There was a compensatory bent to their project, which aimed to show women as persons of accomplishment."[6]

With the ten-year project finally over, Elizabeth Cady Stanton, like Matilda, grew more involved with family, spending time in Europe, where her daughter Harriot lived. Both authors also began new books about the church's oppression of women. Matilda compiled research for *Woman, Church and State*, expanding her chapter from the first volume of the *History of Woman Suffrage* into a full book. Stanton launched *The Woman's Bible*, a book she planned with Matilda, inviting reviewers to interpret the Bible from a woman's point of view.

Susan B. Anthony grew tired of what she called their "church diggings."[7] With Matilda and Stanton otherwise occupied, she shone ever brighter as the star of the women's suffrage movement.

But soon Matilda, with her friend Lillie Devereux Blake, became involved in a new, much publicized protest. In October 1886, when the Statue of Liberty was dedicated, Blake was president and Matilda vice president of the New York State Woman Suffrage Association.

"The Statue of Liberty is a gigantic lie, a travesty, and a mockery," they charged. "It is the greatest sarcasm of the nineteenth century" to represent liberty as a woman, "while not one single woman throughout the length and breadth of the Land is as yet in possession of political Liberty."[8] The statue was a gift to the United States from the nation of France, where women's rights were also denied.

The New York State Woman Suffrage Association made a formal request to be included in the dedication ceremony, but it was declined. "There will be no women in the gathering on the island," the New York *Herald* wrote, "at least it is hoped not. No tickets have been issued to ladies, and if any of the fair sex are present on the island at the unveiling it will be the result of their persistency and diplomacy."[9]

Not surprisingly, these members of the "fair sex" were persistent. Blake appointed a committee to find a boat to rent so that they could sail in the official maritime procession. Then Matilda and others on the executive committee gathered at Blake's apartment at 163 East 49th Street in Manhattan to make plans. Blake welcomed them with her daughter, Katherine Devereux Blake, a twenty-eight-year-old school teacher who lived there, too, with her mother and stepfather.

The cheapest boat available, the committee reported, was a "propeller," the *John Lenox*, a two-story cattle barge with open decks. The captain had promised to have it scoured before they used it. The cost was a hundred dollars a day.

"How much money have we?" President Blake asked the treasurer.

"A little over four dollars," was the reply.

"Then," said Blake, "we'll take the boat."

"For a moment there was silence," Blake's daughter wrote later; the women were "all aghast at her temerity. Then there was a laugh."

"Well, we'll have to work hard," one lady exclaimed.

"But we'll win!" Blake said.[10]

They organized a protest meeting to be held in the Masonic Temple the afternoon before the unveiling and sent out handbills advertising it, as well as notices to newspapers. They also applied to join the official parade of boats, and this request was approved.

The *New-York Tribune* reported that fifty "well-dressed women" attended the protest meeting (the New York *Sun* estimated the crowd at one hundred), where tickets were sold for the next day's boating excursion.[11] The newspaper reported that Lillie Devereux Blake said, "the Statue of Liberty was that of a woman, but that it could just as well be that of a ward politician as it would represent women's liberty just as well."[12]

In her speech, Matilda said, "Ah, women, I wish I could fill your hearts with a desire for liberty like that which burns in my heart."[13]

October 28, 1886, the day of the dedication, dawned "wet and wretched."[14] Despite the captain's promise, the boat had not been cleaned. Several women, overcome by the stench, refused to board, but Matilda, Lillie Devereux Blake, her daughter Katherine, and some two hundred other protestors embarked from the West Twenty-First Street Pier on the Hudson River. Among them were twenty-five men, including Secretary Edward M. Lee of Wyoming Territory, where women had the right to vote, and L. Bradford Prince, soon to become governor of New Mexico Territory, who supported women's suffrage.[15] The passengers, wearing long "water-proofs," coats, and capes, shielded themselves from the rain with umbrellas. At the same time they had to hold tight to rails and posts, as the boat had only a few seats, and the decks were slippery.

Soon the *John Lenox* steamed downriver. A long white pennant flapped from the prow, bearing on it the letters "N.Y.S.W.S.A."—New York State Woman Suffrage Association.[16] Using a megaphone, the passengers called out women's rights slogans to spectators on the shore and on other boats. As the barge reached the choppy bay around Bedloe Island, where the statue stood, Matilda and her friends saw excursion boats, yachts, tugs, and dinghies, all draped in soggy bunting. Some smaller vessels tipped dangerously as people lined the sides offering the best view.

By chance, or perhaps because of a mistake, the *John Lenox* got a prime observation spot in the front row of boats, between two war ships, directly in front of the huge copper figure. Matilda could see the head, its face covered by an enormous French flag. With her colleagues she watched people arriving by steamboats on the island and climbing steps to a wooden grandstand. French and American flags served as decorations.

Several women, the wives of invited dignitaries, did make it onto the island. A noisy gun salute marked President Grover Cleveland's arrival. The *John Lenox* passengers could hear the band playing "Yankee Doodle" and the French national anthem. They watched then as man after man spoke at a podium, but they could not hear what was said.

Lillie Devereux Blake, c. 1886. *Lincoln Memorial University*

The weather worsened, until the top of the statue was covered with clouds and rain. People onshore could not tell when the flag was pulled away from the statue's face, but Matilda and her friends were close enough to see it drop.

Then came a riotous sound of celebration. "The din from the water . . . was deafening," said one newspaper. "The tooting of whistles and the boom of artillery were combined in a contest in which steam and gunpowder alternately predominated."[17]

Lillie Devereux Blake said, "Amid the confusion, I looked into the faces of the tried veterans of our cause who stood about me, and saw how their eyes also glowed with hope."[18] No doubt she meant Matilda, who always took heart from opposition.

After the noise died down, Blake summoned her colleagues to an indignation meeting on the lower deck. "After denouncing the ceremonies just witnessed as a farce," the *New York Times* reported, "she offered resolutions declaring 'that in erecting a statue of Liberty embodied as a woman in a land where no woman has political liberty[,] men have shown a delightful inconsistency which excites the wonder and admiration of the opposite sex.'"[19]

Dedication of the Statue of Liberty, October 28, 1886.
National Park Service

Other, more serious resolutions came from speakers like Matilda. They "recited a litany of unjust laws: fathers alone had custody rights to children, prostitutes were arrested but not their customers, girls at ten were held to be capable of giving consent to intercourse, and the conditions of working women were 'shocking.' Suffrage was needed immediately to give women the power to change these laws, but a New York municipal suffrage law had just been blocked by a governor who 'did not see why the Mothers needed to vote if the Fathers did.'"[20]

The discomforts of that long, wet day seemed worthwhile when Matilda read about their demonstration later in the newspapers.

"They enter a protest," said the headline in *the New York Times.* "Woman suffragists think the ceremonies an empty farce."[21]

When the bills were paid, Matilda and Lillie Devereux Blake celebrated again—they had actually made a few dollars' profit.[22]

21 ✳ The International Council of Women
1887–1888

"Spoke "this afternoon," Matilda wrote proudly to Maud and Helen from Washington on January 26, 1887, "and tell *Frank* [Baum that I] have been greatly complimented, both as to subject-matter and voice."[1]

Her speech, "The Unthought-of Danger," urged the protection of women's right to vote under federal rather than state law. The Washington *National Republican* reported on page one that it had been well received.[2] "My speech will be printed in full in Woman's Tribune, March issue," Matilda wrote.

Matilda had not planned to attend the National's convention, as she could not afford the trip. But the National provided funding,[3] probably at the prompting of Susan B. Anthony, who unofficially controlled donated funds (most bequests were given in her name).[4]

"Even Susan B. says she never heard me speak so well and that I had a 'mission to come,'" Matilda told her daughters. "Met old friends from everywhere.... Wore black silk with lace veil on neck and lace cuffs."[5]

The day before her speech, Matilda sat with fifty other women in the Senate visitors' gallery to hear that organization's first-ever vote on the constitutional amendment to enfranchise women. The amendment, written by Elizabeth Cady Stanton and first introduced in 1878, had been buried in committee for nine years. The National organized a huge petition drive to support the amendment and, in 1887, even the conservative American Woman Suffrage Association and the Woman's Christian Temperance Union joined the campaign. Despite this growing support, while Matilda watched, the amendment was defeated, thirty-four votes to sixteen, with twenty-six members absent.[6]

Still, Matilda felt encouraged. "These Senators begin to feel woman's power and to fear her," she told her daughters. "I tell you there is *great* progress in our reform."[7]

With six colleagues, including Stanton and Susan B. Anthony, Matilda began planning a fortieth-anniversary celebration of the movement, an International Council of Women, to be held in Washington the following year.[8]

In April 1887 Matilda learned that her middle daughter, Julia, had given birth in Dakota to a baby girl, Magdalena. Julia's first child, Harry, was just fifteen months old.

"I feel sorry for her," Matilda wrote to her daughter-in-law Sophie, "with two children so near of an age—scarcely less than twins."[9]

In May Matilda's oldest daughter, Helen, moved with her husband Charly and their daughter Leslie from the Syracuse area to Aberdeen. The Dakota town was too far from Julia's claim for Helen to see her sister often or to help her, and, sad to say, Julia needed help. Her husband had begun drinking heavily. Sometimes he abused her.

Matilda wrote to Helen,

I want [Julia] to understand that she and her babies are welcome to a home with me as long as I possess one, the same as *you all are*, when needed. Of course I see, knowing as I so long have done, the devilish laws that men make for women[,] that care must be used so as not to have that hound, out of spite, keep the children. I don't think he will live until they grow up but that is not now. And if J could live in a village, near neighbors, perhaps it will be the best for her to stay—but I am *bitterly* opposed to a woman's yielding her person to a drunkard and thief.[10]

However, Julia stayed with her husband.

Matilda spent the winter of 1887–1888 in Syracuse with the Baums. Her youngest daughter took care of her through bad colds, the loss of several teeth, dental repairs, and worries about how to pay the dentist. "Maud is very good and lets me sleep late if I choose to," she wrote to Clarkson.[11]

As usual she kept writing. Sometimes her grandsons, age four and almost two, interrupted her. "Both Bun and Rob are in the room," Matilda wrote to Helen, "and talk me wild, and *won't* go down. Rob [the younger] is good to mind, but Bun is self-willed and torments me. I sometimes

Maud and her sons Robin (Robert, at left), and Bun (Frank), 1888. Photo by L. Frank Baum. *Robert A. Baum*

Rob - Mother - Frank

think I shall be obliged to leave, he annoys me so when I am busy and won't quit."[12]

A harsh winter made life difficult across the country. On March 16, 1888, Matilda wrote to Clarkson: "New York has suffered from a dreadful blizzard this week, people perishing *right in the city.* . . . No trains from New York for three days; snow 15 and 20 ft deep. Wires all down. . . . I have already counted up between 40 and 50 deaths from the storm and presume they will mount to hundreds."

Even sea travel was impacted. "I expect Mrs. Stanton and our English delegates are on the ocean," Matilda told Clarkson. "Many vessels have been lost and I am very anxious."[13]

Later that month Elizabeth Cady Stanton and the delegates arrived safely in Washington, as did Matilda, to attend the International Coun-

Delegates to the International Council of Women, with Susan B. Anthony (front row, fourth from left), Elizabeth Cady Stanton (front row, sixth from left), and Matilda Joslyn Gage (front row, seventh from left), 1888. *Nebraska State Historical Society*

cil of Women. Matilda went into debt in order to attend the meeting she helped plan.[14]

The National Woman Suffrage Association sent out ten thousand invitations to women's rights advocates around the world, asking them to join in a celebration commemorating the fortieth anniversary of the Seneca Falls convention. The new Albaugh's Opera House, the largest theater in Washington, was filled to capacity; 1,891 seats and the aisles were packed for each session during the eight-day meeting. One newspaper counted twenty men among the people who had braved bad weather to attend.

Women came from Canada, Denmark, England, France, India, Ireland, and Norway, representing fifty-three organizations: the American Red Cross, the Universal Peace Union, the Woman's National Indian Association, the Christian Women's Board of Missions, book clubs, anti-prostitution workers, missionary groups, and more. Lucy Stone represented the American Woman Suffrage Association, and Frances E. Willard, president of the Woman's Christian Temperance Union, brought women from her organization.

Matilda stayed at the Riggs House hotel. Its owners gave a reception that was packed with Washingtonians who wanted to meet the foreign delegates. President Grover Cleveland and First Lady Frances Cleveland received the delegates at the White House, and Senator Thomas Palmer and his wife Lizzie Palmer hosted a reception for eight hundred people. Senator Leland Stanford and his wife Jane Stanford gave a party honoring forty years of the women's movement and eight of its pioneers: Susan B. Anthony, Clara Barton, Matilda Joslyn Gage, Isabella Beecher Hooker, Julia Ward Howe, Elizabeth Cady Stanton, Lucy Stone, and Frances E. Willard.

The convention opened on Monday morning, March 26, 1888. Later, the fourth volume of the *History of Woman Suffrage* (written without Matilda's or Elizabeth Cady Stanton's input) described the setting: "The vast auditorium . . . was richly decorated with the flags of all nations and of every State in the Union. The platform was fragrant with evergreens and flowers, brilliant with rich furniture, crowded with distinguished women, while soft music with its universal language attuned all hearts to harmony. The beautiful portrait of the sainted Lucretia Mott, surrounded with smilax and lilies of the valley, seemed to sanctify the whole scene and give a touch of pathos to all the proceedings."[15]

Matilda saved a newspaper description:

The scenes during the convention spoke volumes for the progress of the woman's rights movement. In the first place, the appearance of the women assembled, was decidedly unlike that of the old-time gatherings. Here and there were a few sober-looking women dressed in plain Quaker garb. But for the most part the delegates were well-dressed. A majority of them were young women, who wore their sealskin cloaks and soft, bright-colored velvets. Jewels flashed from their hair and hands, and to describe the bonnets would wear out a dictionary of colors.

On the stage sat the old heroines who have carried on the strife against man for the last forty years. Easily first of them all, of course, was Susan B. Anthony. Tall, grim, saturine [sic], she presided over the various meetings with a readiness of speech, a precision of judgment rarely equalled by the Presidents and Speakers who direct affairs in Senate and House. With her sat Mrs. Stanton, her snowy hair and florid face contrasting pleasantly with Miss Anthony's sallow visage. Nearby sat Mrs. Julia Ward Howe, her benign, plain face radiant with good will.

Now and then during the convention, enthusiasm over Mrs. Howe was so great that the audiences instinctively started up the "Battle Hymn of the Republic" [Howe wrote the words to the song.] and sang it through grandly to the end. Matilda Joslyn Gage, another veteran, was a prominent figure throughout the meeting. Her commanding figure and strong oratory made her a most interesting participant.[16]

Matilda and the six other National officers who made up the committee of arrangements wore badges of black and gold, and Matilda was one of thirty-six women and eight men, including Frederick Douglass, entitled to wear the Pioneer's badge—a lavender ribbon with silver letters that spelled out "Pioneer's Day, 1848–1888."[17]

Susan B. Anthony opened the council by introducing Elizabeth Cady Stanton as cofounder of the women's movement. The crowd gave Stanton a standing ovation, clapping, waving their handkerchiefs (for ladies, waving handkerchiefs was considered more polite than cheering), some even weeping.[18]

Susan B. Anthony, as first vice president, presided over many meetings. She used the convention as an opportunity to strengthen her relationships with conservative groups. When she introduced Lucy Stone, who was representing the American Woman Suffrage Association, it was the first time they had been together on a stage in twenty years. Anthony said to the audience:

> I wanted to tell you when I introduced Mrs. Stone how I became converted to woman suffrage. . . . I did not go to that first Worcester convention [in 1850] and I was not at that first convention at Seneca Falls. Do not make any mistakes about my being a pioneer. I am quite a young person. But I did read the New York *Tribune*, and I was converted by the report of the very first of those meetings. Among the speeches was one by Lucy Stone, whom I then had never seen, in which she said the married woman's epitaph was the "relict" of John Smith, or some other man, who had owned her. I then made up my mind that I would be the relict of no man.[19]

"Stanton was speechless," historian Elisabeth Griffith wrote later. "But throughout the week-long meeting she remained publicly gracious and serene."[20] Stanton, like most women in the movement, believed that she had motivated Anthony to take up the cause of women's rights.

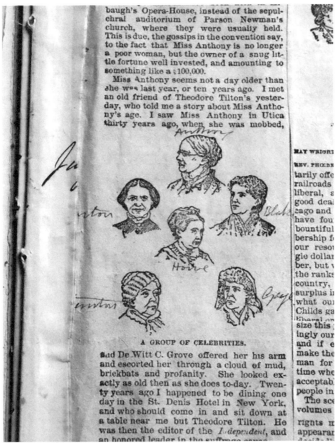

baugh's Opera-House, instead of the sepul-
chral auditorium of Parson Newman's
church, where they were usually held.
This is due, the gossips in the convention say,
to the fact that Miss Anthony is no longer
a poor woman, but the owner of a snug little fortune well invested, and amounting to
something like a $100,000.

Miss Anthony seems not a day older than
she was last year, or ten years ago. I met
an old friend of Theodore Tilton's yesterday, who told me a story about Miss Anthony's age. I saw Miss Anthony in Utica
thirty years ago, when she was mobbed,

A GROUP OF CELEBRITIES.

and De Witt C. Grove offered her his arm
and escorted her through a cloud of mud,
brickbats and profanity. She looked exactly as old then as she does to-day. Twenty years ago I happened to be dining one
day in the St. Denis Hotel in New York,
and who should come in and sit down at
a table near me but Theodore Tilton. He
was then the editor of the *Independent*, and
an honored leader in the suffrage

MAY WRIGHT

REV. PHOEBE
tarily offe
railroads
liberal, a
good dea
cago and
have fou
bountiful
bership f
our reso
gle dollar
ber, but v
the ranks
country,
surplus i
what ou
Childs ga
liberal or
size this
ingly our
and if e
make the
man for
time whe
acceptab
people in
The sce
volumes
rights n
appearar

Then, when Frances E. Willard spoke, she, like Anthony, credited
Lucy Stone with her conversion to the women's rights movement.[21]
Much to Matilda's dismay, Willard proved to be a lively speaker with a
charismatic leadership style.

Later during the convention, Matilda presided at a session on the subject of organization. When she introduced the president of the Woman's
Christian Temperance Union, she kept her remarks brief. "You will now
hear from a lady," she said, "who can surely tell you all there is to tell of
organization, Miss Frances E. Willard."[22]

Matilda spoke several times at the council. On Easter Sunday, the last
day, a murmur went up from the crowd when Susan B. Anthony announced the title of Matilda's final speech, "Woman in the Early Christian Church."[23]

If they were expecting controversy, they got it. All sessions at this convention had begun with prayers offered by women. Commenting on those prayers, Matilda said, "to me, one of the most notable things connected with this Council has been the almost universal unanimity with which the delegates, both ministerial and lay, have ignored the feminine in the Divinity. . . . The almost total ignoring of the Divine Motherhood of God by those who have in any way referred to the Supreme Power, has been to me a subject of profound surprise and astonishment."

"The Divine Motherhood of God" was a shocking concept to some. Others probably dismissed it as pagan talk.

Matilda continued,

All thoughtful persons, and foremost among them should be the women here represented, must be aware of the historical fact that the prevailing religious idea in regard to woman has been the base of all their restrictions. . . . Inasmuch as history teaches us that the rack, the torture, the destruction of human will, the degradation of woman for the past eighteen hundred years, have been dependent upon masculine interpretation of the Bible, based upon belief in a purely masculine divinity, this Council has been to me a dangerous evidence of woman's ignorance upon this most important of questions.

Matilda described how the early church had accepted both masculine and feminine elements of divinity. Displaying a knowledge of Greek and Hebrew, she told how men had eliminated women from the deity to enhance the male image. She explained how women in the early Christian church were ordained into the ministry, officiating as deacons over baptisms and other rites. Citing actions by specific religious councils over the centuries, she described how women were banned from the altar and eventually forbidden even to sing in church.

Matilda ended her talk by calling for a fresh class of clergy. "The religious teachers of the present day," she said, "need to be brave and liberal persons, possessing knowledge of science, history, and the laws of evolution. They need to be persons—they need to be women—who shall dare break away from all the false traditions of the middle ages, fearless in preaching the truth as to the absolute and permanent equality of the feminine with the masculine, not alone in all material, but in all spiritual things."[24]

Frances Willard, c. 1890. Her motto: "The sweetest words are Mother, Home, and Heaven." *Library of Congress*

Her words upset conservative religious women, but they inspired others who believed as she did. Fans hugged her after the meeting, saying that they had been afraid that no one would speak against religion at the council.[25]

Later Matilda told her children that she had rewritten the speech, adding the part about the feminine nature of God,[26] "after I saw the pious way of the council—the ignorant nonsense of some of these women."[27] She meant Frances E. Willard.

Following the council meetings, the National Woman Suffrage Association held a separate convention. There Matilda was appointed to a committee to consider a new proposal from Lucy Stone to merge the National with the American. Susan B. Anthony favored the idea; Matilda did not. Worried that the National was becoming too conservative, she decided to take back some control of the organization by resuming her office as chair of the executive committee.

"As Ch Ex. Com for the N.W.S.A. I need money," she wrote to Clarkson after returning to Fayetteville.

> Our assn. has been steered into an orthodox pit-hole, by Miss Anthony and her aids [sic]—and it needs not only a strong will, but money to put us back. You would scarcely believe that even Mrs Stanton has been dictated to and outrageously treated by Susan and some of her younger aids, she has both *told* me and *written* me in regard to it. . . . I am in the place which requires a strong, steady hand, with money at command. The opposition has money and spends it freely. I have brains, will and the sustaining hand of many.[28]

Increasingly Susan B. Anthony believed that "the opposition," especially the Woman's Christian Temperance Union, with more than 200,000 members, could help the National win votes for women. Frances E. Willard believed that if women could vote, they would vote for prohibition, but her goals went further.

"The Woman's Christian Temperance Union," Willard said, "local, state, national, world-wide, has one vital, organic thought, one all-absorbing purpose, one underlying enthusiasm. It is that Christ shall be this world's King. Yea, verily, this world's king in its realm of cause and effect; king of its courts; its camps; its commerce; king of its colleges and cloisters; king of its customs and constitutions. . . . The kingdom of Christ must enter the realm of law through the gateway of politics."[29]

When Willard was elected president of the National Council of Women, an American organization of women's groups that developed from the International Council, Matilda grew increasingly alarmed. "The great dangerous organization of the movement," she wrote to Elizabeth Cady Stanton, "is the WCTU; and Frances Willard, with her magnetic force, her power of leadership, her desire to introduce religious tests into the government, is the most dangerous person upon the American continent today."

Matilda knew that Stanton agreed with her about the essential need for separation of church and state. "You and I must stand firm," she wrote; "we have a great tide to stem, a great battle yet before us. We must have no religious test for anything. Get ready for a strong fight."[30]

Stanton sent Matilda's letter to the *Woman's Tribune*, the National's official newspaper, saying that it "expresses fully my own ideas," and the editor, Clara Colby, published it.[31]

"I am more vexed than I can tell you," Anthony wrote to Frances E. Willard, "that Mrs. Stanton should send that nonethical scribble of Mrs. Gage's . . . to the Woman's Tribune, and I am chagrined that Mrs. Colby should publish it—even if Mrs. S. did send it to her. . . . It is complimentary to you, in comparison to its fling at 'Susan,' the vulgar way in which it calls me 'Susan' and sites my lack of sight and insight!!"[32]

Matilda spent the summer of 1888 in Fayetteville, joined by Maud and her boys. By then Frank Baum had decided to change their lives and start a new career, and he decided to look—where else?—in Dakota. He may have sold his interest in Baum's Castorine to his uncle, giving him some capital to invest in the West.[33]

Traveling to Aberdeen on his own, Frank found a boom town with more than a hundred buildings under construction. Clarkson's store was thriving. Helen and Charly had bought investment property in town, including store fronts. Frank thought of renting one where he could open a store to sell luxury items, complementing Clarkson's basic goods.

Maud liked the idea of living near her three siblings, especially Helen. In the fall of 1888, Maud, Frank, Bun, and Rob moved to Aberdeen.

"And now to have *the last one*, my baby—go," Matilda wrote to Helen. "It is simply dreadful. . . . I have a bad feeling about my heart, and throat and head. . . . I—am—alone!"[34]

22 ✳ Betrayed 1888–1890

atilda was not alone for long. Following the Baums to Aberdeen, she stayed that winter in their rented house in town and spent time with her other children, too. Helen, Charly, and their daughter, Leslie, lived in an upstairs apartment on Main Street over the ground-floor store they rented to Frank Baum. Clarkson, Sophie, and their daughter, Matilda, had a house just outside Aberdeen. Julia and her family lived seventy miles north on the homestead claim, so Matilda took the train to visit them.

Frank's store opened in October. "Baum's Bazaar is an [Aladdin's] Chamber of wonder and beauty," said the Aberdeen *Evening Republican*, "and the rare novelties, Japanese goods, fine China and crockery, books, frames, albums, ties and candies went like grass before a prairie fire."[1]

Aberdeen had grown since Matilda's previous visit. The streets were still unpaved, but now raised wooden sidewalks elevated pedestrians above the mud after rainstorms and snowfalls. The business district had electric lights and even telephones, some of the first installed outside of New York City. The four thousand residents were well educated, having come from the East (more than fifty from Syracuse and Fayetteville) and several foreign countries. Churches, hotels, an opera house, a school, a small public library, and many community organizations provided an active social life.[2]

Matilda joined in, planning surprises for her grandchildren, sharing the books she read, and hosting séances with Maud and Frank. At these trendy gatherings, people sat around tables in darkened rooms, holding

The building that later housed Baum's Bazaar, with Helen and Charles Gage at windows, Matilda's granddaughters Leslie (*left*) and Matilda on the stairs, c. 1888. Photo by L. Frank Baum. *Alexander Mitchell Library*

hands, trying to contact the dead. Often a "medium," or spiritual leader, led the program. When participants heard mysterious voices, or felt the table tip, or smelled unusual fragrances, some believed, or hoped, like Matilda, that spirits were present.

In December 1888 the National Woman Suffrage Association put out a call for its 1889 Washington convention, signed by President Elizabeth Cady Stanton, Vice President Susan B. Anthony, and Matilda Joslyn Gage, chair of the executive committee. This notice said that the question of uniting the National and the American Woman Suffrage Associations would be considered at the meeting.

What it did not say was that Anthony had met secretly in Boston in with leaders of the American, including Lucy Stone. The two groups had appointed a committee of younger members, including Stone's daughter, Alice Stone Blackwell, and Anthony's "niece," Rachel Foster Avery.

These two women, each secretary of her respective organization, represented younger women in both groups who wanted a merger.

Negotiations continued throughout 1888. One stumbling block was officers: who they should be and how to elect them. The National had many more members than the American (the National had about two thousand members), so a vote by the entire membership would tend to eliminate American candidates.[3] Finally, the American proposed electing officers after the merger if a new constitution and bylaws, which they proposed, were approved by each organization.

Susan B. Anthony was determined to implement this plan at the January 1889 National convention. Matilda, Elizabeth Cady Stanton, and many other National members remained opposed to the union, and Anthony led them to believe that she still agreed with them. Her animosity toward the American, and Lucy Stone in particular, were well known, and she gave no hint to opponents of the merger that she had changed her mind.[4]

The two associations differed on many issues. The National believed that citizens had a natural right to vote and that the federal government should protect this right. The American campaigned within individual states for the right to vote, implying that states had the right to deny it. The American, which focused solely on suffrage, disapproved of the National's controversial campaigns and tactics such as civil disobedience. The American did not want to take on liberal causes like winning equality for women in churches, making divorce easier and fairer for women, or protecting women and children from physical and sexual abuse.[5]

Matilda, anxious to discuss the merger in person, asked for help with expenses to travel from Aberdeen to the convention. In the past she and others had easily obtained funding, but this time Anthony offered only "the most meager travel allowance."[6] Matilda could not afford the trip.

Elizabeth Cady Stanton stayed away, too, probably because she did not want to challenge Anthony directly. Anthony had built such a following in the National that Stanton judged her unstoppable.

"The National Association has been growing politic and conservative for some time," Stanton wrote to a friend. "Lucy [Stone] and Susan alike see suffrage only. They do not see woman's religious and social bondage. Neither do the young women in either association, hence they may as well combine for they have one mind and one purpose."[7]

In Washington on January 21, 1889, in a parlor of the Riggs House

State presidents and officers of the National American Woman
Suffrage Association, 1892. *Bryn Mawr College Library*

hotel, Susan B. Anthony presided in Matilda's absence at a meeting
of the National's executive committee. The group considered the new
proposal from the American, and Anthony took it upon herself to appoint a conference committee to recommend whether or not to accept
it. Two committee members who opposed a merger were asked to re-
sign; two other women who favored the union were appointed (only
one accepted).[8]

Anthony presided in President Elizabeth Cady Stanton's absence,
too, at general sessions, which were held at the Congregational church
on the corner of G and 10th Streets. On the last night of the convention, after most delegates had gone home, the conference committee
addressed a sparsely attended general session. They put forth the new
constitution proposed by the American for the combined associations.
Under this plan, the new organization would have a voting structure
like the American's: people would join through state organizations.
Individual members would no longer be able to vote at national conventions, as National members had always done; that right would be
reserved for state delegates.

The few tired people left in the church voted approval. Then the conference committee took the constitution to the executive committee, which was still meeting, stating that it had just been approved by the National membership. Clara Colby, editor of the *Woman's Tribune*, moved that it be put to a mail vote, to allow input from absent members. Her motion failed.

At midnight the executive committee passed the new constitution by a vote of thirty to eleven, creating the National American Woman Suffrage Association. Susan B. Anthony had campaigned so forcefully that even some women who opposed the union voted in favor of the merger.[9]

In Aberdeen Matilda soon received letters complaining about the merger and the dissolution of the National. Many correspondents asked her to head a protest. She responded with "A Statement of Facts," stating that the limited vote to merge had violated the National's constitution. Even the American, she pointed out, had followed up with a mailed ballot on the issue.

The thirty members of the executive committee who had voted for unification, Matilda said, "violated the principles of a just government, and of the primal woman suffrage demand—individual consent—'the consent of the governed,'—when they thus assumed to control the opinions of the hundreds of individual members of the National Woman Suffrage Association."[10] Five other National officers joined Matilda in signing the statement, which was mailed to all National members. But the deed was done; the weakened National had combined with its old enemy, the American, the new organization supported by the even more conservative Woman's Christian Temperance Union.[11]

The merger pushed Matilda to act on an idea that she had discussed for years with Elizabeth Cady Stanton: starting an antichurch organization. Returning to Fayetteville, she founded the Woman's National Liberal Union (WNLU). She recruited donors, including the Aldriches, a married couple she had met in Rochester, to help her finance a convention for the new organization.

William Farrington Aldrich was a developer of mining and manufacturing in Alabama. He was a social reformer who integrated the living quarters of his black and white workers.[12] His wife, Josephine W. Cables Aldrich, was a spiritualist, a Theosophist, and former editor of the *Occult World*. Her publishing experience would help Matilda to launch a newspaper for the new organization.[13]

Matilda stayed in Fayetteville for the winter of 1889–1890, so she missed Susan B. Anthony's visit to the new state of South Dakota on a speaking tour. In spite of Anthony's differences with Matilda, she stayed with Clarkson while in Aberdeen. She even wrote a letter to the *Woman's Tribune* saying that she had done so.[14]

Matilda also missed the birth of Maud's third son, Harry Neal Baum, on December 18, 1889. By this time Frank Baum's store faced bankruptcy. Luxury items did not sell well in a time of drought, falling wheat sales, and a weakening economy. In January the store closed. Frank sold the remaining goods to his sister-in-law Helen, who reopened the business as the H. L. Gage Bazaar.[15]

Then Frank bought a local newspaper, to be paid for on the installment plan. He published the first weekly issue of the *Aberdeen Saturday Pioneer* on January 25, 1890.[16]

That month Matilda published the first (and only) issue of her newspaper, the *Liberal Thinker*. The first page announced a convention for her

Harry Neal Baum, 1890.
Brenda Baum Turner

new organization, the Woman's National Liberal Union, to be held in Washington, February 24–25, 1890, with Elizabeth Cady Stanton as the featured speaker.

Stanton, however, had decided not to become an officer in the new Union. "I am sick of all organizations and will not pledge myself to do one thing, except to join and speak when you say I must," she wrote to Matilda, in a letter that Matilda published in the paper.[17]

At seventy-four, Stanton was tired, obese, and fed up with politics, but Matilda, who suffered from neuralgia and many other age-related ailments, had lost none of her mental energy. "Again!" Matilda wrote in the *Liberal Thinker*, "this government of the people, by the people, and for the people, seems to be very much limited in the interpretation of the word people; the poor, the women, both married and single, the children, the Indians and other unfortunate inhabitants are not people; the phrase should be changed to read, a government of rich men, by rich men, for rich men."[18]

Matilda went to Washington in February, staying as a guest of the Aldriches in a suite at the Willard Hotel. In public, as usual, she maintained a polite relationship with Susan B. Anthony. On February 15, 1890, she joined two hundred other guests at Anthony's seventieth birthday party, an elegant banquet at the Riggs House hotel. Anthony carried an armful of seventy pink carnations.[19]

Surprisingly Matilda made complimentary after-dinner remarks on "Miss Anthony as a Fellow-worker." Phoebe Couzins toasted "St. Susan," and Elizabeth Cady Stanton spoke on "The Friendships of Women."[20]

In the secret preparations to merge the National and the American, some participants had insisted that Elizabeth Cady Stanton, Susan B. Anthony, and Lucy Stone should take themselves out of the running for president of the combined organization. However, others thought that Stanton, as cofounder of the women's movement, deserved to be president. Still others believed that she had retired from active leadership. Many American members found Stanton's radical ideas, which greatly resembled Matilda's, shocking and unacceptable.

Some people—Susan B. Anthony believed that Matilda was one of them—thought that Anthony wanted to be president, and she probably did. But Anthony decided that she could wait to hold that office. When she addressed a joint meeting of Nationals and Americans on the morning of February 17, 1890, she confronted this issue, and Matilda. "Mrs Gage was present," she wrote afterwards in her diary, "and I made her understand—in my speech on Mrs Stanton for Pres—that all of *her mean efforts* to persuade our members that I favored Union—from ambition to supersede Mrs. Stanton—were fully known to me—and I appealed to all—as they would do me personal honor to vote solid for Mrs Stanton—at the National American union meeting in the afternoon—I was filled with most Rigteous [*sic*] indignation at her."[21]

The joint meeting ended with the election of Elizabeth Cady Stanton as president of the National American, Susan B. Anthony as vice president, and Lucy Stone, who was not present due to illness, as chair of the executive committee. Anthony tried to retain Matilda as a member of the new organization by declaring her an honorary vice president and life member and paying the membership fee herself, but when a list of officers was printed in the *Woman's Tribune*, Matilda's name was not included.[22]

"In all my public life," Matilda wrote later, "I never met so much deceit, vilification, animosity and all uncharitableness as I found in Wash. among my former co-workers."[23]

Matilda and other National loyalists boycotted the first National American convention, which began the next day.[24] However, President Elizabeth Cady Stanton referred to Matilda in her inaugural speech. "I think," Stanton told the crowd, "we should keep our platform as broad as Mrs. Gage and myself desire. It has always been broad. We have discussed upon it everything, and I suppose we always shall. At least I shall, and I suppose Miss Anthony will."[25]

Stanton, who was in poor health, delivered her speech from a sitting position, as she could no longer stand and speak at the same time.[26] Still, she demonstrated her definition of "broad," demanding equality for women in American churches and in divorce law. She urged the new association to reject efforts to introduce the name of God into the constitution. Then she left the convention for New York, where she sailed for Europe the next morning. Clearly she had no intention of speaking at Matilda's convention, which was scheduled to begin six days later.

"Mrs Stanton behaved the worst of them all," Matilda wrote to Clarkson.[27] She had purposely scheduled the Woman's National Liberal Union convention soon after the National American meeting, hoping that some delegates might stay over to attend. Susan B. Anthony warned her supporters not to go, calling the union "ridiculous, absurd, sectarian, bigoted, and too horrible for anything."[28]

Some women did attend both. "Brainy women with advanced views meet in council," the Washington *Critic* reported later. The newspaper described the opening: "Fifty-four ladies in dripping mackintoshes and thirteen gentlemen, accompanying wives and daughters, gathered in Willard Hall." Radical reformers, suffragists, labor organizers, anarchists, Freethinkers, prison reformers, and others had come from twenty-seven states. As they shed their wet wraps, the *Critic* said, "many—nearly all in fact—of the ladies wore little knots of green and yellow ribbon about their dresses, the colors adopted by the Free Thinkers. The green is to represent the earth and the yellow the enlightenment that is bursting over it."[29]

Matilda opened the convention, declaring herself temporary president. Her speech, "The Dangers of the Hour," condemned both Catholic and Protestant churches for trying to expand their powers by breaking down the separation between church and state. She called for a religious revolution to destroy the power of the institutionalized church the same way the American Revolution destroyed the power of monarchy. The convention then passed broad and defiant resolutions against "the Christian Church, of whatever name." Only one speech, by the Reverend Olympia Brown, mentioned suffrage.

Matilda's convention attracted more newspaper coverage in Washington than the National American's had, and it drew national and international attention as well.

"I have been asked for my photo," Matilda wrote to Clarkson a few months later, "to go to Sweden with a sketch of my life. An article of mine is about [to appear] in a Swedish paper. I just received an English Freethought paper containing extracts from my speech at the late convention."[30]

However, the backlash was considerable. Some Freethinkers criticized her for not following parliamentary procedure. Others disapproved of her well-known interest in the occult. The government, taking a dim view of the new organization, intercepted and opened the mail of Matilda and other leaders. Clergymen in Washington, Iowa, and Massachusetts preached against the union.[31]

"I am *glad of it*," Matilda wrote to Clarkson. "I wish to *compel thought* and attract attention to the new step. . . . I am as much as ever, a believer in the *invisible* church—but *not* in this rotten thing known to the world as 'the Christian Church.'"[32]

Soon new supporters, having read about the convention in newspapers, wrote to Matilda asking to join her union. Though Matilda called its convention her "grandest, most courageous work," she could not raise enough money to continue either the organization or its newspaper.[33]

In fact Matilda's financial situation was so dire that she accepted an offer from Susan B. Anthony to buy her out of the *History of Woman Suffrage*. The arrangement led to more bad feelings for Matilda.

"I want to tell you just how Susan cheated me," Matilda wrote to Lillie Devereux Blake.

"I had done a great deal of *advertising* of the History in the *National Citizen* for which I expected pay from Susan, out of the fund she had [been] using for such purpose, and according to her *written guarantee*. Well, after a long time and correspondence I received $160.00[.] Then Susan offered me $1000 for my interest in the History (paid Mrs S, $2000). I needed the money *very greatly*, and finally accepted the $1000.

Susan *demanded a receipt before* she sent the money[.] I forwarded the receipt trusting in her honor and *honesty*, when she sent me $840.00 thus *stealing* $160 from me besides leaving me without payment for all my printing and advertising. That is one specimen. I have kept it to myself but now mean to speak of it—but of course she has got my receipt "locked up in a safe" and I am powerless."[34] As time passed, Stanton appeared ready to make amends. "Well Matilda's convention seemed to go off all right and no one was hurt," she wrote from England to a friend.[35]

"I had [a] recent letter from Mrs Stanton," Matilda wrote to Lillie Devereux Blake, "in which she expressed [her] opinion that the WNLU convention of last winter had been a dignified and successful one, also saying that she was *with me* (a fact I *knew*, only she let her fear of my success,—her cowardice—the intimidation of Susan, &c. cause her to *falsify* and to give lies to the reporter, and to try her utmost for my injury)."

But Matilda still felt wronged. Her letters to Blake, with many words underlined multiple times, reveal her strong feelings at this time.

"Do you suppose I will ever *forget* [Stanton's] course and *Susan's*?" she asked Blake. "I pity them, *so blind*—I have contempt for them, *so unjust*—I have no revengeful feelings, but I *do want them to see* their great mistakes."[36]

Women bicycling through Central Park in New York City, a controversial act at the time, c. 1896.
Library of Congress

23 ✳ Witchcraft and Priestcraft 1891–1893

"Were you at the Council?" Matilda asked Lillie Devereux Blake in a letter written on March 14, 1891. "I hear that Susan and Belva [Lockwood] had a fight. What do you know of it? That Susan accused Belva of face painting, hair dyeing, and riding on a bicycle! What caused the row? When once Susan hates a person for any cause she omits no method of injuring them."[1]

Matilda felt cut off from the movement. She had canceled travel plans in favor of staying in Aberdeen, where the Baums needed her. Frank had undergone three operations, as doctors tried to remove a growth from under his tongue. For a time he was confined to bed, unable to speak. Then, on Matilda's sixty-fifth birthday, March 24, 1891, Maud gave birth to her fourth son, Matilda's eighth grandchild, Kenneth Gage Baum.

As Frank recovered, his newspaper went bankrupt. He decided to make a fresh start in Chicago, a thriving city where a wonderful world's fair was being planned. After traveling there alone, he found work as a newspaper editor but soon switched to a better job selling wholesale china and glassware for the firm of Pitkin and Brooks.[2] He rented a house on the West Side at 34 Campbell Park. While it had no bathroom, running water, or gas hookup, the large front yard faced a pretty street with a parkway of grass and trees down the center. Maud and the boys soon followed Frank to Chicago.

Matilda spent another enjoyable summer in Fayetteville. She remained a member of the Fayetteville Baptist Church, and she attended social events at other churches, too. She visited with friends and sometimes ate dinner at the hotel.

"I forgot to tell you," she wrote to Clarkson, "I have had an offer of marriage and, although I have refused, the gentleman is coming to see me next week. I also forgot to tell you my name has been mentioned for U.S. Senator. . . . I wish I could be elected. I would do a better job than half the men there."[3]

In the fall Matilda's middle daughter Julia arrived in Fayetteville with her eight-year-old niece, Leslie, and her own children, Harry, age five, and Magdalena, four.

Matilda celebrated their arrival. "We had a Garden Party last night," Leslie wrote to her mother and father, Helen and Charly, in Aberdeen. "We had our supper in the summerhouse[.] We had lady's fingers and maccarons [sic] grapes and candy and lemonade[.] The summerhouse was lighted with lanterns out by the spring on the apple tree so it was light around. I wish you and papa could have been here."[4]

The family had probably planned for Leslie to attend school in Fayetteville because her father was seriously ill in Aberdeen. Julia needed medical treatment, too. In October she entered a Syracuse sanitarium for surgery, likely for a gynecological problem.

Matilda took care of the three children, rewarding good behavior and measuring out justice for wrongdoings. "After supper," Leslie wrote to her mother, "I came in the sitting room and was playing with Magdalena, and Harry came up and gave me a blow on the nose with his fist doubled hard as he could. . . . Grandma gave him a good spanking."[5]

That autumn Matilda put up ten pounds of pear preserves. She raked leaves, built bonfires, sewed for her grandchildren, had improvements made on the house, and somehow found time to write to political candidates about women's rights.

She kept up with her granddaughter Matilda, too, writing to her in Aberdeen, "Hallow een night was dark and rainy here, still the children wanted to go into the street, but grandma did not think it best, so she let them go onto the front piazza and holler as loud as they wanted to."[6]

Matilda's daughter Julia came home from the hospital in time for an elaborate Thanksgiving dinner, and in early December she took the children back to South Dakota. The family celebrated in December when Clarkson and Sophie had a second daughter, but the baby lived only a few days.

"Baby has not gone from you," Matilda wrote to Sophie, "but does lie in your arms altho' you cannot see her with your maternal eyes. . . . Her

Matilda's garden, 1888. Photo by L. Frank Baum. *Gage Foundation*

lovely spirit, surrounded by many friends of yours in spirit life, is still with you."[7]

In January 1892 Helen's husband died. "Poor Charley [*sic*]," Matilda wrote to Helen. "There is a certain satisfaction in thinking him free from bodily ills. . . . I want you to remember that my home is always open to you and Leslie. . . . You have done your duty by Charley; let that comfort you. There is the time for all of us to go. Death is as natural as life; it is not a passing out of existence but merely a change of being. Charley still lives, but in a far more comfortable condition than he has for months and years past."[8]

By January 1892 Matilda was back in Chicago, where the Baum family had come to believe that their one-and-a-half-story cottage was haunted. Matilda, whose bedroom was upstairs, said she had to hold tight to the banister as she came down the steps because invisible hands were trying to push her.[9] Unperturbed, she worked on her new book, *Woman, Church and State*. Sometimes she cast horoscopes and read palms for family members.

"She would have us place our palm on an ink pad," her grandson Rob wrote later, "and then make an impression on a piece of paper so she could study the lines of our hands at her leisure. She was also interested in Astronomy and used to take us children out doors at night and point out to us the various stars and constellations."[10]

Despite kidney and other health problems, Matilda kept herself busy and involved. She enjoyed the city life in Chicago, shopping at a store where the tea department was staffed by Chinese clerks with long braids and eating ice cream and strawberries in restaurants. With twenty other people she attended a séance where the medium wore a "beautifully illuminated robe, fixed with phosphorus."[11]

Chicago, according to Matilda, was a great spiritual center. In 1892 Maud and Frank qualified through study to join the Ramayana Theosophical Society; Matilda was already a member. Theosophy continued to attract followers who sought to reconcile new scientific discoveries like evolution or the recalculation of the earth's age with traditional religious beliefs.

Calling herself "an investigator of the occult," Matilda sought out and recorded predictions from astrologers and other spiritual practitioners and checked later to see if they came true.[12] Usually they did not, but she remained hopeful.

Many predictions that Matilda solicited related to business opportunities for her son. When Clarkson wrote from Aberdeen that he felt discouraged, Matilda replied:

> You are rather too young a man to have "lost your ambition." . . . If I had given up when *knocked in the head*, as I have so often been . . . I should have been a poor worthless creature long before this. But I have simply determined that no power on earth, or beyond, should crush me, and here I am, at sixty six, the age at which your father died, holding just as much interest in things as ever. Their character may have changed, but my confidence in myself has not. I can see many things which must be a load on you; but relief is partially in your own hands.[13]

Matilda's self-confidence was evident in February 1893 when she wrote happily to her son, "Even if I should slip out, my chief life-work, my *Woman, Church and State* is done, ready for the printer."[14] "From the toils of the church I hope my book will help free the world," she wrote in another letter, "by giving it new thought."[15]

The book was dedicated, or "inscribed," as Matilda called it, "to the Memory of my Mother, who was at once mother, sister, friend."[16]

She set herself two goals for the book: first, to disprove the myth "that God designed the subjection of woman, and yet her position had been higher under Christianity than ever before,"[17] and second, to inspire women to read history for themselves and dare to draw their own conclusions from its premises.[18]

Matilda, who had a significant library of her own, had also done research at libraries in Syracuse and other cities she visited. She wrote about discoveries from new scholarly fields such as anthropology. "The last half-century has shown great advance in historical knowledge," she wrote; "libraries and manuscripts long inaccessible have been opened to scholars, and the spirit of investigation has made known many secrets of the past, brought many hidden things to light. Buried cities have been explored and forced to reveal their secrets, lost modes of writing have been deciphered, and olden myths placed upon historic foundations."[19]

She told how some societies organized themselves around women, a system she called the matriarchate, citing examples in ancient Egypt, India, Rome, and Scandinavia and in contemporary communities in Africa, Asia, and American Indian confederacies like the Haudenosaunees, or Six Nations. In many pre-Christian or non-Christian societies, and even in the early church, Matilda wrote, women had particular rights and powers.

She believed that Saint Augustine (354–430) had introduced and popularized the doctrine of original sin. Once women were considered contaminated, she said, their very sex became a crime. Eventually male religious leaders, who had come to doubt that women were capable of having souls, banned them from meaningful church participation. In the Middle Ages, Matilda wrote, priests used the teachings of Saint Paul to rule that women had to be silent in church. Some churches created castratos in order to supply choirs with soprano voices. When civil law took over from religious law, the same prejudices prevailed. The idea that women should not speak in public lasted into Matilda's lifetime.

Although the church and government claimed to protect women, Matilda showed that they did not. When she wrote *Woman, Church and State*, the legal age of consent for sexual activity varied from state to state. In Kansas it was twelve. In Delaware it was seven.

"Seven short years of baby life," Matilda raged, "in that state is legally held to transform a girl-infant into a being with capacity to consent to an act of which she neither knows the name nor the consequences, her 'consent' freeing from responsibility or punishment, the villain, youthful or aged, who chooses to assault such baby victim of man-made laws."[20]

In the book's most important and controversial chapter, Matilda expanded her research on witchcraft, citing historical documents that listed expenditures to kill "witches." In Europe burning was the most common and the cheapest method of killing. From around the fifteenth to the eighteenth centuries, the church made such burnings a holiday spectacle.

Witch-hunting, Matilda noted, targeted certain kinds of women. Knowledgeable females were feared most. "Infernally beautiful" women were assumed to possess evil powers over men.[21] Wealthy, independent women were frequent victims. Others included the old, the physically disabled, women with scars or birthmarks, and the mentally ill, their conditions considered proof of a connection to the devil. Relationships with animals were suspect, too: cats were often burned with their owners.

Persecuting witches, Matilda wrote, created a whole industry of jobs for men as clerics, judges, accusers, and torturers in the United States as well as in Europe. Catholics and Protestants alike tormented women who were accused as witches. In colonial Massachusetts, witch-prickers stripped alleged witches naked to see if they had the mark of the devil (a mole) on them or if they responded to being pricked with needles. The tormenters believed that by pricking a "witch-mark," they would render the "witch" unable to speak. "If" Matilda wrote, "under the torture of having every portion of her body punctured by a sharp instrument, the victim became no longer able to cry out, her silence was an accepted proof of finding the witch-mark."[22] And if any victim managed to survive torture, it was believed that she had made a pact with the devil. Trials for witchcraft filled the coffers of the churches, which took the witches' property. Witches were persecuted for 250 years, the practice ending around 1702.

"When for 'witches' we read 'women,'" Matilda said, "we gain fuller comprehension of the cruelties inflicted by the church upon this portion of humanity."[23] "Priestcraft and superstition" were what she called the deadly prejudice against women.[24] Even when witchcraft trials ended, the persecution of women continued. In Matilda's lifetime men could beat, sell, imprison, or even kill their wives with little fear of punishment.

"Looking forward," Matilda wrote at the end of her book, "I see evidence of a conflict more severe than any yet fought by reformation or science. . . . During the ages, no rebellion has been of like importance with that of Woman against the tyranny of Church and State; none has had its far reaching effects. We note its beginning; its progress will overthrow every existing form of these institutions; its end will be a regenerated world."[25]

Woman, Church and State was to be published in July 1893 by a Socialist firm, Charles Kerr of Chicago. The 551-page book would cost two dollars for the cloth edition and three for a half-leather cover. Matilda's son-in-law had an idea for a special edition.

"Frank [Baum] is to have an unbound copy—Has engaged some Frenchman to bind it extra fine," Matilda wrote to Clarkson and Sophie in June, "as a *memorial* volume with my name written etc. He thinks that he can sell a good many also. Has already had orders."[26]

Frank Baum's marketing ideas helped his customers to sell china. After making a sale and waiting for the order to be delivered, he often returned to the store to help arrange the merchandise and perhaps make a new sale.[27] Once he created a window display for a hardware store: instead of simply stacking items, Frank created a man from a boiler torso, stovepipe limbs, a saucepan face, and a funnel hat.[28]

Though grateful for his steady job, Frank hated being away from his family. Lifting heavy boxes of glass and china grew harder each year. On the road he wrote poems to amuse his sons. At home he told stories for his boys and the neighborhood children. Matilda must have enjoyed them, too, as she urged him to write them down and sell them.[29]

To earn extra money, Frank began submitting verses and short stories to contests sponsored by Chicago newspapers. Then he began selling pieces. Matilda wrote proudly to her Dakota relatives about his publishing successes. Eventually Frank sent the manuscript for a children's book to two publishers. *Adventures in Phuniland* was a collection of stories set in a magic land where it rained lemonade and snowed popcorn. Frank's mother offered a hundred dollars to pay for illustrations.

"But if it has as many [pictures] as 'Alice in Wonderland,'" Matilda wrote to Clarkson and Sophie, "it will need sixty engravings. [The

World's Columbian Exposition administration building, evening, 1893. *Brooklyn Museum Archives*

illustrator gets] from $5–$25 an illustration. I hope for Frank's success[.] If his book could get such a run as 'Alice' it would be the literary making of him."[30]

While Matilda and Frank waited to hear about their books, they, along with Maud, the four Baum boys, Frank's mother, who was visiting, and just about everyone else in Chicago, attended the World's Columbian Exposition. This world's fair, covering six hundred acres on the banks of Lake Michigan, was known as "The White City" for its two hundred elaborate white stucco buildings. At night they glowed under electric lights. More than 27 million people attended the fair from May 1 to October 30, 1893.

On June 7, 1893, after five days at the fair, Matilda wrote to Clarkson and Sophie describing its sights: "Saw Tiffany men cutting diamonds," she reported, "and the wasting of diamond dust. . . . I was on the Battle ship yesterday and in the Australian and India Buildings. . . . I met an East Indian High Priest, who is a Theosophist. Carved temple doors, large idols[,] . . . brass work, silver figured punch bowls[,] . . . brass griffins[,] . . . Elegantly carved elephant tusks, sandal wood boxes, gold and silver cloth. . . . Do not begin to give you an idea."[31]

In July Matilda received copies of *Woman, Church and State*. A week later she wrote to Clarkson that the book had gotten a bad review in a Chicago newspaper called the *Inter Ocean*. "I expected savage attacks," she told her son.[32]

Actually, for such a radical book, *Woman, Church and State* was well received. Freethinkers and Theosophists loved it. The *Philadelphia Press, Chicago Times, Boston Transcript*, and *Kansas Farmer* all rated it favorably. The *New York Times* said it would appeal to thinkers.

The Russian author Leo Tolstoy sent Matilda a glowing letter of praise about her book. "It proved a woman could think logically," he said.[33]

24 ✴ Born Criminal 1893–1894

"I have had two more requests from England for my book for review," Matilda wrote to Clarkson from Fayetteville. "One to go to '*Sight*' a prominent spiritual paper, and the other to be used in letters to journals in 'Australia, Tasmania and New Zealand.'"[1] She had sent copies of *Woman, Church and State* to publications in Boston, New York, and India, but the sales she hoped for—and needed badly—did not occur.

Her publisher wanted to advertise the book by promoting Matilda's connection to Elizabeth Cady Stanton and Susan B. Anthony. "I hope that no future mention of either *Mrs Stanton* or *Miss Anthony* will be made," Matilda wrote to Clarkson.

> I have suffered *too much* at their hands to wish to advertise [*sic*] them *in any way*. If W.C. and S. cannot stand on its own merits, let it fall. I have forbidden Mr Kerr to ever mention those women in connection with me—ever again. They have *stabbed* me in reputation, and Susan, at least, has stolen in money from me. They are traitors, also, to woman's highest needs—and Mrs Stanton, especially, I look upon in the woman's battle for freedom, as I do on Benedict Arnold during the war of the Revolution;—she is a traitor to what she knows is right.[2]

But the three of them were inevitably linked. "Mrs. Gage is one of a trio," said a review in the *Truth Seeker*, "Elizabeth Cady Stanton and Susan B. Anthony being the others—whose names are household words among the workers for and supporters of woman suffrage."[3]

In October, Matilda wrote to Clarkson from Fayetteville about a recently passed New York law giving women the right to vote for state school commissioner.

"It is being strenuously combatted," she told him, "and test cases are being made." To her surprise, one case involved her after she registered to vote in the election.

"I had often wondered," she told her son, "how I should feel to be sued, but found out last evening, about six o'clock, when Deputy Sheriff Bennett, of Syracuse, served a Supreme Writ upon me, to appear before Judge M'Lillan [illegible], Monday morning at ten o'clock on petition against my registration."[4]

During her arrest, she said later, "All the crimes which I was *not* guilty of rushed through my mind, but I *failed* to remember that I was a *born* criminal—a woman."[5]

She had no money for a lawyer, but a well-known attorney offered to take the case pro bono because he believed in women's suffrage.

Newspaper coverage of the story amused Matilda, especially a rendering by a courtroom artist.[6] The "Sunday Herald a week since," she wrote to Clarkson, "had what professed to be my likeness [with two other women]. I was represented as a woman weighing 200 pounds, with what looked like a tin basin upside down on my head."[7]

As usual, opposition made her stronger. "Have been in much better *spirits* and *health*, since this warfare began," she wrote to her son. "I think it must end in full suffrage for woman in this state. . . . I had a letter from Susan B Anthony [in] this morning's mail, the first in years but Susan is quick to see anything to her advantage."[8] Anthony wrote to Matilda but left her to face the judicial proceedings on her own.

The court ruled against Matilda, and later she lost an appeal, too. Eventually New York prohibited women's voting in statewide elections in which the jurisdiction extended beyond local school districts.

Soon after this experience, Matilda was adopted into the Wolf Clan of the Mohawk nation. On December 11, 1893, she wrote to Helen from Philadelphia: "While in New York I met Mrs Harriet Maxwell Converse, who has been adopted by the Senecas."[9]

Converse, who was ten years younger than Matilda, came from a family with a great interest in native cultures. Her father and grandfather, both traders, had been adopted by the Seneca nation, her grandfather given the name Ta-se-wa-ya-ee, or "Honest Trader." Harriet Max-

Cartoon from the *Sunday Herald*, 1893. *Gage Foundation*

well Converse, who lived in New York, was a close friend of Ely Samuel Parker, a Seneca attorney and tribal diplomat. With his encouragement, she studied and wrote about the Six Nations, becoming a political advocate for native rights. For her efforts, the Senecas adopted her into the Snipe Clan, and in 1891 they made her a Six Nations chief, the first white woman to achieve this status.[10]

"Mrs Converse . . . proposed our visiting a Mohawk family of women living in New York," Matilda wrote to Helen, "and getting from them an Indian name for me."[11]

The name she received was Ka-ron-ien-ha-wi, Matilda wrote, "or 'Sky Carrier,' or as Mrs. Converse said the Senecas would express it, 'She who holds the sky.' It is a clan name of the wolves." Her Mohawk "sister" said that "this name would admit me to the Council of Matrons, where a vote would be taken, as to my having a voice in the Chieftainship."[12]

Harriet Maxwell Converse shared many interests with Matilda. Both believed, like many other historians, that the United States had, in part, modeled its government after that of the Haudenosaunees. Details of their friendship, and of Matilda's adoption by the Mohawks, are lacking. She must have felt proud and sad at the same time to have voting rights in her adoptive nation but not in the United States.

Matilda spent the hot summer of 1894 in Fayetteville, accompanied by her oldest grandson, who was no longer called Bunting. "I am glad to have Frank with me for errands and to talk with," she wrote to Clarkson. "He . . . seems to have a feeling of responsibility in regard to me."[13] She spent some days in bed with head and stomach problems and suffered also from a pain under her shoulder.

"Have been so debilitated that I reeled like a drunken person at times," she wrote to Helen. The news she sent to her daughter about friends and neighbors included word of many deaths. "*This* is emphatically a place of widows," she wrote.[14]

Across the country, the economy was poor; Matilda worried constantly about money. "Must build a sidewalk next week," she told Helen, "then comes the school tax in two places, &c &c. The pressure upon me is very great and if it does not let up soon, I must go under, I fear; but I *hope* after I get out from under the malign influence of Saturn, that things will be better; they *must* be better."[15]

Her anxieties included Clarkson, too. "I have been looking at your horoscope," she wrote to him, "which I obtained of an astrologer in /86, and I find that *according to astrology*, you are near a very evil time for business, and my advice to you is to settle up your affairs *within this month and next*, or you will be liable to lose all you have."[16]

The family's money problems were real and seemingly permanent, and so were their worries about Julia, Matilda's middle daughter. Her life on the Dakota homestead was harsh; her husband's behavior made everything worse. "I don't know indeed what Julia can do," Matilda wrote to Clarkson, about some unspecified occurrence. "None of us are able to help her. It is a time of trial for us all. *Where* could Frank C. [Julia's husband] take the 'cure' [for alcoholism]?"[17]

When Matilda's health allowed her to work that summer, she sorted out her papers. She wrote her publisher a six-page letter pointing out ways in which he had violated their contract. Although she had taken possession of the plates used to publish *Woman, Church and State*, she still wanted Kerr to sell the copies he had left.

Then she got a surprise. "I want to tell you a most *remarkable* thing," she wrote to Clarkson on August 3, 1894,

that came to my knowledge this morning. When I left home last fall, I put a copy of "*Woman Church and State*" into Dr Wilbur's hands

Matilda's middle daughter, Julia, and her husband, J. D. "Frank" Carpenter, with children Harry and Magdalena, c. 1896. *University of North Dakota*

for presentation to the school library[,] requesting a recognition of the gift, as had not been the case in regard to the *History of Woman Suffrage* which I gave. I got none. I have once or twice spoken to Dr Wilbur in regard to it. This morning I was in there and he asked for a private word. Then, I found that the book went before the [school] board,—that Tom Sheedy, a [Catholic] member of the board, sent the book by express to Anthony Comstock, who sent it back by express with word that he would *prosecute* any school board that put it in their library.[18]

Comstock, secretary of the New York Society for the Suppression of Vice, had gotten Congress to pass the Act for the Suppression of Trade in, and Circulation of, Obscene Literature and Articles of Immoral Use, more commonly called the Comstock Law. This 1873 federal statute outlawed the transportation of obscene materials in the mail; it was based on the New York state law which Comstock used to arrest Victoria Claflin

Anthony Comstock, 1899.
New York Public Library

Woodhull and her sister in 1872 for publishing so-called obscenities in their newspaper. "The incidents of victims of lust told in this book," Comstock wrote, "are such that if I found a person putting that book indiscriminately before the children I would institute a criminal proceeding against them for doing it."[19]

He attacked the book publicly, too. "Unfit to Read," said a headline in the Syracuse *Standard.* "Anthony Comstock condemns a noted suffragist book, *Woman, Church and State.*"[20]

Three days later, Matilda wrote to Clarkson, "the liberal papers and speakers are talking of the Comstock case. If I *had money* I *would prosecute him* for defamation and see how things would turn."[21]

The controversy made national news. Protestants and Catholics alike called for the suppression of Matilda's book. She loved the publicity.

"This is all right splendid for the book," she wrote to Clarkson. "All it now needs is to get into the Papal index Expurgatorius."[22]

Soon a reporter from a local paper came to interview Matilda, who received him while sitting on her front porch. Smiling,[23] she offered her opinion of Anthony Comstock: "I look upon him," she said, "as a man who is mentally and morally unbalanced, not knowing right from wrong or the facts of history from 'tales of lust.' . . . Buddha declared the only sin to be ignorance. If this be true, Anthony Comstock is a great sinner."[24]

Matilda always welcomed criticism. "You wish to know the effect of this Comstock-Catholic attack upon me?" she asked the reporter. "It has acted like a tonic. I have not been well through the summer . . . but the moment I learned of Comstock's letter and read the falsities so freely printed in regard to my book, I grew better and feel myself able to meet all enemies of whatever name or nature."[25]

25 ✳ *The Woman's Bible* 1894–1897

I n 1894 Matilda moved with the Baums to a larger house at 120 Flournoy Street in Chicago. Now they had running water and a bathroom, and the horsecar line to downtown was just a block away.

Surprisingly, Matilda was working with Elizabeth Cady Stanton on a new book. Stanton had asked Matilda in 1886, before their estrangement, to collaborate with her on *The Woman's Bible*. The book would reinterpret the parts of the Bible that referred directly to women, and it would also interpret parts where women were not discussed. Stanton planned to distribute individual books of the Bible to a committee of thirty women, including Matilda, for their comments. Finally, the editors, presumably Elizabeth Cady Stanton and Matilda Joslyn Gage, would combine the work of many into a consistent whole.

Although Matilda still had reservations about her old friend, she liked the idea for this new kind of commentary. "When woman interprets the Bible for herself, it will be in the interest of a higher morality, a purer home," she wrote in *Woman, Church and State*.[1]

Her commentary in *The Woman's Bible* was scathing. "The Christian theory of the sacredness of the Bible has been at the cost of the world's civilization," she wrote.

Its interpretation by the Church, by the State, and by society has ever been prejudicial to the best interests of humanity. . . . From Adam's plaint, "The woman gave to me and I did eat," down to Christ's

L. Frank Baum and his sons (left to right), Frank, Robert, Harry, and Kenneth, at home on Flournoy Street in Chicago, c. 1898. *Alexander Mitchell Library*

"Woman, what have I to do with thee?" the tendency of the Bible has been the degradation of the divinest half of humanity—woman. Even the Christian Church itself is not based upon Christ as a savior, but upon its own teachings that woman brought sin into the world. . . . But our present quest is not what the mystic or spiritual character of the Bible may be; we are investigating its influence upon women under Judaism and Christianity, and pronounce it evil.[2]

Matilda believed that she had created the book's framework and that Stanton had promised to share the copyright with her. Stanton even asked Matilda to apply for the copyright, but in 1895 Matilda learned that Stanton had deleted her from the partnership and asked their friend Clara Colby to submit the application instead.[3]

"Please at once let me know the reason that the copyright of *The Woman's Bible* was not taken out in my name as well as in your own," she wrote to Stanton. "If it was a mistake, perhaps it can be changed even yet as you will not get the copyright papers in some months."[4] Stanton made no change, though she did offer Matilda one hundred dollars to help her in completing the analysis of the Old Testament.[5]

Disappointed and ill, Matilda went home for the summer. In Fayetteville she felt so weak and faint that neighbors checked on her regularly, bringing food and cloth wraps for her chest.

Susan B. Anthony was ailing, too. In August she made national headlines by fainting twice in public. She had to leave the lecture circuit for a month of bed rest. Perhaps the health problems they shared softened Matilda's heart. In September Susan B. Anthony wrote to Elizabeth Cady Stanton, "I had a very sweet letter of sympathy from Matilda yesterday, and I have written her to-day telling her that I hope she will be able to attend your celebration."[6]

Matilda did go to New York for Elizabeth Cady Stanton's eightieth birthday party, sponsored by the National Council of Women. On November 12, 1895, three thousand people gathered at the Metropolitan Opera House to honor the person many considered to be the cofounder of the women's movement. A throne of flowers stood on the stage under an arch of flowers, with the name "Stanton" spelled out in red carnations on a white background.

As Stanton entered the audience rose to salute her, clapping and waving their handkerchiefs. She began a speech, but unable to stand for long or even project her voice, she watched from the seat of honor while a friend delivered most of it.[7]

Afterwards, at a reception at the Savoy Hotel, Stanton, Matilda, and Anthony were honored as pioneers of the women's movement. Later on the trip, Matilda spent a day with Stanton, who now lived in a Manhattan apartment house with an elevator. The two old friends must have reconciled to some extent, as Matilda soon began work on the second volume of *The Woman's Bible*. She must have been pleased when the first volume, published at the same time as the birthday party, sparked a storm of criticism.

Elizabeth Cady Stanton during her eightieth birthday
celebration, 1895. *Rutgers University*

The Washington, D.C., *Evening Times* said, "The volume is made up
of the most caustic criticism of various passages referring to women."[8]

The Saint Paul *Daily Globe* called the book "little less than a hand-
book of infidelity."[9]

Archbishop Patrick William Riordan of San Francisco said, "The
'Woman's Bible' is absurd; preposterous. There is no such thing as
a 'Woman's Bible.' There is but one Bible, and that is for all mankind,
which, of course, includes all womankind as well."[10]

Neither Matilda nor Elizabeth Cady Stanton attended the National
American Woman Suffrage Association's 1896 convention, though Stanton was still president. Many of the association's members complained
there that their president's antireligious new book disgraced the suffrage movement. The convention passed a resolution denying any connection between the association and the "so-called Woman's Bible."[11]

When she heard the news, Stanton was furious. She resigned from
the National American and the women's movement, but she continued
to write.

Back in Chicago, Matilda wrote as her health permitted. She was bedridden for much of 1896 with congestion and stomach, back, and kidney problems. At one point she suffered a near-death experience, carrying on conversations with friends who had died.[12]

In the summer, a brutal heat wave and personal conflict added to her discomfort. "Mrs Baum [Frank's mother] is here for six weeks or so," she wrote to Helen in July, "and behaves like a child. She is terrible;—saps my vitality. I wish I could get away while she is here."[13]

But Matilda could always summon energy to fight with her publisher. "Kerr has refused to pay anything more," she wrote to Helen, "although *acknowledging* an indebtedness of $35.20[.] Besides this, there are 68 books unaccounted for and other things. *He is a thief.* If I could get what he owes me, I might get along."[14]

Sick or well, she worried about family finances. Frank Baum, she believed, had lost the tax receipts from his store in Aberdeen, though he said that he paid the taxes. When he could not prove that he had, Helen, then the owner, thought she was obligated to pay the taxes herself, with money she did not have. It is possible that Helen's poor business skills created this problem; whatever the cause, in September 1896, Matilda sent her $68.45 to pay the debt.

"L. F. [Frank] could have paid these taxes ten times over," Matilda told Helen, "in what he yearly expends for tobacco. He professed to leave off cigars a while since on account of the expense and smoked a pipe. *Now* he uses both."[15]

Even with the taxes paid, Helen's store was failing. The Baums were hard up, too; Frank's china sales had decreased. Matilda urged Helen to enter a writing contest, to take in boarders, and to open an exchange in her store where women could print and sell recipes.

"The *best* of women are now entering *every* kind of business," she wrote to Helen. "Maud is taking embroidery lessons and *expects to give lessons.*"[16]

By Christmas Matilda felt better, writing to her granddaughter Leslie, "the boys hung up stockings and were up at half past four—then had a tree after breakfast. The big boys principally got books, but each one a knife. . . . Aunt Maud gave me a book 'Growth of the Soul'—a Button Boy and recovered my down pillow. Uncle Frank gave me a Chinese Primrose."[17]

Frank Baum's travel created stress for the family. "L.F. comes in Friday," Matilda wrote to Helen in February. "He failed to receive [Maud's] letter for a day or two and telegraphed her—said he wouldn't travel if he didn't hear, &c &c—a perfect baby."[18] But soon she wrote proudly that Frank had earned seventeen dollars for a story published in a magazine.

In her first six weeks of teaching embroidery, Maud enrolled more than twenty students and earned thirty dollars.[19] To help Helen in her Dakota store, Matilda, Maud, and Maud's hired girl, Sigrid, embroidered pieces for her to sell.[20]

In addition to embroidering, seventy-one-year-old Matilda attended lectures, wrote letters, and worked on essays. "Since Jan 1st," she wrote to Helen in April, "I have written or finished up '*The Esotericism of the 1893 National Flag*,' [*sic*] '*The Influence of Food upon Character*,' [next title is illegible], '*Food as Medicine*,' these [last] three all vegetarian and I am to *speak* before the 'West Side Vegetarian Society' next Wednesday."[21]

"So you see," she told Helen, "I *do* a great deal, even if not feeling well. . . . I keep abreast of the world or ahead of the major portion of it even more; it is my nature. I walk quickly as is also my nature, but nevertheless I have arrived at the age—and past—when the Bible says 'the grasshopper is a burden,'—and at seventy, Mrs Stanton wrote me she had found it so. She still lives and works at 81—so perhaps may I."[22]

26 ※ That Word is Liberty 1897–1898

"Frank has had his book, '*Prose Stories of Mother Goose*' accepted by 'Way and Williams' [a publishing firm] of this city," Matilda wrote in June 1897. (This letter was probably to Helen; only a fragment has survived.) "He only took it about a week ago and to-day the letter of acceptance came. It was called 'charming.' 'Way and Williams' are a new house but one that pushes things—(which Kerr never did) and do *fine* work."[1]

The book, later renamed *Mother Goose in Prose*, became L. Frank Baum's first published book for children. Its stories answered questions his sons had asked, such as "why did the mouse run up the clock?" and "how could blackbirds survive being baked in a pie?"

"Let him once make a success with his book," Matilda wrote, "and the way is clear. . . . How many [manuscripts] I have had rejected and the one I had accepted went into the hands of a thief. But such is fate—or karma." Moving on, she started a novel with occult and reform themes.[2]

Feeling better than she had in some time, Matilda spent the summer in Fayetteville. She had the house painted, the windows repaired, and nine dead trees—pear, plum, and cherry—cut down for firewood.[3] Bearing up well under the summer heat, she went through papers, clearing eight bushels of bills, receipts, and letters from the barn. She prepared files of the *National Citizen and Ballot Box* for binding and boxed other newspapers and articles to send to libraries.[4]

In September she wrote to her son, "Have been writing up 'Revelations,' for the 'Woman's Bible.' . . . Have been suffering from indigestion and am using cayenne pepper on my food."[5]

Matilda's Baum grandsons (clockwise from top left), Robert, Frank, Harry, and Kenneth, 1897. *Gage Foundation*

Clarkson had moved with his wife Sophie and daughter Matilda from Aberdeen to Bloomington, Illinois. In the fall he fell ill, hemorrhaging from his bronchial tubes, so Matilda visited him there. When he began to feel better, she returned to the Baums and their busy family life in Chicago.

Sometimes her older grandsons Frank and Rob Baum rode their bicycles into the country. "On one of these trips," Rob wrote later,

> I gathered up several garter snakes, which were a harmless snake about a foot long, and decided to take them home with me as a souvenir of my trip. Having no place to put them, I carefully wrapped them up in my handkerchief and put them in my pocket. When I got home, mother was out but Grandma Gage was up in her room, and I went up to her saying, "Look, Grandma, what I've got." Then I took out the handkerchief and dumped the snakes into her lap. Grandma,

who had been expecting to see some colored stones, or other boyish treasure, was quite startled and none too well pleased. So I had to gather up my snakes and make a hasty retreat to the basement, where I put them in a box.[6]

Snakes aside, Matilda enjoyed surprises and new experiences. "I am going down town after dinner," she wrote to Clarkson, "to hear the Swami Abbapananda on karma. This Swami is a woman. . . . Tell Sophie I have tasted a 'dill pickle[.]' They are the kind that Chicago school children buy for a cent apiece and are very fond of."[7]

After attending a meeting, she wrote to him, "I heard last evening of a South American plant, bearing what is called 'a button,' which if eaten opens the occult senses while not disturbing the normal action of the brain in any way. A high professor in the Homeopathic College here—the largest in the world—told of these buttons and said they would soon be in Chicago. I shall try and see or learn about them and perhaps try them."[8] Whether she ever tried peyote is unknown.

In November, suffering from indigestion and heart palpitations, Matilda had to cancel a talk for the Political Equability Club. Lying in bed, partially propped up on her elbow, she wrote to Clarkson: "I wish you would not worry so much about me. It is entirely unnecessary and hurts both you and me. . . . I am much better this morning[.] My heart beats naturally and I suffer less from indigestion. . . . L.F. [Frank] left this morning to be gone till Friday night. He came in and kissed me good bye, as he always does. He is very kind to me."[9]

Frank, who had long wanted to give up traveling and lugging heavy boxes of china, decided to start a trade journal for window trimmers. The *Show Window* targeted the new department stores that were opening in many cities. After publishing the first issue, on November 1, 1897, Frank resigned from his sales job, but the magazine was never financially successful.

Matilda had a new project, too. The National American Woman Suffrage Association, led by Susan B. Anthony, had invited her to speak at a Chicago convention.

"I am advertized [*sic*] to speak Saturday," she wrote to Clarkson, on November 15, "of '*Suffrage a fundamental right* in a *republican form of government.*' I wish to get well so as to speak. . . . I have got a great ink blot on my best nightdress sleeve in writing this letter."[10]

Maud Gage Baum, c. 1890.
Alexander Mitchell Library

But Matilda was too ill to go. Instead Susan B. Anthony came to visit her.

"Susan seemed to think I looked poorly," Matilda told Clarkson, "but said she had seen me apparently near death many times."[11] During this visit Matilda tried to give Anthony a copy of *Woman, Church and State*, but Anthony "utterly refused."[12]

Matilda had several doctors, one a woman she knew through Chicago spiritualists; Maud called her "a quack."[13] For a time, another doctor visited Matilda daily, heating her spine to help with kidney trouble. He changed her diet frequently, but nothing made her feel better. Even so, she read newspapers and kept up with her family. To her granddaughter Matilda, who now lived in Bloomington, Illinois, she wrote:

Rob and Frank [her older Baum grandsons] . . . have built a house in the back yard near the fence. . . . It is partially shingled, has a window and a door[.] The boys bought a padlock and two keys. . . . They have Aunt Maud's old dining room rug over the top and sides. Uncle Frank had small oil stove, which he let them take. They make toast on the stove and have lots of fun. . . . Aunt Maud did not wish them to have the stove, and I fear they may get burned.[14]

Matilda worried especially about her youngest daughter. "I am a great drag on Maud, who is poorly and has had no *real* rest," she wrote to Helen. "You see, my time is growing short on earth, and I wish it to be if I am not well."[15]

Still she planned to go home in April, in time to start a garden, and to have Helen and Leslie join her in Fayetteville. "My house is large and cool and pleasant," she wrote to Leslie in Aberdeen, "the very pleasantest on the street. I have a hammock—one your mother left—on the front stoop—a beautiful fringed swing on the west end. . . . We will have nice times there; and you will enjoy the . . . red and black currants, plums, pears, apples, grapes, and cherries—a piano you can learn to play on and a nice library. With much love, Grandmother."[16]

In February 1898 in Washington, D.C., the National American Woman Suffrage Association celebrated the fiftieth anniversary of the Seneca Falls convention. Although Matilda had prepared a speech for the convention, "Woman's Demand for Freedom; its Influence upon the World," she was too ill to attend.

"Rev. Anna Shaw made a speech before mine was read," Matilda wrote to Helen, "speaking highly of my work and of *"Woman Church and State"* which must have been a *bomb* in that pious convention. The rule was that no speech should be allowed unless the author was present, but exceptions were made in my case and Mrs Stanton'[s.] The *'Post'* reporter asked for my speech and made a very good report, for all of which I am glad."[17]

Clarkson visited his mother at this time, stopping as he traveled from Bloomington, Illinois, to Aberdeen. On March 9, 1898, she wrote to him in Dakota, "Now do try and see if you cannot sell our lot and Helen's building while there for $1650 or $1600," she urged in several pages of specific advice about money matters. "I have not been well since you left here," she said. "Doctor comes every day and says I have the grip [*sic*]—have great suffering in breathing, but Doctor Smith thinks he can pull me up."[18]

However Dr. Smith could not help his seventy-one-year-old patient. At 6:00 a.m. on Sunday morning, March 13, Matilda fell in the bathroom. The crash woke Maud, who rushed in with Frank and Sigrid, the hired girl. Matilda, who was on the floor, could barely move, but the three of them got her back to bed. Matilda's grandson Frank was sent for the doctor, who diagnosed a stroke.

Matilda, aware at first, tried to help them when they changed her nightdress. She could speak a few words, but gradually she lost that ability and drifted into unconsciousness.[19]

When death seemed certain, Maud wired to her siblings to come. Clarkson and Helen arrived first from Aberdeen. On March 18 Clarkson wrote to his wife Sophie:

Mother's condition is growing weaker and weaker every hour, I did not think this morning she would live the day out but when doctor was here he said she could linger until Sunday. Helen is here and Julia is coming tomorrow night[.] She never will see mother alive. . . . [Mother] can not speak and we all think she is blind in her left eye. I am so glad Sophie that I came here two weeks ago. . . . we had such a nice visit together talking over Fayetteville and family [illegible.] It is all I can do to keep from breaking down in tears, now that the end is so near, nearly every thing I have in this world is done to help from mother.[20]

Matilda died later that evening. "The end," said Helen, "was very quiet and peaceful, just a gradual shortening of her breath."[21]

Julia arrived the next day. "When I first saw Mother," she wrote in her diary, "she lay under a little canopy of white. Later the undertaker came and laid mother on a black leather couch, she was dressed in a dark blue tea gown. . . . We sat in her room most of the time."

For the funeral, the undertaker laid Matilda in a casket in the parlor. Julia said, "The casket and room were filled with flowers. She lay in a *bed of flowers*. American Beauty Roses—of Mother's favorite hue [red] dominated."[22]

Matilda, c. 1895.
Gage Foundation

Maud sobbed over the casket, "Mother, mother, what am I going to do?"[23]

Helen wrote later, "As she lay in her casket, calm, peaceful, . . . I took her hand in mine with reverent love, as I thought how much a few strokes of her pen had done for the welfare of her children, how much it had accomplished for humanity."[24]

Matilda had made plans for her own death. A radical minister presided at her funeral. She had asked to be cremated, an unusual request for the time, and a famous Theosophist spoke at the crematory.

Later Maud took her mother's ashes for burial in the Fayetteville Cemetery. These words are carved on her tombstone: "There is a word sweeter than mother, home, or heaven; that word is liberty."

27 ✳ Erased from History

THE MATILDA EFFECT

n 1888 the *Woman's Tribune* said that the three names of Susan B. Anthony, Elizabeth Cady Stanton, and Matilda Joslyn Gage, "linked together in the authorship of *The History of Woman Suffrage*, will ever hold a grateful place in the hearts of posterity." But this prediction never came true.[1]

Sally Roesch Wagner, the leading expert on Matilda Joslyn Gage, said that "the losers in history are at the mercy of the winners, and Anthony wrote Gage out of the official history of the movement."[2]

Anthony and Stanton, who were both older than Matilda, survived her: Stanton by four years and Anthony by eight. Thus, they had time after her death to shape history the way they wanted it to be. Although there is no evidence that they deliberately plotted together to erase Matilda from collective memory, both women took actions that resulted in that effect. They did this even during her lifetime.

Elizabeth Cady Stanton reminisced about her own life in dozens of pages in the *History of Woman Suffrage*. She also wrote Matilda's biography for the *History*—two paragraphs, plus a footnote. Stanton's brief description of Matilda "rummaging through old libraries"[3] suggested an eccentric rather than the movement's primary historian and scholar. Matilda, who presumably read this passage soon after it was written, likely could have changed it, but she was more interested in reform than in personal fame.

The *History* describes Susan B. Anthony's newspaper, the *Revolution*, in detail. It lasted just two years under Anthony's leadership. Matilda's paper, the *National Citizen and Ballot Box*, which endured for more

Susan B. Anthony and Elizabeth Cady Stanton at
Anthony's home in Rochester, New York, 1891.
Rochester Public Library

than four years as the National's official publication, was described only as a newspaper bought by Matilda and moved to Syracuse.[4]

In April 1888 Matilda answered a letter from Lillie Devereux Blake, who was, apparently, having trouble with Susan B. Anthony. "What did S.B.A. do worse more to you than others?" asked Matilda. "Just think of me, while I was *presiding* [at a convention], she [Anthony] got up and *mentioned* the History which '*she* and *Mrs Stanton* had prepared,'— totally ignoring me-and—there—I—was—in—the—chair!!"[5]

Matilda complained to Blake about many occasions when Anthony kept her from receiving credit, and even payment, for her work. "The various mottos on envelopes, centennial questions and so forth have been mine," she told her friend in 1890,

> although *Susan* has received the *credit* for them, and when "thanked" has not denied the soft impeachment. There is where she is and always has been unjust. Not satisfied with her own powers, her own good work, she has *more than willingly*—robbed others of their just dues. . . . I positively do not think a more *unjust* person to her co-workers lives than Susan B. Anthony. . . . All she cares for is self. . . . She wishes to impress people with the idea that nothing can be done without her finger in the pie. I think she absolutely hates any other person to do work in suffrage that will tend to bring their names before the public.[6]

Anthony asked a journalist, Ida Husted Harper, to write her biography. Harper worked at Anthony's house in Rochester, under Anthony's close supervision. The book, published in 1898, the year Matilda died, as *The Life and Work of Susan B. Anthony*, credited Anthony with most victories in the women's movement.

Harper cited Matilda thirty-one times, while Elizabeth Cady Stanton's autobiography, *Eighty Years and More*, also published in 1898, contained just ten references to Matilda. This selective omission of their many activities together was especially shocking because it was Matilda who encouraged Stanton to write the book; the copyright registration for the title is in Matilda's hand.[7] With this autobiography, Stanton recast her own role in the movement, downplaying her radical opinions and thus rendering herself more acceptable to the mainstream public.

One part of Stanton's book concerned an issue Matilda had complained about to Lillie Devereux Blake. Stanton, Matilda told Blake, "went all over the west, putting *my motto*, one that I *formulated for myself* . . . in autograph albums *as her own.* Came here and told me and *laughed* about it. I asked her if she put it in quotations. She said 'No' and, lo, I found it in Mrs. Bones album, appearing as if *original* with Mrs. Stanton."[8]

In *Eighty Years and More,* Stanton confessed to appropriating Matilda's favorite motto. "I unfortunately used a pet sentiment of Matilda's," Stanton wrote. "So, here and now, I say to my autograph admirers, from New York to San Francisco, whenever you see, 'There is a word sweeter than Mother, Home or Heaven—that word is Liberty,' remember that it belongs to Matilda Joslyn Gage."[9]

Later Stanton's children revised her autobiography, omitting eight references to Matilda, including the story about the autograph. Their cuts left only two mentions of Matilda, the colleague who had most resembled their mother in political and religious beliefs.

Stanton died in 1902, the same year that the fourth volume of the *History of Woman Suffrage,* which covered the years from 1883 to 1900, was published. Susan B. Anthony had kept control of the project, choosing her biographer to do the writing. Ida Husted Harper asked Lillie Devereux Blake for help with the New York chapter.

"I have been hard at work," Blake wrote in her diary, "on a history of what I have done during the years from 1884 to 1900, for Mrs. Harper, who is getting up the fourth volume of Woman Suffrage. As Miss Anthony is directing its writing, I shall probably have small recognition."[10] Blake's premonition came true.

"An uninformed person," Blake's daughter wrote later, "reading the chapter . . . on the work in New York during the years when my mother was its driving force . . . would be convinced that Miss Anthony was ever New York State's leading spirit and that Mrs. Blake's part in the work was negligible. Yet most of the time Miss Anthony was out of the state, working elsewhere, traveling and lecturing."[11]

In Volume 4, Ida Husted Harper named Stanton as the "matchless writer" of the first three volumes and Anthony "the collector of material, the searcher of statistics, the business manager, the keen critic, the detector of omissions, chronological flaws and discrepancies."[12]

"On many occasions," Harper wrote, "they called to their aid for historical facts Mrs. Matilda Joslyn Gage, one of the most logical, scientific and fearless writers of her day." Crediting Matilda with writing only three chapters in Volume 1, one in Volume 2, and none in Volume 3, Harper demoted her from coauthor to helpful assistant.[13]

Volume 4, written entirely by Harper, omitted Matilda from its account of the International Council of Women. Historian Sue Boland says that Matilda never received proper credit for the arrangements she made for this meeting.[14] The official report of the council, however, reveals the major role she played in this convention.

Volume 4 gave a one-paragraph account of the merger of the National Woman Suffrage Association with the American Woman Suffrage Association, omitting any mention of dissent. The book did not list Matilda's Woman's National Liberal Union as a women's organization, though it included lesser groups such as the National Floral Emblem Society. Volume 4 provided detailed coverage of the 1898 National American convention but eliminated Matilda's address, which was her last (read aloud when she was too ill to attend). The printed convention report, however, did include the speech.[15]

Both Clarkson and Helen wrote to Susan B. Anthony, objecting to the small credit their mother received for her work in the books that Anthony had published after Matilda's death.

Anthony responded with a cool letter to Clarkson, beginning "Dear Mr. Gage"; previously she had addressed him as "My Dear Friend."

"I am sorry you were pained at the omission of your mother's name by Mrs. Harper," Anthony wrote. "I think she generally mentions it in connection with the History."[16]

Later she wrote to Helen, "My Dear Girl, . . . I do not know why it was or how it was that the name of Matilda Joslyn Gage was left out of the circular [advertising the *History*] and did not notice it until your brother Clarkson reminded me of it; it shall certainly go back in the next lot that I have printed. But in the preface to the History you will find full credit is given to her for her work on the production . . . of three chapters." Here Anthony decreased Harper's chapter count by one, adding that Matilda's "help *on many other* chapters was *truly great.*"

"I think," she continued, "you will find no other place where her name has not been mentioned, *except in the circular*, and I am very sorry for that, and, as I say, when I get more printed I will have her name inserted."[17]

Lillie Devereux Blake's daughter Katherine Devereux Blake became a well-known suffrage and peace activist. In 1943 she cowrote a book about her mother, in which she also described Matilda:

> Mrs. Gage was a tireless student, a fine research worker, thorough in all she undertook; she had a deep sense of justice and at times an appalling frankness of speech—which I loved! One was never in doubt as to where Mrs. Gage stood, and she was invariably fair to others. She prepared many important suffrage documents, not always getting credit for them. . . . She was absolutely honest in all her dealings and I would take her word at any time as against anybody else's. I always loved and admired her greatly. I think in many ways she was the greatest of these four women [including Anthony, Blake, and Stanton]. Someone should write an adequate life of this great leader.[18]

Harriot Stanton Blatch, the daughter of Elizabeth Cady Stanton and a feminist leader in her own right, wrote a memoir with coverage of her mother, too. But none of Matilda's children wrote books about her, and she left no autobiography or diary. Her granddaughter Matilda Jewell Gage preserved about five hundred letters which were passed down to her from her father, Clarkson, and her cousin Leslie Gage.

Few letters survive from what must have been an extensive correspondence among the three women, Matilda Joslyn Gage, Elizabeth Cady Stanton, and Susan B. Anthony.[19] Both Stanton and Anthony burned their letters near the end of their lives, and Anthony burned the rest of her papers as well, ensuring that their accounts of history would stand as written. In time, Anthony's biography, Stanton's autobiography, and the *History of Woman Suffrage* became the unquestioned history of the women's movement.

One author did not forget Matilda: her son-in-law, L. Frank Baum. After Matilda died, he kept *Woman, Church and State* in print while he continued to write children's stories. His 1900 book *The Wonderful Wizard of Oz* featured a self-confident American heroine named Dorothy. Baum went on to write thirteen more Oz books; Matilda's influence can be seen throughout. In the second volume, the rightful ruler of Oz, a fairy princess named Ozma, comes to power. For the rest of the series, Oz is a feminist utopia, ruled by women.[20]

By the time women got the vote in 1920, Matilda Joslyn Gage had been forgotten. Even the memory of Elizabeth Cady Stanton was fading; the

L. Frank Baum, c. 1911. Like his mother-in-law Matilda, Baum always used the word "suffragist," never the demeaning term "suffragette." Photo by George Steckel. *UCLA Library*

Nineteenth Amendment, which enfranchised women, was known by then as the Anthony Amendment, even though Stanton had written it.

Male historians and publishers, who controlled the study of history, lost interest in women's rights as the country moved through two world wars and the post–World War II boom of economic growth.

Not until the 1960s, during the American Civil Rights movement, did a second-wave women's rights movement surface. Although women could vote at this time, they still faced inequality in many areas. Job discrimination was blatant, with separate want ads for men and women. Only men were considered suitable doctors, engineers, or pilots. Fewer than 50 percent of women worked outside the home, most in comparatively low-paying positions such as secretaries, waitresses, or teachers.[21] Though many women played prominent roles in the Civil Rights movement, they were often excluded from formal leadership positions. Few women were elected or appointed to high offices in state and national government.

In the 1960s, working women had to meet requirements about height, weight, or age in jobs where those qualities were irrelevant. They had to wear skirts, never slacks, to school and work. Some jobs even required makeup. Enduring lewd remarks or unwanted touching from male coworkers was "just part of the job." Abortion was illegal. Qualified women were denied jobs because they had young children. Working women who got pregnant could be fired. Flight attendants had to give up their jobs if they married. Married women had to take their husband's surnames.

In 1964 a landmark U.S. Civil Rights Act prohibited discrimination because of race, color, religion, national origin, and, for the first time, sex. But society was slow to change its unfair requirements for women. The Equal Employment Opportunity Commission, created to enforce the statute, did little until women began suing for equal rights on the job—and winning.

Outraged that women's rights were still routinely denied, activists founded the National Organization of Women in 1966. Meanwhile books like *The Second Sex* (1953) by Simone de Beauvoir, *The Feminine Mystique* (1963) by Betty Friedan, Kate Millet's *Sexual Politics* (1969), Germaine Greer's *The Female Eunuch* (1970), and Barbara Seaman's *Free and Female* (1972), as well as *Ms.* magazine, founded in 1972 by Gloria Steinem and Dorothy Pitman Hughes, showed that women's common experiences had been submerged and never studied.[22]

Around the world women began rallying to a new cry, "The personal is political," and working on grassroots issues like shelters for battered women, rape crisis centers, and childcare cooperatives. Women academics, gaining ground in universities, founded departments to study the culture of women.

An Australian activist, Dale Spender, described this time: "In the late 1960s an over-riding issue in my life was to find out whether other women felt and thought as I did in a male-dominated society. It soon became apparent that I was not alone. As many of us began to talk to each other . . . we experienced a feeling of elation that goes with finding a more meaningful and positive way of viewing the world and ourselves. But then many of us began to ask whether we were the first generation of women to have felt this way."[23]

In 1972 the U.S. Congress finally passed the Equal Rights Amendment, which began with the words "Equality of rights under the law shall not be denied or abridged by the United States or by any State on account of sex." But the law that Matilda had worked so hard to put in place failed to win ratification by thirty-eight states as needed in the time allotted. It is still not part of the Constitution.

Sally Roesch Wagner (left) with Matilda Jewell Gage on Gage's porch
in Aberdeen, 1975. Photo from collection of Sally Roesch Wagner.

More encouragingly, in 1972, a federal law known as Title IX went
into effect, saying: "No person in the United States shall, on the basis of
sex, be excluded from participation in, be denied the benefits of, or be
subjected to discrimination under any education program or activity
receiving Federal financial assistance." Title IX opened major opportunities for women in higher education programs, especially women
athletes.

Sally Roesch Wagner, one of the first scholars in the United States to
receive a doctorate in women's studies, chose Matilda as the subject of
her 1978 dissertation. Wagner founded one of the first women's studies
programs in the country at California State University, Sacramento. For
more than forty years, she has studied Matilda Joslyn Gage.

Wagner grew up in Aberdeen, South Dakota, where she knew Matilda's granddaughter, Matilda Jewell Gage. The two women worked together as Wagner recorded many Gage family stories. Eventually Wagner convinced the granddaughter to leave her grandmother's papers to the Schlesinger Library on the History of Women in America at Radcliffe University. Wagner has published a number of monographs and articles about Matilda, and she encouraged publishers to reissue Matilda's work.

When *Woman, Church and State* was republished in 1972, feminist scholars rediscovered Matilda Joslyn Gage. In her book *Gyn/Ecology* (1978), American scholar Mary Daly focused on practices like foot-binding in China, female genital mutilation in Africa, and witch burning in Europe. Her study of this last topic led her to Matilda's work.

"It is infuriating," Daly wrote then, "to discover that this foresister, and others like her, had already gathered and analyzed materials which feminist scholars are just beginning to unearth again."[24] She wondered if the new round of feminist scholarship would be similarly forgotten.

Dale Spender included a thirty-six-page biographical sketch of Matilda in her book *Women of Ideas: And What Men Have Done to Them* (1982). "As I go over these words of Gage," she wrote, "again and again I have to try to make sense of all the contradictions: Written in Victorian times? Encompassing some of the most radical insights of contemporary times? All that scholarship? Why didn't I know?"[25]

In a 1980 foreword to a new edition of *Woman, Church and State*, Mary Daly called Matilda "a major radical feminist theoretician and historian whose written work is indispensable for an understanding of the woman's movement today. . . . She made the connections which others feared to make. She prophesied, and she named the enemy. Consequently, of course, her stature has never been acknowledged."[26]

Dale Spender wrote, "It is one of the greatest tragic ironies that this woman who understood so much about the process, who put such energy into exposing and subverting it, should herself be the one to 'disappear', should have her work wiped away. Could it be that she was the most dangerous?"[27]

In 1993 Margaret W. Rossiter, a professor of the history of science, invented the term "the Matilda effect" to describe "women scientists who have been ignored, denied credit or otherwise dropped from sight." Rossiter found so many cases, both historical and contemporary, "that a sex-linked phenomenon seems to exist as has been documented to be the case in other fields, such as medicine, art history and literary criticism." She named this effect for Matilda because Matilda "was aware of, and denounced, the tendency of men to prohibit women from reaping the fruits of their own toil, and in fact noticed that the more woman worked the more men around her profited and the less credit she got."[28]

In 1999 scholars studying witch trials endorsed Matilda's view that victims had died terrible deaths for what she called "a crime which never existed—save in the imagination of those persecutors, and which grew in their imagination from a false belief in woman's extraordinary wickedness—based upon a false theory as to original sin."[29] These modern historians praised Matilda's work. Based on new research, they greatly reduced her estimate of how many women had been killed for the crime of witchcraft (she said 9 million; new estimates are fifty thousand to one hundred thousand), but still they respected her analysis.[30]

That same year, Sally Roesch Wagner went to see Matilda's house, which had been divided into apartments. Relocating to Fayetteville, Wagner founded the Matilda Joslyn Gage Foundation and began raising money to buy and renovate the house. Wagner recruited key supporters such as Gloria Steinem—then and still the best-known leader in the modern women's movement.

Steinem said, "Matilda was ahead of the women who were ahead of her time." She wrote that Matilda defined marriage in a way that foreshadowed an equal partnership, marrying across racial lines, and marriage between members of the same sex.[31]

A scholarly book by Leila R. Brammer, *Excluded from Suffrage History: Matilda Joslyn Gage, Nineteenth-Century American Feminist*, was published in 2000. It described Matilda's work, but not her family life.

In 2007 the National Women's History Project honored Matilda as one of fourteen women in a program called "Generations of Women Moving History Forward."

In 2011 Sally Roesch Wagner led the celebration when the Gage House in Fayetteville opened as a participatory museum and a center for social justice dialogue (matildajoslyngage.org). The Gage House, which attracts thousands of visitors each year, is a stop on the Votes for Women Trail and also on the Freethinkers' Trail. It is recognized by the New York and federal governments as a site on the Underground Railroad.

Women from New York picketing at the White House, 1917.
Library of Congress

The second wave of the women's rights movement helped to restore Matilda Joslyn Gage's reputation, though not to the extent that her contributions justified. In part this may be because people tend to simplify history as time passes. They select individuals to represent movements—Martin Luther King for civil rights, César Chávez for farmworkers' rights, and Susan B. Anthony for women's rights. These leaders certainly changed the world but not by themselves.

Other contributions, large and small, have been lost to history. While writing this book I told many people about Matilda. I was pleased when some responded with their own stories. "My grandmother, Elizabeth Selden Rogers, was arrested in 1914 for picketing in front of the White

House," my friend Anthony H. Horan told me. "She was sentenced to sixty days in a workhouse, but Woodrow Wilson pardoned her after just three days."

Researchers can add to history while honoring Matilda and other pioneers by investigating members of their own families and communities, people who fought for women's rights or other rights, and then they can record these stories.

The *History of Woman Suffrage* is available free from online sources like Project Gutenberg and Google Books. Students and scholars could trace the ninety-three women Matilda profiled in the first chapter, many of whom have been forgotten. They include people like Lady Mary Wortley Montagu (Matilda spelled the name *Montague*) who, in the 1720s, introduced smallpox inoculation to western medicine after seeing it practiced in Turkey; Frances Wright, who in 1825 created a settlement in Tennessee where slaves could work to earn their freedom; and Jane Marcet, a British educator whose book, *Conversations on Chemistry*, served as a textbook in British and American schools for much of the nineteenth century ("and from it various male writers filched their ideas," Matilda wrote).[32]

Other subjects to study include men who supported the women's movement, such as Samuel May, Parker Pillsbury, and George Francis Train. A paper on the antisuffrage movement might also prove enlightening. The index of almost any modern book about a reform movement will reveal a culturally diverse group of people and causes.

Documenting the present is important, too. In 2017 a major scandal developed worldwide as powerful men in entertainment, media, politics, and other fields lost their jobs and paid millions of dollars in damages to women they had harassed or assaulted. Criminal charges resulted for some; the story was still unfolding as this book went to press. In response to the many offenses reported, actress Alyssa Milano launched an internet campaign to promote the #MeToo movement, urging women who had been harassed or assaulted to come forward on social media. Later she credited Tarana Burke for founding the movement in 2006. Both women emphasized that the campaign was designed to focus on victims rather than perpetrators.[33] The response was overwhelming and it included women from many walks of life—service industries, farm workers, universities, and more.

Given that millions of U.S. women still face harassment and even assault on the job, it is not surprising to note that they do not yet receive equal pay for equal work. In addition, restrictions on sex education, birth control, and abortion prevent them from controlling their own bodies. Around the world, religious organizations exclude women from positions of leadership or equality. Some religions support governments in limiting women's freedom of movement, access to education and health care, and life choices about marriage and work. In 2017 millions of women were literally enslaved and others lived in conditions close to slavery.

Brave reporters like Nicholas D. Kristof and Sheryl WuDunn reveal these conditions. "The global statistics on the abuse of girls are numbing," they wrote in their 2009 book, *Half the Sky*, describing how girls are killed by murder, abortion (boy babies are preferred), or neglect. "It appears that more girls have been killed in the last fifty years," they said, "precisely because they were girls, than men were killed in all the battles of the twentieth century." They offer ideas for ways in which individuals can make a difference, as Matilda did.

Kristof and WuDunn put this women's rights issue into perspective. "In the nineteenth century," they wrote, "the central moral challenge was slavery. In the twentieth century, it was the battle against totalitarianism. We believe that in this century the paramount moral challenge will be the struggle for gender equality in the developing world."[34]

To help the oppressed, we need to study and appreciate the efforts of many people to bring justice into the world. Matilda worked all her life to record women's accomplishments and to make the world a better place for everyone. Recent scholars have built on her efforts by bringing her work to light again. New historians are still needed to document the past, the present, and what will become our future.

Hillary Rodham Clinton said recently, "Women's rights are human rights."

Matilda Joslyn Gage said, "The longer I work, the more I see that woman's cause is the world's cause."[35] Matilda died in 1898. Her cause continues.

❋ Notes

The following abbreviations appear throughout the notes and sources.

MJG	Matilda Joslyn Gage
HLG	Helen Leslie Gage (Matilda's oldest daughter; her married name was also Gage)
TCG	Thomas Clarkson Gage (Matilda's son)
LDB	Lillie Devereux Blake (Matilda's friend)
Blake Papers	Lillie Devereux Blake Papers, 1847–1986, Missouri Historical Society, Saint Louis
Gage Papers	Matilda Joslyn Gage Papers, 1840–1974, Arthur and Elizabeth Schlesinger Library on the History of Women in America, Radcliffe Institute for Advanced Study, Harvard University
HOWS	*History of Woman Suffrage*, edited by Elizabeth Cady Stanton, Susan B. Anthony, and Matilda Joslyn Gage (New York: Source Book Press, 1970), 3 vols.
NCBB	*National Citizen and Ballot Box* (Syracuse, N.Y.), newspaper on microfilm, available at Arthur and Elizabeth Schlesinger Library on the History of Women in America, Radcliffe Institute for Advanced Study, Harvard University
LC Scrapbook	Matilda Joslyn Gage's woman suffrage scrapbook, 1850–1898, held at Library of Congress, call no. JK1901.G16.

INTRODUCTION

1. Sally Roesch Wagner, introduction to Matilda Joslyn Gage (MJG), *Woman, Church and State: The Original Exposé of Male Collaboration against the Female Sex* (Watertown, Mass.: Persephone Press, 1980), p. xxiii.

CHAPTER 1. RISKING ARREST, JULY 4, 1876

1. *HOWS* 3:18.

2. Sally Roesch Wagner, *A Time of Protest: Suffragists Challenge the Republic, 1870–1887* (Aberdeen, S.Dak.: Sky Carrier Press, 1992), p. 53, cites the Gage scrapbook of writings, Matilda Joslyn Gage Papers, 1840–1974, Arthur and Elizabeth Schlesinger Library on the History of Women in America, Radcliffe Institute for Advanced Study, Harvard University.

3. This form of the title is used on a handbill advertising a meeting at the Unitarian Church, July 4, 1876, LC Scrapbook. *HOWS* 3:27 calls it "a declaration of rights of the women of the United States, and articles of impeachment against the government."

4. MJG to TCG, July 6, 1876, Gage Papers.

5. "City of the Declaration," *New York Times*, July 6, 1876.

6. Unattributed newspaper article, LC Scrapbook.

7. *HOWS* 3:41.

8. This account of Couzins's actions, and the quotation, are from Katherine Devereux Blake and Margaret Louise Wallace, *Champion of Women: The Life of Lillie Devereux Blake* (New York: Fleming H. Revell Company, 1943), p. 125. Blake said of Couzins: "she went away from our unsafe proximity." In her speech later that day, Couzins said that she had been on the platform and participated in the "overt act." (*HOWS* 3:36).

9. *HOWS* 3:30.

10. Blake and Wallace, *Champion of Women*, p. 125.

11. MJG to TCG, July 6, 1876, Gage Papers.

12. Blake and Wallace, *Champion of Women*, p. 125.

13. *New York Semi-Weekly Tribune*, untitled article, July 21, 1876, in LC Scrapbook.

14. MJG to TCG, July 6, 1876, Gage Papers. "Order, order" is quoted in *HOWS* 3:30.

15. Blake and Wallace, *Champion of Women*, p. 126.

16. MJG to TCG, July 6, 1876, Gage Papers.

17. *HOWS* 3:31.

18. MJG to TCG, July 6, 1876, Gage Papers.

CHAPTER 2. A FAMILY SECRET, 1826–1836

1. Sally Roesch Wagner, "That Word Is Liberty: A Biography of Matilda Joslyn Gage" (PhD diss., University of California, Santa Cruz, 1978), p. 3.

2. "Judgment Day, Part 4: 1831–1865, People and Events, The Underground Railroad, c. 1780–1862," PBS, pbs.org.

3. Frederick Douglass, *Narrative of the Life of Frederick Douglass, An American Slave, Written by Himself* (Cambridge, Mass.: Belknap Press of Harvard University Press, 1960), pp. 28–30.

4. Vanessa Johnson, a Griot (storyteller) and consultant to the Gage Foundation's Underground Railroad Room, used the term "freedom seeker" in connection with MJG.

5. Sally Roesch Wagner in discussion with the author, May 1, 2011. Wagner was a close friend of Matilda Jewell Gage, a niece of Matilda Joslyn Gage (MJG), who provided Wagner with an "exhaustive knowledge of family history and stories" (Wagner, "That Word Is Liberty," p. ix). Wagner states that MJG had blue eyes in "Oral History as a Biographical Tool," in *Women's Oral History: The Frontiers Reader*, ed. Susan Hodge Armitage, Patricia Hart, and Karen Weathermon (Lincoln: University of Nebraska Press, 2002).

6. MJG, speech in *Report of the International Council of Women, Assembled by the National Woman Suffrage Association, Washington, D.C., U.S. of America, March 25 to April 1, 1888* (Washington, D.C.: Rufus H. Darby, 1888), 1:347.

7. "The First Piano in Onondaga County, New York" (*Syracuse Herald*, August 15, 1915), cited in Wagner, "That Word Is Liberty," p. 15.

8. Wagner, "That Word Is Liberty," p. 8.

9. Ibid., p. 28.

10. Ibid., p. 17.

11. Ibid., p. 19.

12. Ibid., p. 27.

13. Ibid., pp. 10–12.

14. W. S. Cee, "Mrs. Isaac Cody: The 'New Woman' of her Period" (newspaper article, Syracuse, ca. 1910), cited in Wagner, "That Word Is Liberty," p. 11.

15. Wagner, "That Word Is Liberty," p. 8.

16. Typescript of letter from MJG to LDB, May 11, 1890, Lillie Devereux Blake Papers, Missouri Historical Society, Saint Louis. Some handwritten pages of this letter are missing.

17. Ibid.

18. Wagner, "That Word Is Liberty," p. 16.

19. Typescript of letter from MJG to LDB, May 11, 1890, Blake Papers.

20. Wagner, "That Word Is Liberty," p. 36.

21. Ibid., pp. 42–43.

CHAPTER 3. THINK FOR YOURSELF, 1837–1845

1. Typescript of letter from MJG to LDB, May 11, 1890, Lillie Devereux Blake Papers, Missouri Historical Society, Saint Louis. Some handwritten pages are missing.

2. Sally Roesch Wagner, "That Word Is Liberty: A Biography of Matilda Joslyn Gage" (PhD diss., University of California, Santa Cruz, 1978), pp. 52–53.

3. Ann Preston, speech for the Woman's Rights Convention at Westchester, Penn., printed in the Seneca Falls *Lily*, August 1852, p. 1.

4. MJG, speech in *Report of the International Council of Women, Assembled by the National Woman Suffrage Association, Washington, D.C., U.S. of America, March 25 to April 1, 1888* (Washington, D.C.: Rufus H. Darby, 1888), 1:347.

5. Elizabeth Cady Stanton, Susan B. Anthony, and Matilda Joslyn Gage, *HOWS* 1:466.

6. Ibid. 1:81.

7. MJG, "Address of Matilda Joslyn Gage," in *The Proceedings and Addresses at the Freethinkers' Convention Held at Watkins, N.Y., 1878* (New York: Da Capo Press, 1970), p. 213.

8. *New York Sunday Morning News*, quoted in Samuel J. May, *Some Recollections of Our Antislavery Conflict* (New York: Arno Press and *New York Times*, 1968), p. 167.

9. Wagner, "That Word Is Liberty," p. 49.

10. Hezekiah Joslyn to Helen Leslie Joslyn, November 11, 1841, in the Gage family scrapbooks of family history items and newspaper clippings, cited in Wagner, "That Word Is Liberty," p. 81, as part of the Matilda Jewell Gage Collection, probably now part of the Matilda Joslyn Gage Papers, 1840–1974, Arthur and Elizabeth Schlesinger Library on the History of Women in America, Radcliffe Institute for Advanced Study, Harvard University.

11. MJG to Leslie Gage, February 5, 1896, Gage Papers.

12. MJG to TCG, November 14, 1897, Gage Papers.

13. Wagner, "That Word Is Liberty," p. 85.

14. "The Clinton Liberal Institute," Fort Plain Free Library, New York Heritage Digital Collections, cdm16694.contentdm.oclc.org.

15. MJG to Helen Leslie Joslyn, [April] 24, 1842, Gage Papers.

16. Wagner, "That Word Is Liberty," p. 86.

17. MJG to Helen Leslie Joslyn, [April] 24, 1842, Gage Papers.

18. *Syracuse Post Standard*, April 13, 1917, cited in Wagner, "That Word Is Liberty," p. 90.

19. Mary E. Paddock Corey, "Matilda Joslyn Gage: Woman Suffrage Historian, 1852–1898" (PhD. diss., University of Rochester, 1995), p. 5.

CHAPTER 4. DEFYING THE LAW, 1845–1850

1. Sally Roesch Wagner, "That Word Is Liberty: A Biography of Matilda Joslyn Gage" (PhD diss., University of California, Santa Cruz, 1978), p. 95.

2. Matilda Joslyn Gage (MJG), speech in *Report of the International Council of Women, Assembled by the National Woman Suffrage Association, Washington, D.C., U.S. of America, March 25 to April 1, 1888* (Washington, D.C.: Rufus H. Darby, 1888), 1:347.

3. Barbara S. Rivette, *Fayetteville's First Woman Voter: The Story of Woman Suffrage Leader Matilda Joslyn Gage Including her 1880 Writings about the New York School Vote Campaign* (Fayetteville, N.Y.: Matilda Joslyn Gage Foundation, 2006), p. 15.

4. Wagner, "That Word Is Liberty," pp. 100–103.

5. Ads in *Syracuse Standard*, June 18 and December 3, 1845, cited in Wagner, "That Word Is Liberty," p. 107.

6. Wagner, "That Word Is Liberty," p. 106.

7. Ibid., pp. 107–8.

8. MJG to TCG, May 29, 1885, Gage Papers.

9. Wagner, "That Word Is Liberty," pp. 108–10.

10. Frederick Douglass, *Narrative of the Life of Frederick Douglass, An American Slave, Written by Himself* (Cambridge, Mass.: Belknap Press of Harvard University Press, 1960), appendix, pp. 156–57.

11. Wagner, "That Word Is Liberty," p. 115.

12. Ibid., pp. 120–21.

13. Barbara S. Rivette, "Fayetteville's First Woman Voter," p. 11.

14. Ibid.

15. Ibid., p. 125.

16. Elizabeth Cady Stanton, Susan B. Anthony, and Matilda Joslyn Gage, *HOWS* 1:63–64.

17. MJG to TCG, July 15, 1886, Gage Papers.

18. Wagner, "That Word Is Liberty," p. 127.

19. Ibid., p. 133.

20. MJG, speech in *Report of the International Council of Women*, 1:347.

21. Rheta Childe Dorr, *Susan B. Anthony: The Woman Who Changed the Mind of a Nation* (New York: AMS Press, 1970), p. 51.

22. *Mechanic's Advocate* (Albany, N.Y.), cited in *HOWS* 1:802-3.

23. MJG to TCG and Sophie Jewell Gage, December 19, 1891, Gage Papers.

24. [MJG], "Old Times and New," *NCBB* (Syracuse, N.Y.), May 1880, pp. 3-4.

CHAPTER 5. BOLD AND DARING, 1851-1852

1. Elizabeth Cady Stanton, Susan B. Anthony, and Matilda Joslyn Gage, *HOWS* 1:465.

2. Geoffrey C. Ward, *Not for Ourselves Alone: The Story of Elizabeth Cady Stanton and Susan B. Anthony, an Illustrated History* (New York: Alfred A. Knopf, 1999), p. 70. No source given.

3. Elizabeth Cady Stanton, *Eighty Years and More (1815-1897), Reminiscences of Elizabeth Cady Stanton* (London: T. Fisher Unwin, 1898), p. 201.

4. Sally Roesch Wagner, "That Word Is Liberty: A Biography of Matilda Joslyn Gage" (PhD diss., University of California, Santa Cruz, 1978), p. 193.

5. Ibid., p. 335.

6. MJG, speech in *Report of the International Council of Women, Assembled by the National Woman Suffrage Association, Washington, D.C., U.S. of America, March 25 to April 1, 1888* (Washington, D.C.: Rufus H. Darby, 1888), 1:347.

7. Wagner, "That Word Is Liberty," p. 213.

8. MJG, speech in *Report of the International Council of Women*, 1:347.

9. *HOWS* 1:519.

10. Ibid. 1:520.

11. MJG, speech in *Report of the International Council of Women*, 1:347.

12. Leila R. Brammer, *Excluded from Suffrage History: Matilda Joslyn Gage, Nineteenth-Century American Feminist* (Westport, Conn.: Greenwood Press, 2000), pp. 4-5.

13. MJG, speech, *The Proceedings of the National Woman's Rights Convention, Held at Syracuse, September 8th, 9th, and 10th* (Syracuse: Printed by J. Masters, 1852), p. 38. The following excerpts and descriptions of this speech are taken from pages 38-45. *HOWS* 1: 528-29 uses the word *lords* instead of *lord* in the first quotation.

14. Unattributed newspaper article, Gage Papers.

15. MJG, speech in *Report of the International Council of Women*, 1:347.

16. *Syracuse Journal*, quoted in *HOWS* 1:526.

17. "National Woman's Rights Convention," *New-York Daily Tribune*, September 14, 1852, p. 6.

18. Ibid., p. 6.

19. *Syracuse Daily Journal*, September 13, 1852, quoted in *HOWS* 1:543.

20. *Syracuse Daily Star*, September 11, 1852, quoted ibid. 1:852.

21. Sally Roesch Wagner, introduction to MJG, *Woman, Church and State: The Original Exposé of Male Collaboration against the Female Sex* (Watertown, Mass.: Persephone Press, 1980), p. xv, cites *Syracuse Star*, October 1852.

22. Barbara S. Rivette, *Fayetteville's First Woman Voter: The Story of Woman Suffrage Leader Matilda Joslyn Gage Including her 1880 Writings about the New York School Vote Campaign* (Fayetteville, N.Y.: Matilda Joslyn Gage Foundation, 2006), p. 5.

23. Typescript of letter from MJG to LBD, May 11, 1890, Lillie Devereux Blake Papers, Missouri Historical Society, Saint Louis. Some handwritten pages are missing.

CHAPTER 6. A WOMAN OF NO ORDINARY TALENTS, 1853–1854

1. The certificate and analysis of Matilda Joslyn Gage are in the Gage Papers.

2. Elizabeth Cady Stanton, Susan B. Anthony, and Matilda Joslyn Gage, *HOWS* 1:465–66.

3. Sally Roesch Wagner, "That Word Is Liberty: A Biography of Matilda Joslyn Gage" (PhD diss., University of California, Santa Cruz, 1978), p. 288.

4. *HOWS* 1:546.

5. Ibid. 1:547.

6. Ibid. 1:549.

7. *New-York Daily Tribune*, September 8, 1853, p. 5.

8. *HOWS* 1:567.

9. Ibid. 1:567–68.

10. Ibid. 1:567.

11. Alice Stone Blackwell, *Lucy Stone: Pioneer of Women's Rights* (Boston: Little, Brown, 1930), p. 105.

12. Wagner, "That Word Is Liberty," p. 333.

13. Barbara S. Rivette, *Fayetteville's First Woman Voter: The Story of Woman Suffrage Leader Matilda Joslyn Gage, Including her 1880 Writings about the New York School Vote Campaign* (Fayetteville, N.Y.: Matilda Joslyn Gage Foundation, 2006), p. 3.

14. Sally Roesch Wagner reports that when the floor in this area of the Gage house was taken up during reconstruction, no such cellar was found. Telephone interview with the author, May 11, 2011.

15. Helen Leslie Gage, quoted in Sally Roesch Wagner, "Underground Railroad Room," Matilda Joslyn Gage Foundation, matildajoslyngage.org.

16. Susan B. Anthony, "Matilda Joslyn Gage: Work of the Dead Suffrage Leader Recalled by Susan B. Anthony," *Rochester Democrat and Chronicle*, March 28, 1898, cited in "What Others Say," Matilda Joslyn Gage Foundation,matildajoslyngage.org

17. *Daily Saratogian*, August 19, 1854, quoted in *HOWS* 1:622.

18. *HOWS* 1:622.

19. Anthony, "Matilda Joslyn Gage," *Rochester Democrat and Chronicle*, March 28, 1898.

20. Lucretia Mott to MJG, October 5, 1854, Gage Papers.

21. Wagner, "That Word Is Liberty," p. 352.

CHAPTER 7. LIBERTY FOR ALL, 1855–1865

1. Sally Roesch Wagner, "That Word Is Liberty: A Biography of Matilda Joslyn Gage" (PhD diss., University of California, Santa Cruz, 1978), pp. 242–43.

2. Ibid., p. 150.

3. TCG, "Reminiscences," July 1931, Matilda Joslyn Gage Center, quoted in Wagner, "That Word Is Liberty," pp. 184–85.

4. MJG, "Julia's Lessons," ca. 1855, in possession of Jocelyn Birch Burdick, Fargo, N.Dak., quoted in Wagner, "That Word Is Liberty," p. 375.

5. Sally Roesch Wagner, "Underground Railroad Room," Matilda Joslyn Gage Foundation, matildajoslyngage.org.

6. Wagner, "That Word Is Liberty," p. 373.

7. Ibid., p. 405.

8. MJG to Helen Leslie Joslyn, March 29, 1857, Gage Papers.

9. Wagner, "That Word Is Liberty," p. 432.

10. Ibid., p. 436.

11. Ibid., p. 447–48.

12. MJG to TCG, Sunday, August 7, [1858 or 1859], Gage Papers. The date 1858 has been penciled in on this letter, but August 7 was a Sunday in 1859.

13. MJG, "Uncle Tom," [1861?], typescript, Gage Papers.

14. Wagner, "Underground Railroad Room," Gage Foundation website (about the store); "How I Decorated on the Fourth," *NCBB* (Syracuse, N.Y.), July 1879, p. 2 (about the house).

15. MJG, "Uncle Tom."

16. "The Civil War and Central New York," cnycivilwar.com.

17. Joseph [second two names illegible], 122nd Regiment, to MJG, January 16, 1863, Gage Papers.

18. Barbara S. Rivette, *Fayetteville's First Woman Voter: The Story of Woman Suffrage Leader Matilda Joslyn Gage, Including her 1880 Writings about the New York School Vote Campaign* (Fayetteville, N.Y.: Matilda Joslyn Gage Foundation, 2006), pp. 5–6.

19. Wagner, "Underground Railroad Room."

20. *Syracuse Onondaga Standard*, September 4, 1862, quoted in Sally Roesch Wagner, introduction to Matilda Joslyn Gage, *Woman, Church and State: The Original Exposé of Male Collaboration against the Female Sex* (Watertown, Mass.: Persephone Press, 1980), p. xvii.

21. "Emancipation Proclamation," *Syracuse Journal*, January 2, 1863, cited in Sally Roesch Wagner, "Matilda Joslyn Gage House: A Station on the Underground Railroad," pacny.net.

22. MJG to HLG, [November 1897], fragment, Gage Papers.

23. [MJG], "How I Decorated on the Fourth," *NCBB*, July 1879, p. 2.

CHAPTER 8. THE NEGRO'S HOUR?, 1866–1869

1. Susan B. Anthony, speech to the Eleventh National Woman's Rights Convention, New York, May 10, 1866, in Elizabeth Cady Stanton and Susan B. Anthony, *Se-*

lected Papers of Elizabeth Cady Stanton and Susan B. Anthony, ed. Ann D. Gordon (New Brunswick, N.J.: Rutgers University Press, 1997), 1:585.

2. Susan B. Anthony, speech to the Woman's Rights Convention, May 10, 1866, quoted in Ida Husted Harper, *Life and Work of Susan B. Anthony, Including Public Addresses, Her Own Letters and Many from her Contemporaries during Fifty Years* (New York: Arno, 1969), 1:260.

3. MJG, "Is Woman Her Own?," *Revolution*, April 9, 1868, p. 215.

4. MJG to Susan B. Anthony, *Revolution*, January 14, 1869, p. 20.

5. TCG to MJG, March 21, 1869, Gage Papers.

6. Henry Hill Gage to TCG, May 9, 1869, Gage Papers.

7. Elizabeth Cady Stanton, speech to the Equal Rights Association, May 12, 1869, in Elizabeth Cady Stanton, Susan B. Anthony, and Matilda Joslyn Gage, *HOWS* 2:350. *HOWS* identifies this as the speech that Stanton gave to a December 1868 conference; Elizabeth Cady Stanton and Susan B. Anthony, *Selected Papers of Elizabeth Cady Stanton and Susan B. Anthony*, ed. Ann D. Gordon (New Brunswick, N.J.: Rutgers University Press, 2000), 2:198, says that Stanton misidentified the speech in *HOWS* as she adapted it only after the passage of the Fifteenth Amendment in February 1869, after which she called for a Sixteenth Amendment.

8. Elizabeth Cady Stanton, "Manhood Suffrage," *Revolution*, December 24, 1868, p. 392.

9. *HOWS* 2:353 says that this speech was from the January 1869 Woman Suffrage Convention, but the first footnote in the *Selected Papers of Elizabeth Cady Stanton and Susan B. Anthony*, 2:198, says that Stanton mistakenly published it as her January speech in *HOWS*. It was actually her May 1869 version of the speech that was published in *HOWS*. The May speech is not quoted in the *Selected Papers*, only in *HOWS*.

10. *HOWS* 2:351, with the same caveat as in note 9 above. This information is from her May speech.

11. *HOWS* 2:382.

12. Ibid.

13. Alice Stone Blackwell, *Lucy Stone: Pioneer of Women's Rights* (Boston: Little, Brown, 1930), 2:384.

14. Ibid.

15. M. V. Longley, "Anniversary of the Equal Rights Association," *Dayton Women's Advocate* (Ohio), May 29, 1869, pp. 4–5, in Ellen Carol DuBois, *Feminism and Suffrage: The Emergence of an Independent Women's Movement in America, 1848–1869* (Ithaca: Cornell University Press, 1978), p. 191.

CHAPTER 9. THE NATIONAL WOMAN SUFFRAGE ASSOCIATION, 1869

1. Alma Lutz, *Susan B. Anthony: Rebel, Crusader, Humanitarian* (Boston: Beacon Press, 1959), p. 160.

2. George Ellington, *The Women of New York or the Under-World of the Great City* (New York: Arno Press, 1972), pp. 31, 38.

3. Ibid., pp. 46–47.

4. *HOWS* 2:400–401.

5. Ibid.

6. Lana Rakow and Cheris Kramarae, eds., *The Revolution in Words: Righting Women, 1868–1871* (New York: Routledge, 1990), p. 68.

7. MJG, "Letter from Mrs. Gage," *Revolution*, January 6, 1870, p. 4.

CHAPTER 10. STRONG-MINDED WOMEN, 1869–1871

1. Celia Burleigh, "Fashionable Moments: When Flora McFlimsey Looked in the Face of Susan B. Anthony and Did Not Turn to Stone," 1896 article in *The Woman Citizen*, vol. 3, by Alice Stone Blackwell, Leslie Woman Suffrage Commission, 1918, p. 896.

2. Mary E. Paddock Corey, "Matilda Joslyn Gage: Woman Suffrage Historian, 1852–1898" (PhD. diss., University of Rochester, 1995), p. 7.

3. MJG, "Appeal to the Friends of Woman Suffrage in the State of New York," *Revolution*, July 29, 1869, p. 49.

4. Ibid.

5. MJG, letter to the editor, *Revolution*, December 9, 1869, p. 364.

6. "Woman in Washington," ibid., February 17, 1870, p. 102.

7. MJG to TCG, January 19, 1860, Gage Papers.

8. Washington University in Saint Louis was the first law school in the country to admit women. Phoebe Couzins, born between 1839 and 1843 (sources vary), entered in 1869, graduating in 1871. Because other law schools also began accepting women students around this same time, Couzins was the third woman law student in the country to graduate, following Ada Kapley, who graduated from the Union College of Law in 1870, and Sara Kilgore Wertman, who graduated from the Michigan University Law School two months before Couzins graduated in Missouri. Karen L. Tokarz, "Commemoration: A Tribute to the Nation's First Women Law Students," *Washington University Law Review*, January 1990, pp. 94–95, openscholarship.wustl.edu.

9. "Woman in Washington," *Revolution*, February 17, 1870, p. 102.

10. *HOWS* 2:415.

11. "Woman in Washington," *Revolution*, February 17, 1870, p. 102.

12. MJG to TCG, January 19, 1860, Gage Papers.

13. MJG, "The Moral Aspect," *Revolution*, February 10, 1870, p. 92.

14. "Mrs. Joslyn Gage in Virginia," ibid., May 19, 1870, p. 314, says this happened on May 6, 1870. *HOWS* 2:435 says it happened in April 1870.

15. "Suffrage Conventions," *Revolution*, July 7, 1870, p. 26.

16. Lana Rakow and Cheris Kramarae, eds., *The Revolution in Words: Righting Women, 1868–1871* (New York: Routledge, 1990), pp. 18–19.

17. MJG to Martha Coffin Wright, June 10, 1870, Garrison Family Papers, Sophia Smith Collection and Archives, Smith College, Northampton, Mass.

18. "Woman's Suffrage Books," *Revolution*, February 24, 1970, p. 127.

19. Gloria Steinem, "Introduction: Victoria Woodhull through Modern Eyes," in *The Woman Who Ran for President: The Many Lives of Victoria Woodhull*, by

Lois Beachy Underhill (Bridgehampton, N.Y.: Bridge Works Publishing, 1995), p. xiii.

20. Underhill, *Woman Who Ran for President*, p. 77.

21. Victoria C. Woodhull, "The Memorial of Victoria C. Woodhull," *HOWS* 2:448–49.

22. "Reflections and Incidents—The Washington Convention," *Revolution*, January 19, 1871, p. [6].

23. Ida Husted Harper, *Life and Work of Susan B. Anthony, Including Public Addresses, Her Own Letters and Many from her Contemporaries during Fifty Years* (New York: Arno, 1969), 2:375.

24. *HOWS* 2:485.

25. Emanie Sachs, *"The Terrible Siren": Victoria Woodhull (1838–1927)* (New York: Harper and Brothers, 1928), p. 80.

26. MJG, "Woman's Rights Catechism," *Fayetteville Weekly Recorder*, July 27, 1871, LC Scrapbook.

27. Sally Roesch Wagner, *Sisters in Spirit: Haudenosaunee (Iroquois) Influence on Early American Feminists* (Summertown, Tenn.: Native Voices, 2001), p. 79.

28. MJG to LDB, July 8, 1884, Lillie Devereux Blake Papers, Missouri Historical Society, Saint Louis.

CHAPTER 11. THE UNITED STATES ON TRIAL, 1871–1873

1. *Syracuse Journal*, May 7, 1871, quoted in Sally Roesch Wagner, *Matilda Joslyn Gage: She Who Holds the Sky*, 2nd ed. (Aberdeen, S.Dak.: Sky Carrier Press, 2002), p. 3; Barbara S. Rivette, *Fayetteville's First Woman Voter: The Story of Woman Suffrage Leader Matilda Joslyn Gage, Including her 1880 Writings about the New York School Vote Campaign* (Fayetteville, N.Y.: Matilda Joslyn Gage Foundation, 2006), p. 6 (no source given in Rivette).

2. Elizabeth Cady Stanton and Susan B. Anthony, *Selected Papers of Elizabeth Cady Stanton and Susan B. Anthony*, ed. Ann D. Gordon (New Brunswick, N.J.: Rutgers University Press, 2000), 2:xxiv–xxv.

3. MJG to TCG, January 15, 1872, Matilda Joslyn Gage Papers, 1840–1974, Arthur and Elizabeth Schlesinger Library on the History of Women in America, Radcliffe Institute for Advanced Study, Harvard University (hereafter Gage Papers).

4. Unattributed, LC Scrapbook.

5. "Wanted—Our Rights," *Washington Daily Patriot*, January 11, 1872, ibid.

6. Lucia Patrick, "Religion and Revolution in the Thought of Matilda Joslyn Gage, 1826–1898" (PhD diss., Florida State University, 1996), p. 127.

7. All details and quotations in this and the preceding paragraph are from MJG to TCG, January 15 and 21, 1872, Gage Papers.

8. Rheta Childe Dorr, *Susan B. Anthony: The Woman Who Changed the Mind of a Nation* (New York: AMS Press, 1970), pp. 249–50.

9. Ibid.

10. Ibid., p. 251.

11. Emanie Sachs, *"The Terrible Siren": Victoria Woodhull (1838–1927)* (New York: Harper & Brothers, 1928), pp. 191, 215.

12. Dorr, *Susan B. Anthony*, p. 253.

13. Sally Roesch Wagner, "The Susan B. Anthony Window in the Home of Matilda Joslyn Gage," *New York History Review*, March 29, 2012, nyhrarticles.blogspot.com.

14. Ida Husted Harper, *Life and Work of Susan B. Anthony, Including Public Addresses, Her Own Letters and Many from her Contemporaries during Fifty Years* (New York: Arno, 1969), 1:423.

15. John Hooker, "Judge Hunt and the Right of Trial by Jury," in *An Account of the Proceedings on the Trial of Susan B. Anthony, on the Charge of Illegal Voting, at the Presidential Election in Nov., 1872, and on the Trial of Beverly W. Jones, Edwin T. Marsh and William B. Hall, The Inspectors of Election by whom her Vote was Received* (Rochester, N.Y.: *Daily Democrat* and Chronicle Book Print, 1874).

16. Dorr, *Susan B. Anthony*, p. 254.

17. *HOWS* 2:629. I assume that this description, and subsequent comments about the case, were written by Matilda. The writing sounds like hers. Elizabeth Cady Stanton did not attend the trial, but later she and Susan B. Anthony revised the chapter that Matilda had written.

18. Ibid. 2:630.

19. MJG, "The United States on Trial; Not Susan B. Anthony," speech, in *An Account of the Proceedings of the Trial of Susan B. Anthony*.

20. *HOWS* 2:647.

21. Ibid.

22. Alma Lutz, *Susan B. Anthony: Rebel, Crusader, Humanitarian* (Boston: Beacon Press, 1959), p. 209.

23. *HOWS* 2:647.

24. Ibid.

25. Ibid., pp. 675, 679.

26. Ibid., p.700.

27. Harper, *Life and Work of Susan B. Anthony*, 1:441.

28. MJG, "Women without a Country," *NCBB* (Syracuse, N.Y.), March 1879, p. 4.

CHAPTER 12. TO US AND OUR DAUGHTERS FOREVER, 1873–1876

1. Leila R. Brammer, *Excluded from Suffrage History: Matilda Joslyn Gage, Nineteenth-Century American Feminist* (Westport, Conn.: Greenwood Press, 2000), p. 47, cites Gage Papers.

2. MJG, "Colorado," *Revolution*, February 17, 1870, p. 106.

3. Susan B. Anthony to Isabella Beecher Hooker, May 12, 1873, in Elizabeth Cady Stanton and Susan B. Anthony, *Selected Papers of Elizabeth Cady Stanton and Susan B. Anthony*, ed. Ann D. Gordon (New Brunswick, N.J.: Rutgers University Press, 2000), 2:608.

4. Brammer, *Excluded from Suffrage History*, p. 8, cites Barbara S. Rivette, *Fayetteville's First Woman Voter: The Story of Woman Suffrage Leader Matilda Joslyn*

Gage, Including her 1880 Writings about the New York School Vote Campaign (Manlius, N.Y.: League of Women Voters, 1970), p. 7.

5. Sally Roesch Wagner, *Matilda Joslyn Gage: She Who Holds the Sky*, 2nd ed. (Aberdeen, S.Dak.: Sky Carrier Press, 2002), p. 16.

6. Wagner, *Matilda Joslyn Gage*, pp. 34–35.

7. "The Suffrage Movement," *Washington National Republican*, January 29, 1876, p. 1, Chronicling America Historic American Newspapers, Library of Congress, chroniclingamerica.loc.gov.

8. Ibid., p. 4.

9. Brammer, *Excluded from Suffrage History*, p. 9, cites "Freethinkers Past and Present: Matilda Joslyn Gage," Gage Papers, MC 377, Folder 49.

10. MJG to TCG, February 8, 1876, Gage Papers.

11. Sue Boland, "Matilda Joslyn Gage (March 24, 1826–March 18, 1898)," in *Dictionary of Literary Biography Complete Online: American Radical and Reform Writers, Second Series*, vol. 345 (Detroit: Gale, 2009), p. 148.

12. *HOWS* 3:21.

13. MJG to TCG, May 22, 1876, Gage Papers.

14. Brammer, *Excluded from Suffrage History*, p.37.

15. MJG to TCG, [May 22 or 23], 1876, Gage Papers.

16. Ida Husted Harper, *Life and Work of Susan B. Anthony, Including Public Addresses, Her Own Letters and Many from her Contemporaries during Fifty Years* (New York: Arno, 1969), 1:475.

17. MJG to TCG, June 4, 1876, Gage Papers.

18. Uncredited newspaper article, LC Scrapbook.

19. MJG to TCG, [undated but 1876], Gage Papers.

20. MJG to TCG, June 20, 1876, ibid.

21. MJG to TCG, June 16, 1896, ibid.

22. Ibid.

23. MJG to TCG, June 20, 1876, Gage Papers.

24. Ibid.

25. MJG, "The United States on Trial; Not Susan B. Anthony," speech, in *An Account of the Proceedings on the Trial of Susan B. Anthony, on the Charge of Illegal Voting, at the Presidential Election in Nov., 1872, and on the Trial of Beverly W. Jones, Edwin T. Marsh and William B. Hall, The Inspectors of Election by whom her Vote was Received* (Rochester, N.Y.: *Daily Democrat* and Chronicle Book Print, 1874).

26. *HOWS* 3:34.

CHAPTER 13. A HUNDRED YEARS HENCE: JULY 1876

1. MJG to TCG, July 6, 1876, Gage Papers.

2. *HOWS* 3:35–36.

3. Uncredited newspaper article, Gage Papers.

4. Frances Dana Gage, "One Hundred Years Hence," 1852, in *HOWS* 3:38–39.

5. MJG to TCG, July 6, 1876, Gage Papers.

6. Ibid.

7. Rheta Childe Dorr, *Susan B. Anthony: The Woman Who Changed the Mind of a Nation* (New York: AMS Press, 1970), 283.

8. Katharine Anthony, *Susan B. Anthony: Her Personal History and Her Era* (Garden City, N.Y.: Doubleday, 1954), 329.

9. *New York Semi-Weekly Tribune*, July 21, 1876, LC Scrapbook.

10. Uncredited article, ibid.

11. "Woman's Rights," *New York Times*, July 5, 1876, p. 5.

12. Uncredited article, July 6, 1876, "Times" handwritten at bottom, Gage Papers.

CHAPTER 14. THE *HISTORY OF WOMAN SUFFRAGE*, 1876–1878

1. MJG to Harriet Robinson, February 28, 1879, Papers of Harriet Jane Hanson Robinson and Harriette Lucy Robinson Shattuck, 1833–1937, Arthur and Elizabeth Schlesinger Library on the History of Women in America, Radcliffe Institute for Advanced Study, Harvard University, cited in Sally Roesch Wagner, *Matilda Joslyn Gage: She Who Holds the Sky*, 2nd ed. (Aberdeen, S.Dak.: Sky Carrier Press, 2002), p. 20.

2. Susan B. Anthony to Martha Coffin Wright, January 1, 1873, in Elizabeth Cady Stanton and Susan B. Anthony, *Selected Papers of Elizabeth Cady Stanton and Susan B. Anthony*, ed. Ann D. Gordon (New Brunswick, N.J.: Rutgers University Press, 2000), 2:547.

3. Ida Husted Harper, *Life and Work of Susan B. Anthony, Including Public Addresses, Her Own Letters and Many from her Contemporaries during Fifty Years* (New York: Arno, 1969), 1:480.

4. [MJG], "The Woman Suffrage History," *NCBB* (Syracuse, N.Y.), November 1880, p. 2.

5. Margaret Stanton Lawrence, "As a Mother," *New Era*, November 1885, p. 323.

6. The wording of this contract is pieced together from two sources. Mary E. Paddock Corey, "Matilda Joslyn Gage: Woman Suffrage Historian, 1852–1898" (PhD. diss., University of Rochester, 1995), p. 118, quotes most of it, leaving ellipses; her citation does not say where the "Partnership Agreement for Preparation and Publication of History of Woman Suffrage, signed: Elizabeth Cady Stanton, Matilda Joslyn Gage and Susan B. Anthony, November 15, 1876," is located. Sally Roesch Wagner fills in some of the ellipses in *Matilda Joslyn Gage*, p. 20, citing Harper Papers, Huntington Library.

7. Elinor Rice Hayes, *Morning Star: A Biography of Lucy Stone, 1818–1893* (New York: Octagon Books, 1978), p. 288.

8. *HOWS* 1:51.

9. Harper, *Life and Works of Susan B. Anthony*, 2:530.

10. *HOWS* 3:61, 66.

11. "They Want to Vote," *Washington National Republican*, January 17, 1877, p. 1.

12. Susan B. Anthony, diary, January 21, 1877, in Elizabeth Cady Stanton and Susan B. Anthony, *Selected Papers of Elizabeth Cady Stanton and Susan B. Anthony*, ed. Ann D. Gordon (New Brunswick, N.J.: Rutgers University Press, 2003), 3:283.

13. Susan B. Anthony, diary, March 21, 1877, ibid., p. 298.

14. Wagner, *Matilda Joslyn Gage*, pp. 14–15.

15. *HOWS* 3:60.

16. Leila R. Brammer, *Excluded from Suffrage History: Matilda Joslyn Gage, Nineteenth-Century American Feminist* (Westport, Conn.: Greenwood Press, 2000), p. 11.

17. *HOWS* 3:72.

18. [MJG], "A Lost Opportunity," *NCBB*, December 1879, p. 2.

19. *HOWS* 3:72.

20. Ibid., pp. 71, 75.

21. *Washington Union*, January 11, 1878, *HOWS* 3:71.

22. *HOWS* 3:71.

23. MJG, speech to the Senate Committee on Privileges and Elections, January 11 or 12, 1878, *HOWS* 3:94–95.

24. *Washington Evening Star*, January 11, [1877]; *HOWS* 3:97–98—the date printed in the book, 1876, is likely a mistake.

CHAPTER 15. THE *NATIONAL CITIZEN AND BALLOT BOX*, 1878–1880

1. Mary E. Paddock Corey, "Matilda Joslyn Gage: Woman Suffrage Historian, 1852–1898" (PhD. diss., University of Rochester, 1995), p. 71.

2. Sally Roesch Wagner, *Matilda Joslyn Gage: She Who Holds the Sky*, 2nd ed. (Aberdeen, S.Dak.: Sky Carrier Press, 2002), p. 26.

3. [MJG], "Editorial Notes," *NCBB* (Syracuse, N.Y.), April 1880, p. 3.

4. [MJG], *NCBB*, May 1878, p. 1.

5. [MJG], "What the Press Say of Us," ibid., July 1878, p. 3.

6. [MJG], "Indian Citizenship," ibid., May 1878, p. 1.

7. *HOWS* 3:117.

8. [MJG], "National Woman's Suffrage Association—Anniversary Day," *NCBB*, August 1878, p. 2.

9. *HOWS* 3:122.

10. Ibid., p.123.

11. [MJG], "National Woman's Suffrage Association—Anniversary Day," *NCBB*, August 1878, pp. 2–3.

12. [MJG], *NCBB*, June 1879, p. 2.

13. *HOWS* 3:125.

14. *New York World*, quoted in "Press Comments upon the Resolutions," *NCBB*, August 1878, p. 4.

15. [MJG], "The Clergy against Us," ibid., August 1878, p. 4.

16. Elizabeth B. Warbasse, "Gage, Matilda Joslyn," in *Notable American Women 1607–1950: A Biographical Dictionary* (Cambridge: Belknap Press of Harvard University Press, 1971), 2:5.

17. *The Proceedings and Addresses at the Freethinkers' Convention Held at Watkins, N.Y., 1878* (New York: Da Capo Press, 1970), p. 15.

18. Ezra Heywood, "Cupid's Yokes," 1877, described by National Coalition Against Censorship, wiki.ncac.org.

19. MJG, "Address of MJG," *Proceedings and Addresses at the Freethinkers' Convention*, pp. 212–13.

20. Ibid., p. 213.

21. *New York Herald*, 1878, in Wagner, *Matilda Joslyn Gage*, pp. 38, 40.

22. [MJG], "Presenting the Case to the President," *NCBB*, February 1879, p. 7.

23. *HOWS* 3:129.

24. Corey, "Matilda Joslyn Gage," pp. 82–83.

25. [MJG], "How I Decorated on the Fourth," *NCBB*, July 1879, p. 2.

26. [MJG], "A Lost Opportunity," ibid., December 1879, p. 2.

27. [MJG], "Presidential Candidates," ibid., July 1880, p. 4.

CHAPTER 16. FAYETTEVILLE'S FIRST WOMAN VOTER, 1880–1881

1. [MJG], "The Political Outlook," NCCB, September 1879, p. 2.

2. HOWS 3:422.

3. [MJG], "Robinson's Defeat," *NCBB*, November 1879, p. 2.

4. Sue Boland, introduction to appendix, in Barbara S. Rivette, *Fayetteville's First Woman Voter: The Story of Woman Suffrage Leader Matilda Joslyn Gage, Including her 1880 Writings about the New York School Vote Campaign* (Fayetteville, N.Y.: Matilda Joslyn Gage Foundation, 2006), p. ii.

5. Rivette, *Fayetteville's First Woman Voter*, p. 8.

6. [MJG,] "School Suffrage in Fayetteville," *NCBB*, October 1880, p. 2.

7. Ibid., p. 3.

8. Susan B. Anthony to MJG, November 18, 1880, Gage Papers.

9. Elizabeth Cady Stanton, *Eighty Years and More (1815–1897), Reminiscences of Elizabeth Cady Stanton* (London: T. Fisher Unwin, 1898), pp. 326–27.

10. MJG to Laura de Force Gordon, December 29, 1880, "Laura [de Force] Gordon Papers, 1856–82," Box 1, Bancroft Library, University of California, Berkeley.

11. Mary E. Paddock Corey, "Matilda Joslyn Gage: Woman Suffrage Historian, 1852–1898" (PhD. diss., University of Rochester, 1995), p. 73.

12. Rivette, *Fayetteville's First Woman Voter*, p. 12.

13. MJG to HLG, January 17, 1892, Gage Papers.

14. Hartford Courant, 1881, *HOWS* 3:192–93.

15. *HOWS* 1:7.

16. Ibid., p. 18.

17. Ibid., p. 762.

18. Ibid., p. 765.

19. Ibid., p. 767.

20. MJG to LDB, July 13, 1881, Lillie Devereux Blake Papers, Missouri Historical Society, Saint Louis.

21. *New York Times*, quoted in "Press Notices," *NCBB*, August 1881, p. 1.

22. *New York Tribune*, quoted ibid.

23. [MJG], "The End Not Yet," *NCBB*, October 1881, p. 2.

CHAPTER 17. INTOLERABLE ANXIETY, 1881–1883

1. MJG, to TCG, October 2, 1881, Gage Papers.

2. Ibid.

3. Ibid.

4. Ibid., October 10, 1881.

5. Ibid., November 19, 1881.

6. Ibid.

7. Ibid.

8. Ibid.

9. Ibid.

10. MJG to Laura de Force Gordon, December 29, 1880, "Laura [de Force] Gordon Papers, 1856–82," Box 1, Bancroft Library, University of California, Berkeley.

11. Michael Patrick Hearn, introduction to *The Annotated Wizard of Oz*, by L. Frank Baum (New York: W.W. Norton & Company, 2000), p. xviii.

12. Ibid., p. xix.

13. Michael Patrick Hearn, lecture, on bus tour of sites near Fayetteville and Rochester, New York, October 8, 2010.

14. MJG to Laura de Force Gordon, December 29, 1880, Gordon Papers, Box 1.

15. Frank Joslyn Baum and Russell P. MacFall, *To Please a Child: A Biography of L. Frank Baum* (Chicago: Reilly & Lee, 1961), pp. 43–44.

16. MJG to TCG, August 28, 1882, Gage Papers.

17. Lisa Tetrault, *The Myth of Seneca Falls: Memory and the women's Suffrage Movement, 1848–1898* (Chapel Hill: University of North Carolina Press, 2014), pp. 139–40.

18. MJG to LDB, July 8, 1884, Lillie Devereux Blake Papers, Missouri Historical Society, Saint Louis.

19. MJG to TCG, September 29, 1882, Gage Papers.

20. Michael Patrick Hearn to author, May 20, 2016.

21. Sally Roesch Wagner, *Matilda Joslyn Gage: She Who Holds the Sky*, 2nd ed. (Aberdeen, S.Dak.: Sky Carrier Press, 2002), pp. 20–21.

22. MJG, "Woman As Inventor," *North American Review*, May 1883, p. 468.

23. MJG to TCG, March 5, 1883, Gage Papers.

24. Ibid., January 25, 1883.

25. Ibid., February 15, 1883.

26. Ibid.

CHAPTER 18. BROKEN UP, 1883–1884

1. MJG to TCG, March 5, 1883, Papers.

2. Ibid., January 25, 1883.

3. Michael Patrick Hearn to author, May 20, 2016. This information, based on a letter Hearn owns from Frank Baum to his father in May 1882, contradicts earlier accounts (including those by Hearn) that say that Frank Baum replaced himself in the show when Maud got pregnant.

4. Nancy Tystad Koupal, introduction to L. Frank Baum, *Our Landlady*, ed. Nancy Tystad Koupal (Lincoln: University of Nebraska Press, 1996), p. 3.

5. Leila R. Brammer, *Excluded from Suffrage History: Matilda Joslyn Gage, Nineteenth-Century American Feminist* (Westport, Conn.: Greenwood Press, 2000), p. 15.

6. MJG to LDB, June 29, 1883, Lillie Devereux Blake Papers, Missouri Historical Society, Saint Louis.

7. Ibid.

8. Julia Gage Carpenter, "Diary, 1882–1907, Followed by Genealogical Information," University of North Dakota Library, OGLMC #0520, July 15, 1883, pp. 33–34.

9. Ibid.

10. Ibid.

11. Nancy Tystad Koupal, "Marietta Bones: Personality and Politics in the South Dakota Suffrage Movement," in *Feminist Frontiers: Women Who Shaped the Midwest*, ed. Yvonne J. Johnson (Kirksville, Mo.: Truman State University Press, 2010), p. 73.

12. MJG, letter to the Women of Dakota, 1883, in *HOWS* 3:664.

13. MJG, letter to the Dakota constitutional convention, 1883, ibid., p. 665.

14. Alan C. Elms, *Uncovering Lives: The Uneasy Alliance of Biography and Psychology* (New York: Oxford University Press, 1994), p. 151.

15. MJG to TCG, May 26, 1884, Gage Papers.

16. MJG to LDB, July 8, 1884, Blake Papers.

17. MJG to TCG, August 11, 1884, Gage Papers.

18. Ibid., [September 1884].

19. MJG to LDB, September 20, 1884, Blake Papers.

CHAPTER 19. A COURAGEOUS, FATEFUL WOMAN, 1884–1886

1. MJG to LDB, June 29, 1883, Lillie Devereux Blake Papers, Missouri Historical Society, Saint Louis.

2. MJG to TCG, May 20, 1885, Gage Papers.

3. MJG to TCG and Sophia Jewell Gage, June 8, 1885, ibid.

4. MJG to Sophia Jewell Gage, June 28, 1885, ibid.

5. Mary E. Paddock Corey, "Matilda Joslyn Gage: Woman Suffrage Historian, 1852–1898" (PhD. diss., University of Rochester, 1995), pp. 151–52.

6. MJG to TCG and Sophia Jewell Gage, January 1, 1886, Gage Papers. The description of Christmas in the paragraphs above comes from this letter.

7. "The Theosophical Society in America," theosophical.org.

8. "Who is Helena Blavatsky? A Sketch of Her Life and Work," Blavatsky Study Center, blavatskyarchives.com.

9. MJG to TCG, December 19, 1885, Gage Papers.

10. Ibid., [December 1885].

11. Ibid., July 15, 1886.

CHAPTER 20. PROTESTING LADY LIBERTY, 1886

1. MJG to HLG, August 18, 1886, Gage Papers.

2. Ibid., August 20, 1886.

3. Ibid.

4. Ibid., August 23, 1886.

5. *HOWS* 3:iv.

6. Lisa Tetrault, *The Myth of Seneca Falls: Memory and the Women's Suffrage Movement, 1848–1898* (Chapel Hill: University of North Carolina Press, 2014), pp. 142–43.

7. Mary E. Paddock Corey, "Matilda Joslyn Gage: Woman Suffrage Historian, 1852–1898" (PhD. diss., University of Rochester, 1995), p. 184.

8. Sally Roesch Wagner, *Matilda Joslyn Gage: She Who Holds the Sky*, 2nd ed. (Aberdeen, S.Dak.: Sky Carrier Press, 2002), p. 28.

9. *New York Herald*, October 28, 1883, p. 3, in Sally Roesch Wagner, *A Time of Protest: Suffragists Challenge the Republic: 1870–1887* (Aberdeen, S.Dak.: Sky Carrier Press, 1992), p. 112, and in Corey, "Matilda Joslyn Gage," p. 10.

10. Katherine Devereux Blake and Margaret Louise Wallace, *Champion of Women: The Life of Lillie Devereux Blake* (New York: Fleming H. Revell Company, 1943), p. 165.

11. "Some Things the Woman Suffragists Want," *New York Sun*, October 28, 1886, p. 2, Chronicling America Historic American Newspapers, Library of Congress.

12. "Women Express Their Preferences," *New-York Tribune*, October 28, 1886, p. 2.

13. Ibid.

14. Grace Farrell, *Lillie Devereux Blake: Retracing a Life Erased* (Amherst: University of Massachusetts Press, 2002), p. 155.

15. "Early Suffrage Protests," interview with Katherine Devereux Blake, *New York Times,* July 11, 1915. Although Blake called Lee the lieutenant governor of Wyoming; he was actually secretary to the governor of the territory, second in command, according to Phil Roberts, *A New History of Wyoming*, chapter 5, uwyo.edu.

16. LDB, "Our New York Letter," *Woman's Journal*, November 6, 1886, p. 357.

17. "Unveiling the Goddess," *New-York Tribune*, October 29, 1886.

18. LDB, "Our New York Letter."

19. "They Enter a Protest," *New York Times*, October 29, 1886.

20. Wagner, *A Time of Protest*, p. 114.

21. "They Enter a Protest," *New York Times*, October 29, 1886.

22. Blake and Wallace, *Champion of Women*, p. 165.

CHAPTER 21. THE INTERNATIONAL COUNCIL OF WOMEN, 1887–1888

1. MJG to HLG and Maud Gage Baum, January 27, 1887, Gage Papers.

2. "The Nineteenth Century," *Washington National Republican*, January 27, 1887, p. 1, gives the title. Lucia Patrick, "Religion and Revolution in the Thought of Matilda Joslyn Gage, 1826–1898" (PhD diss., Florida State University, 1996), p. 186, describes the talk.

3. Leila R. Brammer, *Excluded from Suffrage History: Matilda Joslyn Gage, Nineteenth-Century American Feminist* (Westport, Conn.: Greenwood Press, 2000), p. 15.

4. Sally Roesch Wagner, *Matilda Joslyn Gage: She Who Holds the Sky*, 2nd ed. (Aberdeen, S.Dak.: Sky Carrier Press, 2002), p. 51.

5. MJG to HLG and Maud Gage Baum, January 27, 1887, Gage Papers.

6. *HOWS* 3:110.

7. MJG to HLG and Maud Gage Baum, January 27, 1887.

8. A flyer for "Fortieth Anniversary of the Woman Suffrage Movement, International Council of Women," Gage Papers, lists the committee members.

9. MJG to Sophia Jewell Gage, April 9, 1887, Gage Papers.

10. MJG to HLG, September 29, 1887, ibid.

11. MJG to TCG, January 1, 1888, ibid.

12. MJG to HLG, January 21, 1888, ibid.

13. MJG to TCG, March 16, 1888, ibid.

14. Ibid. Matilda wrote to her son that she thought she would have to sell something, that she was already "running in debt so as to go suitably to Washington." Brammer, *Excluded from Suffrage History*, p. 15, says that Matilda had to sell property in order to attend this meeting.

15. Susan B. Anthony and Ida Husted Harper, eds., *History of Woman Suffrage*, Volume 4, 1883–1900 (Rochester, N.Y.: Susan B. Anthony, 1902), 4:133.

16. "Washington Letter," uncredited newspaper article in LC Scrapbook.

17. *Report of the International Council of Women, Assembled by the National Woman Suffrage Association, Washington, D.C., U.S. of America, March 25 to April 1, 1888* (Washington, D.C.: Rufus H. Darby, 1888), 1:352, 456.

18. Alexandra Gripenberg, *Alexandra Gripenberg's A Half Year in the New World: Miscellaneous Sketches of Travel in the United States* (Newark: University of Delaware Press, 1954), p. 15.

19. Susan B. Anthony, speech, *Report of the International Council of Women*, 1:47.

20. Elisabeth Griffith, *In Her Own Right: The Life of Elizabeth Cady Stanton* (New York: Oxford University Press, 1984), p. 193.

21. *Report of the International Council of Women*, 1:47.

22. MJG, ibid. 1:222.

23. Wagner, *Matilda Joslyn Gage*, p. 43.

24. MJG, "Woman in the Early Christian Church," speech in *Report of the International Council of Women*, 1:400–407.

25. Wagner, *Matilda Joslyn Gage*, p. 45.

26. Sue Boland, "Matilda Joslyn Gage (March 24, 1826–March 18, 1898)," in *Dictionary of Literary Biography Complete Online: American Radical and Reform Writers, Second Series*, vol. 345 (Detroit: Gale, 2009), p. 151.

27. Wagner, *Matilda Joslyn Gage*, p. 45, cites Gage Papers.

28. MJG to TCG, May 26, 1888, Gage Papers.

29. Frances E. Willard, presidential address, National Woman's Christian Temperance Union Convention, Nashville, Tenn., 1887, quoted in Douglas Morgan,

"A Clash of Millennialisms on Capitol Hill," *Liberty Magazine* (November/ December 2009), libertymagazine.org.

30. MJG to Elizabeth Cady Stanton, July 13, 1888, Elizabeth Cady Stanton and Susan B. Anthony, *Selected Papers of Elizabeth Cady Stanton and Susan B. Anthony*, ed. Ann D. Gordon (New Brunswick, N.J.: Rutgers University Press, 2009), 5:128–29.

31. Ibid. 5:129.

32. Susan B. Anthony to Frances E. Willard, August 23, 1888, National Woman's Christian Temperance Union Archives, Evanston, Illinois, cited in Kathi Kern, *Mrs. Stanton's Bible* (Ithaca: Cornell University Press, 2001), p. 125.

33. Michael Patrick Hearn to the author, May 20, 2016.

34. MJG to HLG, undated, [September 1888], Gage Papers.

CHAPTER 22. BETRAYED, 1888–1890

1. Quoted in Nancy Tystad Koupal, ed., *Baum's Road to Oz: The Dakota Years* (Pierre: South Dakota Historical Society Press, 2000), p. 11.

2. Nancy Tystad Koupal, preface and introduction to L. Frank Baum, *Our Landlady* (Lincoln: University of Nebraska Press, 1996), pp. x, 3.

3. Leila R. Brammer, *Excluded from Suffrage History: Matilda Joslyn Gage, Nineteenth-Century American Feminist* (Westport, Conn.: Greenwood Press, 2000), p. 99.

4. Ibid., pp. 97–98.

5. Sally Roesch Wagner, *A Time of Protest: Suffragists Challenge the Republic: 1870–1887* (Aberdeen, S.Dak.: Sky Carrier Press, 1992), pp. 12–13.

6. Mary E. Paddock Corey, "Matilda Joslyn Gage: Woman Suffrage Historian, 1852–1898" (PhD. diss., University of Rochester, 1995), p. 216.

7. Elizabeth Cady Stanton to Olympia Brown, May 8, 1888, Olympia Brown Papers, Arthur and Elizabeth Schlesinger Library on the History of Women in America, Radcliffe Institute for Advanced Study, Harvard University.

8. MJG, et al., "A Statement of Facts. Private. To the Members of the NWSA Only," 1889, p. 5, signed also by Olympia Brown, Charlotte F. Daley, and Marietta M. Bones, Gage Papers.

9. Sally Roesch Wagner, introduction to Matilda Joslyn Gage, *Woman, Church and State: The Original Exposé of Male Collaboration against the Female Sex* (Watertown, Mass.: Persephone Press, 1980), pp. xxxiv–xxxv.

10. MJG et al., "A Statement of Facts," p. 5, Gage Papers.

11. Wagner, introduction, p. xxxv.

12. Lucia Patrick, "Religion and Revolution in the Thought of Matilda Joslyn Gage, 1826–1898" (PhD diss., Florida State University, 1996), p. 231.

13. Elizabeth Cady Stanton and Susan B. Anthony, *Selected Papers of Elizabeth Cady Stanton and Susan B. Anthony*, ed. Ann D. Gordon (New Brunswick, N.J.: Rutgers University Press, 2009), 5:224–25.

14. Susan B. Anthony to the editor, Woman's Tribune, December 23, 1889, in Stanton and Anthony, *Selected Papers*, 5:226.

15. Koupal, *Baum's Road to Oz*, p. 41.

16. Ibid., p. 42.

17. Elizabeth Cady Stanton to MJG, October 19, 1889, in Stanton and Anthony, *Selected Papers*, 5:214–15.

18. MJG, "Public Defenders," *Liberal Thinker*, January 1890, p. 3, in Melissa Ryan, "Others and Origins: 19th Century Suffragists and the 'Indian Problem,'" presented at "Susan B. Anthony and the Struggle for Equal Rights," conference at University of Rochester, 2006, p. 12.

19. Ida Husted Harper, *Life and Work of Susan B. Anthony, Including Public Addresses, Her Own Letters and Many from her Contemporaries during Fifty Years* (New York: Arno, 1969), 2:671.

20. Ibid. 2:665–67.

21. Susan B. Anthony, diary, February 17, 1890, in Stanton and Anthony, *Selected Papers*, 5:248.

22. Elizabeth Cady Stanton, "Mrs. Stanton's Remarks, 1890," Papers of Harriet Jane Hanson Robinson and Harriette Lucy Robinson Shattuck, 1833–1937, Arthur and Elizabeth Schlesinger Library on the History of Women in America, Radcliffe Institute for Advanced Study, Harvard University.

23. MJG to Harriet H. Robinson, March 11, 1890, ibid.

24. Sally Roesch Wagner, email to author, June 1, 2016.

25. Stanton, "Mrs. Stanton's Remarks, 1890."

26. Stanton and Anthony, *Selected Papers*, 5:249.

27. MJG to TCG, February 22, 1890, Gage Papers.

28. Susan B. Anthony to Eliza Wright Osbourne, February 5 and March 5, 1890, Garrison Papers, Sophia Smith Library, Smith College; Anthony to LDB, February 6, 1890, Lillie Devereux Blake Papers, Missouri Historical Society, Saint Louis, cited in Sally Roesch Wagner, *Matilda Joslyn Gage: She Who Holds the Sky*, 2nd ed. (Aberdeen, S.Dak.: Sky Carrier Press, 2002), p. 56.

29. "Free-Thinkers' Ideas. Brainy Women with Advanced Views Meet in Council," Washington *Critic*, February 24, 1890, p. 1.

30. MJG to TCG, August 13, 1890, cited in Wagner, *Matilda Joslyn Gage*, p. 59.

31. Wagner, *Matilda Joslyn Gage*, pp. 58–59.

32. MJG to TCG, March 7, 1890, Gage Papers.

33. Wagner, *Matilda Joslyn Gage*, p. 59.

34. MJG to LDB, May 2, 1890, Blake Papers.

35. Elizabeth Cady Stanton to Clara Bewick Colby, March 21, 1890, Stanton and Anthony, *Selected Papers*, 5:278.

36. MJG to LDB, November 15, 1890, Blake Papers.

CHAPTER 23. WITCHCRAFT AND PRIESTCRAFT, 1891–1893

1. MJG to LDB, March 14, 1891, Lillie Devereux Blake Papers, Missouri Historical Society, Saint Louis (hereafter Blake Papers).

2. Michael Patrick Hearn, "Introduction to the Wizard of Oz," p. xxiv.

3. MJG to TCG, [fragment, c. 1890], Gage Papers.

4. Leslie Gage to HLG and Charly Gage, September 27, 1891, ibid.

5. Leslie Gage to HLG, October 1891, ibid.

6. MJG to Matilda Jewell Gage, November 7, 1891, ibid.

7. MJG to Sophia Jewell Gage, January 17, 1891, ibid. Matilda had eight grandchildren who survived to adulthood. Sophia and Clarkson lost their second and third babies, both girls, and later Julia lost her third child, a boy who died at the age of eight months.

8. MJG to HLG, January 17, 1892, ibid.

9. Michael Patrick Hearn, lecture, Fayetteville and Syracuse, N.Y., October 8, 2010.

10. R. S. [Robert Stanton] Baum, "That's My Dad: An Autobiography," p. 6, unpublished manuscript provided by Matilda's great-great-grandson, also named Robert Baum.

11. MJG to TCG, March 9, 1892, Gage Papers.

12. Ibid., December 16, 1891.

13. Ibid., June 9, 1892.

14. Ibid., February 1, 1893.

15. Ibid., July 18, 1892.

16. Matilda Joslyn Gage, *Woman, Church and State: A Historical Account of the Status of Woman through the Christian Ages, with Reminiscences of the Matriarchate* (Chicago: Charles H. Kerr & Company, 1893), p. [3].

17. Ibid., p. [5].

18. Ibid., p. 535.

19. Ibid., p. 12.

20. Ibid., p. 210.

21. Ibid., p. 224.

22. Ibid., p. 248.

23. Ibid., p. 291.

24. Ibid., p. 469.

25. Ibid., p. 545.

26. MJG to TCG and Sophia Jewell Gage, June 7, 1893, Gage Papers.

27. Harry Neal Baum, "My Father was 'The Wizard of Oz,'" *Baum Bugle* 29, (Autumn 1985):8.

28. Joseph Haas, "A Little Bit of 'Oz' in Northern Indiana" (interview with Harry Neal Baum) *Indianapolis Times*, May 3, 1965, cited in Michael Patrick Hearn, introduction to *The Annotated Wizard of Oz* (New York: W.W. Norton & Company, 2000), p. xxvii.

29. Ibid., p.88.

30. MJG to TCG and Sophia Jewell Gage, June 7, 1893, Gage Papers.

31. Ibid.

32. MJG to TCG, July 18, 1893, ibid.

33. Barbara S. Rivette, *Fayetteville's First Woman Voter: The Story of Woman Suffrage Leader Matilda Joslyn Gage, Including her 1880 Writings about the New York School Vote Campaign* (Fayetteville, N.Y.: Matilda Joslyn Gage Foundation, 2006), p. 11.

CHAPTER 24. BORN CRIMINAL, 1893–1894

1. MJG to TCG, 22 October 1893, Gage Papers.

2. Ibid., July 11, 1893.

3. *Truth Seeker*, July 1, 1893, cited in Sally Roesch Wagner, *Matilda Joslyn Gage: She Who Holds the Sky*, 2nd ed. (Aberdeen, S.Dak.: Sky Carrier Press, 2002), p. 61.

4. MJG to TCG, October 22, 1893, Gage Papers.

5. Sally Roesch Wagner, introduction to Matilda Joslyn Gage, *Woman, Church and State: The Original Exposé of Male Collaboration against the Female Sex* (Watertown, Mass.: Persephone Press, 1980), p. xxiii. No source given.

6. Michael Patrick Hearn to author, May 20, 2016.

7. MJG to TCG, November 7, 1893, Gage Papers.

8. Ibid.

9. MJG to HLG, December 11, 1893, ibid.

10. "The Biography of Harriet Maxwell Converse," pbs.org.

11. MJG to HLG, December 11, 1893, Gage Papers.

12. Ibid. Sally Roesch Wagner, *Sisters in Spirit: Haudenosaunee (Iroquois) Influence on Early American Feminists* (Summertown, Tenn.: Native Voices, 2001), p. 32, and Wagner, *Matilda Joslyn Gage*, 34, quote this letter, but on the microfilm of the Gage Papers, the letter ends abruptly, before reaching this part.

13. MJG to TCG, July 8, 1894, Gage Papers.

14. MJG to HLG, June 29, 1894, ibid.

15. Ibid.

16. MJG to TCG, July 8, 1894, ibid.

17. Ibid.

18. MJG to TCG, August 3, 1894, ibid.

19. Wagner, epilogue to Gage, *Woman, Church and State*, 247, cites *Fayetteville Recorder* and *Syracuse Onondaga Standard*, August 16–23, 1894.

20. "Unfit to Read. Anthony Comstock Condemns a Noted Suffragist Book, Woman, Church and State," *Syracuse Standard*, August 12, 1894, cited in Lucia Patrick, "Religion and Revolution in the Thought of Matilda Joslyn Gage, 1826–1898" (PhD diss., Florida State University, 1996), p. 296.

21. MJG to TCG, August 6, 1894, Gage Papers.

22. Ibid., August 3, 1894.

23. Barbara S. Rivette, *Fayetteville's First Woman Voter: The Story of Woman Suffrage Leader Matilda Joslyn Gage Including her 1880 Writings about the New York School Vote Campaign* (Fayetteville, N.Y.: Matilda Joslyn Gage Foundation, 2006), p. 11.

24. "Mrs. Gage's Book: A Statement of Her Side of the Case," *Fayetteville Weekly Recorder* and *Syracuse Onondaga Standard*, August 16–23, 1894, cited in Wagner, *Matilda Joslyn Gage*, pp. 61–62.

25. Ibid., p. 62.

CHAPTER 25. *THE WOMAN'S BIBLE*, 1894–1897

1. Matilda Joslyn Gage, *Woman, Church and State: A Historical Account of the Status of Woman through the Christian Ages, with Reminiscences of the Matriarchate* (Chicago: Charles H. Kerr & Company, 1893), p. 424.

2. Elizabeth Cady Stanton, *The Woman's Bible*, Parts I and II (New York: Arno Press, 1972), 2:209.

3. Sally Roesch Wagner, *Matilda Joslyn Gage: She Who Holds the Sky*, 2nd ed. (Aberdeen, S.Dak.: Sky Carrier Press, 2002), p. 64.

4. MJG to Elizabeth Cady Stanton, May 28, 1895, Colby Papers, Archives Divisionm Wisconsin Historical Society, cited in Wagner, *Matilda Joslyn Gage*, p. 64.

5. Kathi Kern, *Mrs. Stanton's Bible* (Ithaca: Cornell University Press, 2001), p. 170.

6. Susan B. Anthony to Elizabeth Cady Stanton, September 30, 1895, in Elizabeth Cady Stanton and Susan B. Anthony, *Selected Papers of Elizabeth Cady Stanton and Susan B. Anthony*, ed. Ann D. Gordon (New Brunswick, N.J.: Rutgers University Press, 2009), 5:710.

7. Stanton and Anthony, *Selected Papers*, 5:719.

8. *Washington Evening Times*, November 18, 1895, p. 4, in LC Scrapbook.

9. *St. Paul Evening Globe*, November 26, 1895, p. 6.

10. "The Woman's Bible Here," *San Francisco Call*, November 4, 1895, p. 25.

11. Ida Husted Harper, *Life and Work of Susan B. Anthony, Including Public Addresses, Her Own Letters and Many from her Contemporaries during Fifty Years* (New York: Arno, 1969), 2:853.

12. Leila R. Brammer, *Excluded from Suffrage History: Matilda Joslyn Gage, Nineteenth-Century American Feminist* (Westport, Conn.: Greenwood Press, 2000), p. 19.

13. MJG to HLG, undated letter fragment, probably summer 1896, Gage Papers.

14. Ibid.

15. Ibid., September 14, 1896.

16. Ibid., September 19, 1896.

17. MJG to Leslie Gage, December 29, 1896, ibid.

18. MJG to HLG, February 18, 1897, ibid.

19. Ibid.

20. Ibid., September 19, 1896.

21. Ibid., April 10, 1897.

22. Ibid., undated letter fragment, probably 1897.

CHAPTER 26. THAT WORD IS LIBERTY, 1897–1898

1. MJG to unknown correspondent, [June 10, 1897], Gage Papers.

2. Ibid.

3. MJG to TCG, July 15, 1897, ibid.

4. MJG to HLG, September 9, 1897, ibid.

5. MJG to TCG, September 22, 1897, Gage Papers.

6. R. S. [Robert Stanton] Baum, "That's My Dad: An Autobiography," p. 17, unpublished manuscript provided by Matilda's great-great-grandson, also named Robert Baum.

7. MJG to TCG, October 1897, Gage Papers.

8. Ibid.

9. Ibid., November 15, 1897.

10. Ibid.

11. Ibid., November 22, 1897.

12. Mary E. Paddock Corey, "Matilda Joslyn Gage: Woman Suffrage Historian, 1852–1898" (PhD. diss., University of Rochester, 1995), p. 243.

13. Michael Patrick Hearn to author, May 20, 2016.

14. MJG to Matilda Jewell Gage, 1897 or 1898, Gage Papers.

15. MJG to HLG, [undated, 1898?], ibid.

16. MJG to Leslie Gage, January 24, 1898, ibid.

17. MJG to HLG, February 24, 1898, ibid.

18. MJG to TCG, March 9, 1898, ibid.

19. Julia Gage Carpenter, "Diary, 1882–1907, Followed by Genealogical Information," University of North Dakota Library, OGLMC #0520, March 1898, p. 126.

20. TCG to Sophia Jewell Gage, March 18, 1898, Gage Papers.

21. Sally Roesch Wagner, *Matilda Joslyn Gage: She Who Holds the Sky*, 2nd ed. (Aberdeen, S.Dak.: Sky Carrier Press, 2002), p. 66. No source given.

22. Carpenter, "Diary, 1882–1907,".

23. Michael Patrick Hearn, lecture, on bus tour of sites near Fayetteville and Rochester, New York, October 8, 2010.

24. [HLG], "MJG," unattributed newspaper obituary signed "A loving tribute from one of her daughters. Aberdeen, S. D.," in LC Scrapbook.

CHAPTER 27. ERASED FROM HISTORY: THE MATILDA EFFECT

1. *Woman's Tribune*, 1888, quoted in Sally Roesch Wagner, afterword to Matilda Joslyn Gage, *Woman, Church and State: A Historical Account of the Status of Woman through the Christian Ages, with Reminiscences of the Matriarchate* (Aberdeen, S.Dak.: Sky Carrier Press, 1998), p. 329.

2. Wagner, ibid., p. 330.

3. *HOWS* 1:466.

4. Leila R. Brammer, *Excluded from Suffrage History: Matilda Joslyn Gage, Nineteenth-Century American Feminist* (Westport, Conn.: Greenwood Press, 2000), p. 112.

5. MJG to LDB, April 21, 1888, Lillie Devereux Blake Papers, Missouri Historical Society, Saint Louis.

6. MJG to LDB, May 2, 1890, Blake Papers.

7. Michael Patrick Hearn to author, May 20, 2016.

8. MJG to LDB, May 2, 1890, Blake Papers.

9. Elizabeth Cady Stanton, *Eighty Years and More (1815–1897): Reminiscences of Elizabeth Cady Stanton* (London: T. Fisher Unwin, 1898), pp. 328–29.

10. Katherine Devereux Blake and Margaret Louise Wallace, *Champion of Women: The Life of Lillie Devereux Blake* (New York: Fleming H. Revell Company, 1943), p. 211.

11. Ibid.

12. *HOWS* 4:133.

13. Ibid. 4:v.

14. Sue Boland, "Matilda Joslyn Gage (March 24, 1826–March 18, 1898)," in *Dictionary of Literary Biography Complete Online: American Radical and Reform Writers, Second Series*, vol. 345 (Detroit: Gale, 2009), p. 151.

15. Sally Roesch Wagner, *Matilda Joslyn Gage: She Who Holds the Sky*, 2nd ed. (Aberdeen, S.Dak.: Sky Carrier Press, 2002), p. 68.

16. Susan B. Anthony to TCG, April 8, 1903, Gage Papers.

17. Susan B. Anthony to HLG, June 16, 1903, ibid.

18. Blake and Wallace, *Champion of Women*, p. 115.

19. Sally Roesch Wagner, "That Word Is Liberty: A Biography of Matilda Joslyn Gage" (PhD diss., University of California, Santa Cruz, 1978), says that only fourteen letters survived, but more have probably been found since then.

20. Michael Patrick Hearn called Oz a matriarchy in "L. Frank Baum and the 'Modernized Fairy Tale,'" in *Wizard of Oz*, by L. Frank Baum (New York: Schocken Books, 1983), p. 286.

21. Gillian Thomas, *Because of Sex: One Law, Ten Cases, and Fifty Years That Changed American Women's Lives at Work* (New York: St. Martin's Press, 2016), p. 3.

22. In a letter to the author, May 20, 2016, Michael Patrick Hearn noted that *Ms.* magazine published an early feminist analysis of Oz by Noah Seaman and his mother, Barbara Seaman, "Munchkins, Ozophiles, and Feminists, Too," *Ms.* 2 (January 1974):93.

23. Dale Spender, *Women of Ideas and What Men Have Done to Them* (London: Pandora, 1988), p. 2.

24. Mary Daly, *Gyn/Ecology: The Metaethics of Radical Feminism* (Boston: Beacon Press, 1978), p. 216.

25. Spender, *Women of Ideas*, p. 330.

26. Mary Daly, foreword to Matilda Joslyn Gage, *Woman, Church and State: The Original Exposé of Male Collaboration against the Female Sex* (Watertown, Mass.: Persephone Press, 1980), p. vii.

27. Spender, *Women of Ideas*, p. 323.

28. Margaret W. Rossiter, "The ~~Matthew~~ Matilda Effect in Science," *Social Studies of Science* 23 (May 1, 1993):336–37.

29. Matilda Joslyn Gage, *Woman, Church and State: A Historical Account of the Status of Woman through the Christian Ages, with Reminiscences of the Matriarchate* (reprint ed.; Aberdeen, S.Dak.: Sky Carrier Press, 1998), p. 124.

30. Ronald Hutton, *The Triumph of the Moon: A History of Modern Pagan Witchcraft* (Oxford: Oxford University Press, 1999), p. 141. Figures seen in introduction to Matilda Joslyn Gage, *Woman, Church and State: A Historical Account of the Status of Woman through the Christian Ages, with Reminiscences of the Matriarchate* (Chicago: Charles H. Kerr & Company, 1893), available at sacred-texts.com.

31. Gloria Steinem, "Meet the Woman Who Was Ahead of the Women Who Were Ahead of Their Time" (Fayetteville, N.Y.: Matilda Joslyn Gage Foundation, 2008).

32. *HOWS* 1:34.

33. Sandra E. Garcia. "The Woman Who Created '#MeToo' Long Before Hashtags." New York Times, October 20, 2017.

34. Nicholas D. Kristof and Sheryl WuDunn, *Half the Sky: Turning Oppression into Opportunity for Women Worldwide* (New York: Alfred A. Knopf, 2009), p. xvii.

35. MJG, "Letter from Mrs. Gage," *Revolution*, January 6, 1870, p. 4.

❊ Sources: *An Annotated Bibliography*

PRIMARY SOURCES

An Account of the Proceedings of the Trial of Susan B. Anthony, on the Charge of Illegal Voting, at the Presidential Election in Nov., 1872, and on the Trial of Beverly W. Jones, Edwin T. Marsh and William B. Hall, The Inspectors of Election by whom her Vote was Received (Rochester, N.Y.: Daily Democrat and Chronicle Book Print, 1874).

Anthony, Susan B. "Library and papers of Susan B. Anthony." Library of Congress. Anthony gave this collection to the library in 1903; 349 images can be seen at loc.gov.

———. *The Trial of Susan B. Anthony*. Introduction by Lynn Sherr. Amherst, N.Y.: Humanity Books, 2003.

Anthony, Susan B., and Ida Husted Harper, eds. *History of Woman Suffrage*. Vol. 4, 1883–1900. Rochester, N.Y.: Susan B. Anthony, 1902.

Baum, Frank Joslyn, and Russell P. MacFall. *To Please a Child: A Biography of L. Frank Baum*. Chicago: Reilly and Lee, 1961.

Baum, L. Frank. *The Annotated Wizard of Oz, Centennial edition. The Wonderful Wizard of Oz* by L. Frank Baum. Pictures by W. W. Denslow. Edited with an introduction and notes by Michael Patrick Hearn. New York: W. W. Norton, 2000, 1973. Includes a brief biography of Baum. Hearn is the primary expert on Baum.

———. *Our Landlady*. Edited and annotated by Nancy Tystad Koupal. Lincoln: University of Nebraska Press, 1996.

Baum, Robert Stanton. "That's My Dad: An Autobiography." Unpublished. No date. Photocopy of a typescript owned by the author's grandson and namesake, Robert A. Baum.

Blackwell, Alice Stone. *Lucy Stone: Pioneer of Women's Rights*. Boston: Little Brown, 1930. A biography of Stone written by her daughter.

Blake, Katherine Devereux, and Margaret Louise Wallace. *Champion of Women: The Life of Lillie Devereux Blake*. New York: Fleming H. Revell Company, 1943. A biography of Blake, cowritten by her daughter.

Blake, Lillie Devereux. *Fettered for Life, or, Lord and Master: A Story for Today*. New York: Feminist Press at the City University of New York, 1996. Blake's 1874 novel about a working girl in New York, includes a cross-dressing character.

———. Papers, 1847–1908. Archives and Manuscripts Collections, Missouri Historical Society Repository, Saint Louis.

———. *Woman's Place To-Day*. New York: John W. Lovell Company, 1883. Lectures on the need for full equality for women.

Blavatsky, H. P. *The Secret Doctrine*. Abridged and annotated by Michael Gomes. New York: Jeremy P. Tarcher/Penguin, 2009. Originally published in 1888. MJG was a Theosophist; this book is the classic Theosophist text.

Bloomer, D. C. *Life and Writings of Amelia Bloomer*. New York: Schocken Books, 1975. Reprinted from the Arena Press edition of 1895. Includes firsthand accounts by Amelia Bloomer, though her husband is credited as primary author.

Carpenter, Julia Gage. "Diary, 1882–1907, Followed by Genealogical Information." University of North Dakota Library, OGLMC #0520.

Douglass, Frederick. *Narrative of the Life of Frederick Douglass, An American Slave, Written by Himself.* Cambridge, Mass.: Belknap Press of Harvard University Press, 1960.

———. *Narrative of the Life of Frederick Douglass, An American Slave, Written by Himself.* San Francisco: City Lights Books, 2010.

Gage, Matilda Joslyn. "Address of Mrs. Gage." In *The Proceedings and Addresses at the Freethinkers' Convention Held at Watkins, N.Y., 1878*. New York: Da Capo Press, 1970, pp. 212–17. Reprint of 1878 edition.

———. *The Dangers of the Hour*. Edited with an introduction by Sally Roesch Wagner. Fayetteville, N.Y.: Matilda Joslyn Gage Foundation, 2004. Originally published as *Speech of Matilda Joslyn Gage at the Woman's National Liberal Union Convention, February 24, 1890*.

———. "An Incident of the Centennial Fourth." A signed but uncredited newspaper article by MJG in her scrapbook at the Library of Congress. Probably from the *New York Evening Post*, July 1876.

———. Papers. Arthur and Elizabeth Schlesinger Library on the History of Women in America, Radcliffe Institute for Advanced Study, Harvard University. Handbills, photos, publications, letters to MJG and hundreds of letters written by her, mostly to her son, many to her daughter Helen.

———. Speech. National Woman's Rights Convention, Syracuse, N.Y., 1852. Matilda Joslyn Gage Foundation, matildajoslyngage.org. MJG's speech from her first women's rights convention.

———. *Who Planned the Tennessee Campaign of 1862?* National Citizen Tract No. 1, 1873.

———. *Woman, Church and State: A Historical Account of the Status of Woman through the Christian Ages, with Reminiscences of the Matriarchate.* Chicago: Charles H. Kerr and Company, 1893.

———. *Woman, Church and State: The Original Exposé of Male Collaboration against the Female Sex.* Watertown, Mass.: Persephone Press, 1980. Foreword by Mary Daly; introduction and epilogue by Sally Roesch Wagner.

———. "Woman as Inventor." *North American Review* 136, no. 318 (May 1883), pp. 478–89.

———. "Woman in the Early Christian Church," speech, in *Report of the International Council of Women*. Assembled by the National Woman Suffrage Association. Washington, D.C.: Rufus H. Darby, 1888.

———. "Woman's Rights Catechism." *Fayetteville Weekly Recorder*, July 27, 1871. Gage Papers.

———. Woman Suffrage Scrapbook, 1850–1898, 4 vols. Library of Congress, call no. JK1901.G16. MJG's daughter Maud Gage Baum may have compiled the scrapbooks after her mother died. They include articles by MJG and others, flyers, letterhead stationery, handbills, etc.

Gordon, Laura [de Force]. Papers, 1856–82. Bancroft Library, University of California, Berkeley.

Ingram, J. S. *The Centennial Exposition, Described and Illustrated, Being a concise and graphic description of this grand enterprise commemorative of this First Centenary of American Independence.* Philadelphia: Hubbard Bros., 1876.

Lumsden, Linda J. *Rampant Women: Suffragists and the Right of Assembly.* Knoxville: University of Tennessee Press, 1997. Quotes Matilda on p. xxix.

May, Samuel J. *Some Recollections of our Antislavery Conflict.* Boston: Fields, Osgood, 1869.

"The Metropolitan Fair Buildings." *Harper's Weekly, A Journal of Civilization* 8 (April 9, 1864). sonofthesouth.net. MJG attended this fair.

Mott, Lucretia. *Lucretia Mott: Her Complete Speeches and Sermons.* Edited by Dana Greene. New York: Edwin Mellen Press, 1980.

———. *Selected Letters of Lucretia Coffin Mott.* Edited by Beverly Wilson Palmer. Urbana: University of Illinois Press, 2002.

———. *Slavery and "The Woman Question": Lucretia Mott's Diary of her Visit to Great Britain to Attend the World's Anti-Slavery Convention of 1840.* Edited by Frederick B. Tolles. Haverford, Penn.: Friends' Historical Association, 1952.

The Proceedings of the National Woman's Rights Convention, Held at Syracuse, September 8th, 9th, and 10th. Syracuse: Printed by J. Masters, 1852.

Rakow, Lana, and Cheris Kramarae, eds. *The Revolution in Words: Righting Women, 1868–1871.* New York: Routledge, 1990. Selections from the newspaper; includes several pieces by MJG.

Report of the International Council of Women, Assembled by the National Woman Suffrage Association, Washington, D.C., U.S. of America, March 25 to April 1, 1886. Vol. 1. Washington, D.C.: Rufus H. Darby, 1888. Condensed from the Stenographic Report made by Mary F. Seymour and Assistants for the *Woman's Tribune*, published daily during the council.

Revolution. Newspaper published by Susan B. Anthony, edited by Elizabeth Cady Stanton and Parker Pillsbury. MJG made a name for herself with articles she wrote for this feminist newspaper.

"The Revolution, 1868–1872." In *Papers of Elizabeth Cady Stanton and Susan B. Anthony*, edited by Patricia G. Holland and Ann D. Gordon. Series 1. Wilmington, Del.: Scholarly Resources, 1989, microfilm.

Rivette, Barbara. *Glimpses of Fayetteville.* Fayetteville, N.Y.: Sesquicentennial Committee, 1994. Booklet with historical photos.

Saunders, Frederick, ed. *Our Quadrennial and Centennial Jubilee. Addresses Historical and Patriotic, Centennial and Quadrennial, delivered in the Several States of the Union, July 4, 1876–1883*. New York: E. B. Treat, 1893.

Sewall, May Wright. *Genesis of the International Council of Women and the Story of its Growth, 1888–1893*. No publisher. Compiler's note dated April 1914.

Stanton, Elizabeth Cady. *Eighty Years and More: Reminiscences 1815–1897.* New York: T. Fisher Unwin, 1898. A charming autobiography that downplays MJG's role in the movement and makes Stanton seem less radical, and more mainstream, than she really was. Later editions, edited by her children, omitted most of Stanton's original references to MJG. This edition can be seen at "A Celebration of Woman Writers," digital.library.upenn.edu.

——. *Elizabeth Cady Stanton As Revealed in Her Letters, Diary and Reminiscences.* This is Stanton's autobiography as edited by her children, Theodore Stanton and Harriot Stanton Blatch, omitting most items about MJG that were in *Eighty Years and More*. New York: Arno and *New York Times*, 1969.

——. *The Woman's Bible, Parts I and II*. New York: Arno Press, 1972.

Stanton, Elizabeth Cady, and Matilda Joslyn Gage. "The Declaration of the Rights of Women of the United States and Articles of Impeachment against the Government of the United States." National Woman Suffrage Association, July 4, 1876. MJG alone wrote the section on rights.

Stanton, Elizabeth Cady, and Susan B. Anthony. *The Elizabeth Cady Stanton–Susan B. Anthony Reader: Correspondence, Writings, Speeches*. Revised edition. Edited with a critical commentary by Ellen Carol DuBois. Boston: Northeastern University Press, parts 1–3, 1981; part 4, 1992. MJG is cited three times in the index.

——. *The Papers of Elizabeth Cady Stanton and Susan B. Anthony: Guide and Index to the Microfilm Edition*. Edited by Patricia G. Holland and Ann D. Gordon. Wilmington, Delaware: Scholarly Resources, 1992. Dozens of entries in the index refer to MJG. Her children and granddaughter are also cited.

——. *The Selected Papers of Elizabeth Cady Stanton and Susan B. Anthony*. Edited by Ann D. Gordon. 5 vols. New Brunswick, N.J.: Rutgers University Press, 1997–2009. MJG is cited 4 times in the index to vol. 1, 29 times in vol. 2, 101 times in vol. 3, 34 times in vol. 4, 41 times in vol. 5, 6 times in vol. 6.

Stanton, Elizabeth Cady, Susan B. Anthony, and Matilda Joslyn Gage, eds. *History of Woman Suffrage*. 3 vols. New York: Source Book Press, 1970. Unabridged republication of the 1899 Rochester edition published by Charles Mann. Still the definitive history of the early women's movement.

Stanton, Elizabeth Cady, Susan B. Anthony, Matilda Joslyn Gage, and Ida Husted, eds. *The Concise History of Woman Suffrage: Selections from the Classic Work of Stanton, Anthony, Gage, and Harper*. Edited by Mari Jo Buhle and Paul Buhle. Urbana: University of Illinois Press, 1978.

Stanton, Elizabeth Cady, and Matilda Joslyn Gage. "The Declaration of Rights for Women," also known as the "Woman's Declaration of Rights and Articles of Impeachment against the Government of the United States." The National

Woman Suffrage Association, July 4, 1876. MJG alone wrote the section on rights.

U.S. Congress. House of Representatives Committee on the Judiciary. *Woman Suffrage: Hearings on Woman Suffrage*. March 3, 1914.

Willard, Frances E. *Glimpses of Fifty Years: The Autobiography of an American Woman*. New York: Source Book Press, 1970. Originally published by the Woman's Temperance Publication Association and H. J. Smith and Co., 1889. No index.

SECONDARY SOURCES

Anderson, Bonnie S. *Joyous Greetings: The First International Women's Movement, 1830–1860*. New York: Oxford University Press, 2000.

Anthony, Katharine. *Susan B. Anthony: Her Personal History and Her Era*. Garden City, N.Y.: Doubleday, 1954. MJG is cited nine times in the index but not mentioned in the text until 1872.

Artz, Don. *A Tour of L. Frank Baum's Aberdeen*. Memories Incorporated, 1997. Includes information on MJG and her family.

Bacon, Margaret Hope. *Mothers of Feminism: The Story of Quaker Women in America*. San Francisco: Harper and Row, 1986.

Barry, Kathleen. *Susan B. Anthony: A Biography of a Singular Feminist*. New York: New York University Press, 1988. MJG is cited twelve times in the index.

The Baum Bugle: A Journal of Oz. Published by the International Wizard of Oz Club from 1957 to the present. Includes scholarly and popular articles about Oz and everything related to it, such as Baum's family. MJG lived with the Baums at the end of her life. For many years the *Bugle* was the only source of information about Baum.

Boland, Sue. "Matilda Joslyn Gage (March 24, 1826–March 18, 1898)." In *Dictionary of Literary Biography Complete Online: American Radical and Reform Writers, Second Series. Vol. 345*. Detroit: Gale, 2009, pp. 141–54. This biographical essay covers MJG's life, professional and personal, includes a five-page list of her publications.

Bordin, Ruth. *Frances Willard: A Biography*. Chapel Hill: University of North Carolina Press, 1986.

Borzone, Beth. "Upstate New York to Offer 'Votes for Women' Trail." "American History @ suite 101," beth-borzone.suite101.com. MJG's home is the easternmost site on this trail, which in 2017 was still under development.

Brammer, Leila R. *Excluded from Suffrage History: Matilda Joslyn Gage, Nineteenth-Century American Feminist*. Westport, Conn.: Greenwood Press, 2000. The author grew up in Aberdeen, South Dakota. She found MJG in the local museum but not in any histories. This scholarly book focuses on MJG's professional activities. Brammer concludes that Stanton and Anthony, who outlived MJG, chose to minimize her contributions to the women's movement, distancing themselves and the movement from her radical opinions and creating a flattering image of themselves and the movement.

Burns, Ken, and Paul Barnes. *Not for Ourselves Alone: The Story of Susan B. Anthony and Elizabeth Cady Stanton.* PBS documentary. Washington, D.C.: Florentine Films and WETA, 1999. MJG gets just a brief mention here. Sally Roesch Wagner appears in the production. The book of the same name listed below under author Geoffrey Ward is a companion to this documentary. Resources for teachers are available at the companion website, pbs.org.

Carpenter, Angelica Shirley, and Jean Shirley. *L. Frank Baum: Royal Historian of Oz.* Minneapolis: Lerner Publications, 1992. This book was the first modern biography (no invented dialogue) of Baum.

"Catherine Littlefield Greene." *UXL Encyclopedia of World Biography.* UXL, 2003.

Colman, Penny. *Elizabeth Cady Stanton and Susan B. Anthony: A Friendship That Changed the World.* New York: Henry Holt, 2011. A joint biography written for young adults. Cites MJG seven times in the index.

Corey, Mary E. Paddock. "Matilda Joslyn Gage: Woman Suffrage Historian, 1852–1898." PhD diss., University of Rochester, 1995.

Daly, Mary. *Gyn/Ecology: The Metaethics of Radical Feminism.* Boston: Beacon Press, 1978.

Dorr, Rheta Childe. *Susan B. Anthony: The Woman Who Changed the Mind of a Nation.* New York: AMS Press, 1970. Reprint of the 1928 edition. MJG is cited five times in the index.

DuBois, Ellen Carol. *Feminism and Suffrage: The Emergence of an Independent Women's Movement in America, 1848–1869.* Ithaca: Cornell University Press, 1978.

DuBois, Ellen Carol, and Lynn Dumenil. *Through Women's Eyes: An American History with Documents.* Boston: Bedford/St. Martin's, 2009.

Ellington, George [pseud.]. *The Women of New York, or the Under-World of the Great City.* New York, Arno Press, 1972. Reprint of the 1869 edition.

Farrell, Grace. "Beneath the Suffrage Narrative," *Canadian Review of American Studies* (July 1, 2006):45–65.

Farrell, Grace. *Lillie Devereux Blake: Retracing a Life Erased.* Amherst: University of Massachusetts Press, 2002. Farrell argues that Blake was erased from feminist and American history for many of the same reasons that MJG was.

Ferrara, Susan. *The Family of the Wizard: The Baums of Syracuse.* Bloomington, Ind.: Xlibris, 2000.

Fisher, Katharine. *Lucretia and Elizabeth: London 1840–Seneca Falls 1848.* N.P., [ca. 1923]. Introductory note says "Compliments of Dr. Frances Dickinson to the National Woman's Party in Session at Seneca Falls, N.Y., July 20, 1923."

Frisken, Amanda. *Victoria Woodhull's Sexual Revolution: Political Theater and the Popular Press in Nineteenth-Century America.* Philadelphia: University of Pennsylvania Press, 2004.

Gabriel, Mary. *Notorious Victoria: The Life of Victoria Woodhull, Uncensored.* Chapel Hill: Algonquin, 1998.

Gaylor, Annie Laurie, ed. *Women without Superstition: "No Gods—No Masters,"* *The Collected Writings of Women Freethinkers of the Nineteenth and Twentieth Centuries.* Madison, Wisc.: Freedom From Religion Foundation, 1997.

Gordon, Anna. *The Beautiful Life of Frances Willard*. Chicago: Woman's Temperance Publishing Association, 1898.

Graeber, Carey, and Sally Roesch Wagner. "Rediscovering Dorothy in the Wonderful Mother of Oz." Talk for "Oz: The Books" conference cosponsored by the International Wizard of Oz Club and The Arne Nixon Center for the Study of Children's Literature, California State University, Fresno, May 14, 2010.

Griffith, Elisabeth. *In Her Own Right: The Life of Elizabeth Cady Stanton*. New York: Oxford University Press, 1984. MJG is cited six times in the index.

Halstead, Rachel. "The New Myth of the Witch." *Trouble and Strife* 2 (Spring 1984):10–17.

Hare, Lloyd C. M. *The Greatest American Woman: Lucretia Mott*. New York: Negro Universities Press, 1970. Originally published by the American Historical Society, Inc., 1937.

Harper, Ida Husted. *The Life and Work of Susan B. Anthony, Including Public Addresses, Her Own Letters and Many from her Contemporaries during Fifty Years*. New York: Arno and *the New York Times*, 1969. Originally published in Indianapolis by the Hollenbeck Press, vols. 1–2, 1898; vol. 3, 1908. Anthony's biography, written with her participation by her approved biographer cites MJG thirty times in the index to the first two volumes, four times in the index to vol. 3.

Harper, Judith E. *Susan B. Anthony: A Biographical Companion*. Santa Barbara: ABC-CLIO, 1998. MJG gets a two-page entry.

Hays, Elinor Rice. *Morning Star: A Biography of Lucy Stone, 1818–1893*. New York: Octagon Books, 1978; originally published 1961. Hays says that Lucy Stone's achievements are virtually unknown to Anthony and Stanton. "There is room in the heavens for a third star of equal magnitude. This third is Lucy Stone." MJG is cited twice in the index.

Hearn, Michael Patrick. Introduction to *The Annotated Wizard of Oz*, by L. Frank Baum. Edited by Michael Patrick Hearn. New York: W.W. Norton and Company, 2000.

———. "L. Frank Baum and the 'Modernized Fairy Tale.'" In *The Wizard of Oz*, by L. Frank Baum. New York: Schocken Books, 1983.

———. Lectures on L. Frank Baum, October 8–9, 2010, Syracuse and Fayetteville, N.Y.

Hollihan, Kerrie Logan. *Rightfully Ours: How Women Won the Vote*. Chicago Review Press, 2012.

Hutton, Ronald. *The Triumph of the Moon: A History of Modern Pagan Witchcraft*. Oxford University Press, 1999.

Johnston, Johanna. *Mrs. Satan: The Incredible Saga of Victoria C. Woodhull*. New York: G. P. Putnam's Sons, 1967.

Kern, Kathi. *Mrs. Stanton's Bible*. Ithaca, N.Y.: Cornell University Press, 2001. MJG is cited thirty-four times in the index.

Kirkley, Evelyn A. *Rational Mothers and Infidel Gentlemen: Gender and American Atheism, 1865–1915*. Syracuse, N.Y.: Syracuse University Press, 2000.

Koupal, Nancy Tystad, ed. *Baum's Road to Oz: The Dakota Years*. Pierre: South Dakota Historical Society Press, 2000.

———. "Marietta Bones: Personality and Politics in the South Dakota Suffrage Movement." In *Feminist Frontiers: Women Who Shaped the Midwest*, edited by Yvonne J. Johnson. Kirksville, Mo.: Truman State University Press, 2010. Pp. 69–82.

Kristof, Nicholas D. and Sheryl WuDunn. *Half the Sky: Turning Oppression into Opportunity for Women Worldwide*. New York: Alfred A. Knopf, 2009.

Linder, Doug. "The Trial of Susan B. Anthony for Illegal Voting." 2001. law2.umkc. edu.

Loncraine, Rebecca. *The Real Wizard of Oz: The Life and Times of L. Frank Baum*. New York: Gotham Books, 2009. MJG is cited twenty-six times in the index.

Lumsden, Linda J. *Rampant Women: Suffragists and the Right of Assembly*. Knoxville: University of Tennessee Press, 1997.

Lurie, Alison. "The Oddness of Oz." *New York Review of Books* 47 (December 21, 2000):16–17, 20–24.

Lutz, Alma. *Susan B. Anthony: Rebel, Crusader, Humanitarian*. Boston, Beacon Press, 1959. MJG is cited twelve times in the index.

Mannix, Daniel P. "The Father of the Wizard of Oz." *American Heritage* 16, no. 1 (December 1964):36–47.

"Matilda Joslyn Gage: The Forgotten Feminist." Retrospective exhibit prepared by the Matilda Joslyn Gage Center for the Fayetteville Free Library, Fayetteville, N.Y., October 2010.

Million, Joelle. *Woman's Voice, Woman's Place: Lucy Stone and the Birth of the Woman's Rights Movement*. Westport, Connecticut: Praeger, 2003.

Moreno, Barry. *The Statue of Liberty Encyclopedia*. New York: Simon and Schuster, 2000.

Mosley, Shelley, and John Charles. *The Suffragists in Literature for Youth: The Fight for the Vote*. Lanham, Md.: Scarecrow Press, 2006. MJG is included as a major figure of the movement.

Newman, Daisy. *A Procession of Friends: Quakers in America*. Garden City, N.Y. Doubleday, 1972.

Norgren, Jill. *Belva Lockwood: The Woman Who Would Be President*. New York: New York University Press, 2007.

Patrick, Lucia. "Religion and Revolution in the Thought of Matilda Joslyn Gage, 1826–1898." PhD diss., Florida State University, 1996. UMI no. 9700190.

Rivette, Barbara S. *Fayetteville's First Woman Voter: The Story of Woman Suffrage Leader Matilda Joslyn Gage Including her 1880 Writings about the New York School Vote Campaign*. Manlius, N.Y.: League of Women Voters, 1970. Reprinted in 2006 by the Matilda Joslyn Gage. This booklet is the first biography of MJG.

Rogers, Katharine M. *L. Frank Baum, Creator of Oz: A Biography*. New York: St. Martin's Press, 2002. *Baum Bugle* was Rogers's main source; she read it at the Library of Congress. Until Michael Patrick Hearn finishes biography of Baum, this biography is the most complete. MJG is cited twenty-four times in the index.

Rossiter, Margaret W. "The ~~Matthew~~ Matilda Effect in Science." *Social Studies of Science* 23, no. 2 (May 1, 1993), pp. 325–41.

Ryan, Melissa. "Others and Origins: 19th Century Suffragists and the 'Indian Problem.'" Presented at "Susan B. Anthony and the Struggle for Equal Rights" conference at University of Rochester, 2006. urresearch.rochester.edu.

Sachs, Emanie. *"The Terrible Siren": Victoria Woodhull (1838–1927)*. New York: Harper and Brothers, 1928.

Sanders, Matthew J. "An Introduction to Phoebe Wilson Couzins." Final paper, Women in the Legal Profession, Autumn 2000, Professor Barbara A. Babcock. Women's Legal History website, Womenslegalhistory.stanford.edu.

Schwartz, Evan I. "Matilda Joslyn Gage—The Unlikely Inspiration for the Wizard of Oz." Historynet. September 24, 2009. historynet.com.

Seaman, Noah, and Barbara Seaman. "Munchkins, Ozophiles, and Feminists, Too." *Ms.* 2 (January 1974):93.

Sehgal, Parul. "Fighting 'Erasure.'" *New York Times Magazine.* February 2, 2016. Another version of this article appeared as "Memory Lapse," in the "First Words" series, *New York Times Magazine*, February 7, 2016, pp. 15–17.

Sherr, Lynn. *Failure is Impossible: Susan B. Anthony in her own Words.* New York: Times Books and Random House, 1995. MJG is cited three times in the index.

Spender, Dale. *Women of Ideas and What Men Have Done to Them.* London: Pandora, 1982. MJG, cited thirty-one times in the index, receives extensive coverage.

Steinem, Gloria. "Meet the Woman Who Was Ahead of the Women Who Were Ahead of Their Time." Fayetteville, N.Y.: Matilda Joslyn Gage Foundation, 2008.

———. *My Life on the Road.* New York: Random House, 2015.

Stern, Madeleine B. *Heads and Headliners: The Phrenological Fowlers.* Norman: University of Oklahoma Press, 1971.

———, comp. *A Phrenological Dictionary of Nineteenth-Century Americans.* Westport, Conn.: Greenwood Press, 1982.

Tetrault, Lisa. *The Myth of Seneca Falls*: *Memory and the Women's Suffrage Movement, 1848–1898.* Chapel Hill: University of North Carolina Press, 2014.

Thomas, Gillian. *Because of Sex: One Law, Ten Cases, and Fifty Years That Changed American Women's Lives at Work.* New York: St. Martin's Press, 2016.

Underhill, Lois Beachy. *The Woman Who Ran for President: The Many Lives of Victoria Woodhull.* Bridgehampton, N.Y.: Bridge Works Publishing, 1995.

Wagner, Sally Roesch. "Matilda Joslyn Gage." In *Women Public Speakers in the United States, 1800–1925: A Bio-critical Sourcebook*, edited by Karlyn Kohrs Campbell. Westport, Conn.: Greenwood Press, 1993. Pp. 279–93.

———. "Matilda Joslyn Gage, 1826–1898." New York History Net. nyhistory.com.

———. "The Matilda Joslyn Gage House: A Station on the Underground Railroad." pacny.net.

———. *Matilda Joslyn Gage: She Who Holds The Sky.* 2nd ed. Aberdeen, S.Dak.: Sky Carrier Press, 2002.

———. "One Woman, One Vote." *NWSA Journal* 12 (Summer 2000):181.

———. "Oral History as a Biographical Tool." In *Women's Oral History: The Frontiers Reader*, edited by Susan Hodge Armitage, Patricia Hart, and Karen Weathermon. Lincoln: University of Nebraska Press, 2002, pp. 115-24.

———. *Sisters in Spirit: Haudenosaunee (Iroquois) Influence on Early American Feminists*. Summertown, Tenn.: Native Voices, 2001.

———. Telephone interviews with the author, May 1, 2011, July 19, 2013. Wagner offered suggestions, corrections, etc., which I have incorporated.

———. "That Word Is Liberty: A Biography of Matilda Joslyn Gage." PhD diss., University of California at Santa Cruz, 1978.

———. "The Susan B. Anthony Window in the Home of Matilda Joslyn Gage." *New York History Review* 6 (December 2012):16-22. Seen as a typescript sent by Wagner.

———. *A Time of Protest: Suffragists Challenge the Republic: 1870-1887*. Aberdeen, S.Dak.: Sky Carrier Press, 1992.

———. *The Wonderful Mother of Oz*. Fayetteville, N.Y.: Matilda Joslyn Gage Foundation, 2003.

———, and Deborah Hughes. Dialogue about the conflict and communalities between MJG and Anthony. Susan B. Anthony House, Rochester, N.Y., October 8, 2010.

Warbasse, Elizabeth B. "Gage, Matilda Joslyn." In *Notable American Women 1607-1950: A Biographical Dictionary*. Cambridge: Belknap Press of Harvard University Press, 1971. 2:4-6.

Ward, Geoffrey C. *Not For Ourselves Alone: The Story of Elizabeth Cady Stanton and Susan B. Anthony*. New York: Alfred A. Knopf, 1999.

Weatherford, Jack. *Indian Givers: How the Indians of the Americas Transformed the World*. New York: Fawcett Columbine, 1988.

Wellman, Judith, and Sally Roesch Wagner. "From the Underground Railroad to Women's Writes," lecture and tour, Fayetteville and Rochester, N.Y. October 8, 2010.

Wheeler, Marjorie Spruill, ed. *One Woman, One Vote: Rediscovering the Woman Suffrage Movement*. Troutdale, Ore.: New Sage Press, 1995.

White, Donald F., comp. and ed. *Exploring 200 Years of Oneida County History*. Utica, N.Y.: Oneida County Historical Society, 1998.

Willard, Frances E., and Mary A. Livermore, eds. *A Woman of the Century: fourteen hundred-seventy biographical sketches accompanied by portraits of leading American women in all walks of life*. Buffalo: Charles Wells Moulton, 1893. Republished by Gale Research Company, Book Tower, Detroit, 1967.

Women in a Changing World: The Dynamic Story of the International Council of Women since 1888. London: Routledge and Kegan Paul, 1966.

SELECTED WEBSITES

"Anna Ella Carroll." Maryland Women's Hall of Fame, Maryland State Archive, 2001. msa.md.gov. This website agrees with MJG that Carroll was a strategist for Lincoln in the Civil War but that her involvement was kept secret.

The Arthur and Elizabeth Schlesinger Library on the History of Women in America, Radcliffe Institute for Advanced Study, Harvard University. radcliffe.edu. This collection documents women's lives and endeavors from the early nineteenth century to the present. In addition to MJG's papers, the holdings include manuscripts, books, periodicals, photographs, etc. Includes a link to the library's catalog and information about exhibitions. More helpful to researchers than to young readers.

Blavatsky Study Center. blavatskyarchives.com.

"The Biography of Harriet Maxwell Converse." PBS. pbs.org.

The Elizabeth Cady Stanton and Susan B. Anthony Papers Project. Edited by Ann D. Gordon. Rutgers University. ecssba.rutgers.edu. Includes biographies, information for students, sample documents.

Elizabeth Cady Stanton Trust. elizabethcadystanton.org. The Stanton Trust bought a collection of three thousand items related to women's suffrage. Some may be seen on the website. There is also some information on Stanton and related subjects.

Erie Canal Museum, Syracuse, N.Y. eriecanalmuseum.org.

The Freethought Trail. freethought-trail.org. This project of the Council for Secular Humanism showcases west-central New York as a hotbed of social, political, and religious innovation. MJG, who believed in the Freethinker movement and wrote for its publications, is featured prominently. The trail is described in words and photographs, by cause, person, and location.

Matilda Joslyn Gage Foundation. Fayetteville, N.Y. matildajoslyngage.org. This website, constantly updated, is an invaluable resource for information about MJG and her time. The foundation has an admirable public relations campaign that promotes programs and fundraising through links to the website. The museum has won awards for its participatory style: visitors can write messages on a wall in the house, or they can write virtual messages via the website.

"Old Fulton NY Post Card Website, New York State Historical Photos and Newspapers, 1795–2007." fultonhistory.com. A searchable repository of old newspapers; many of them are from very old microfilm that is impossible to read. MJG is cited 768 times; many citations are for articles she wrote.

Susan B. Anthony Museum and House website. susanbanthonyhouse.org. The house is in Rochester, N.Y., about fifty miles from MJG's house in Fayetteville.

"Teaching with Documents: Woman Suffrage and the 19th Amendment." National Archives. archives.gov. Includes lesson plans and activities based on original documents.

"The Theosophical Society in America." theosophical.org.

"Votes for Women: Selections from the National American Woman Suffrage Association, 1848–1921." American Memory Project. Library of Congress. Texts here are linked to illustrative materials at memory.loc.gov, "By Popular Demand: 'Votes for Women' Suffrage Pictures, 1850–1920." MJG gets a mention in the text section. Photos of others from the movement can be found here.

Women's Heritage Trail. New York State Office of Parks, Recreation, and Historic Preservation. nysparks.com. MJG's house is part of this trail.

Women's Rights National Historical Park. New York. nps.gov. This national park in Seneca Falls, about fifty miles from MJG's home in Fayetteville, includes the church where the first women's rights convention was held in 1848, a visitor center, and the house where Elizabeth Cady Stanton lived. Invites the reader to join on Facebook or Twitter.

✳ Questions

1   Have you ever signed a petition? If yes, was it online or in person? What was it for? If no, have you seen petitions being offered for people to sign? What about? What petition might you sign right now?

2   Should men and women be educated together? Should teenage boys and girls be educated together? Why or why not?

3   Matilda taught her audiences about women's accomplishments throughout history. Have you heard of the women she praised: Semiramis, Sappho, Helena Lucretio Cornaro, Maria Cunitz, Caroline Herschel, Anna Maria van Schurman, Queen Victoria, Jenny Lind, and Harriet Beecher Stowe? Which woman do you most admire?

4   Matilda felt energized by opposition. How do you react to opposition? Give an example of how you responded when someone criticized you or tried to stop you from doing something you thought was right.

5   Matilda's favorite slogans included "No taxation without representation" and "There is a word sweeter than mother, home, or heaven—that word is 'liberty.'" What are your favorite political slogans from the past and from today? What do they mean to you?

6   Matilda viewed prostitution as an economic problem. She felt that many women were unable to find other jobs that could support them and their children. Do you think women choose prostitution today, or are they coerced into it? Find research to support your opinion.

7   What progress remains to be made in the women's movement in the United States?

8   True or false: today's family courts tend to favor mothers over fathers in custody cases. What sources can you give to support your belief?

9   Matilda said, "When men begin to *fear* the power of women, their voice and their influence, then we shall secure justice, but not before." Do men fear the power of women now? Do you agree with Matilda's argument?

10 Matilda believed that the enfranchisement of women was the most important demand of the nineteenth century. Do you agree? What was the most important demand of the twentieth century? And the twenty-first century?

11 Matilda thought that the prolonged slavery of women was the darkest page in human history. Do you agree? If not, what would you say was the worst crime in human history?

12 Scholars have said that the *History of Woman Suffrage* was a new kind of history: social history. Define social history. Name some current books and movies that might be considered social history.

13 In 1888 Matilda said, "Frances Willard, with her magnetic force, her power of leadership, her desire to introduce religious tests into the government, is the most dangerous person upon the American continent" in her time. Who would she think is the most dangerous person today?

14 Do modern churches now treat women and men more equally than they did in Matilda's lifetime?

15 Has the United States achieved separation of church and state? How do you think that the current situation will change?

16 Matilda tried to stay abreast of new developments in biology. What recent issues in biology might interest her?

17 What is the legal age of consent in your state? What rights are associated with this status?

18 In Europe from the late fifteenth through the late eighteenth centuries, witch burnings were sometimes part of public holidays. What rites in the world today resemble this custom?

19 Who controls history now?

20 Why was Matilda written out of history? Who stood to gain from her exclusion?

21 Define this slogan from the second wave of the women's movement: "The personal is political."

22 Is the United States still a male-dominated society?

23 Recently the Los Angeles City Council voted to replace Columbus Day with Indigenous Peoples Day. Would Matilda have approved? What other changes might she suggest in holidays or historical statues?

✳ Activities

1   Make an herbarium of plants from your area. Which ones are native and which are imported? Find directions at diynatural.com /diy-herbarium.

2   Matilda began her career by writing letters to the editors of newspapers, expressing her views on political issues. Look up your local newspaper's rules for submitting letters to the editor. Write one on an issue you think is important. If you feel strongly enough, submit it to the newspaper.

3   Women's clothes were heavy and cumbersome in Matilda's lifetime. Find out how this felt by making and wearing a long, heavy skirt, then carrying "a baby" and "a candle" up a staircase. If this seems too dangerous, try going up and down without holding anything extra. Do not try this without adult supervision.

Equipment needed:
1   An old sheet, double size or bigger
2   A hula hoop
3   20 large safety pins or packing tape
4   15–20 hardback books (a typical adult hardback weighs about a pound)
5   Plastic bags with handles
6   A strong belt that fits loosely around your waist
7   A length of rope to hold up the skirt
8   A baby or a doll
9   A battery candle or flashlight
10 A helpful assistant

Directions:
1   Fold sheet in half crosswise.
2   Thread a rope through the fold. This will be the top of the skirt, at your waist.

3   Pin or tape a hula hoop (make a casing for it) to the inside of the sheet, near the bottom. The top part of the sheet should cover it.

4   Place the skirt on the ground in a ring, open in the middle.

5   Put 15–20 books into plastic bags, string the bags on a belt, and buckle it around your waist.

6   Step into the skirt, pull it the top part up to your waist, over the books, and tie the rope behind you.

7   Pick up your doll and light.

8   Try to climb upstairs. Hold your skirt, the banister, the doll, and the light.

9   Warning: This is dangerous, there is a risk of tripping, and sometimes the sheet does not survive. Be careful!

4   Search the internet for information about the women's protest in Philadelphia on July 4, 1876. Report on the articles that you find. Do they mention Matilda? For more articles, try searching the Library of Congress's Chronicling America newspaper collection at chroniclingamerica.loc.gov.

5   Search the internet for information about the World Anti-Slavery Convention in London in 1840. Report on the articles that you find. Do they mention the issue of women's rights?

6   Search the internet for paintings of the World Anti-Slavery Convention in London in 1840 (where are women seated?); the dedication of the Statue of Liberty (do you see any women?); and a portrait of Lincoln and his advisors with an empty chair (Do you think that the empty chair represents Anna Ella Carroll?).

7   Research recent studies about biological differences between men and women.

8   Who were some foresisters (historical women's rights activists) in your community? Identify some modern women's rights activists in your area.

9   Interview your family members about your family's involvement in or feelings about the women's rights movement.

Angelica Shirley Carpenter practiced climbing stairs in her own homemade skirt with a doll and a battery-powered candle a few times before she got the hang of it. *Carpenter Collection*

10 Make a chart comparing specific women's rights (voting, education, driving, birth control, etc.) in the United States to the same rights in other countries.

11 Class project: create a newspaper with articles or editorials on some of the single topics listed below, plus others inspired by Matilda's life. Or if you're reading on your own, write an article, editorial, or speech about one of the following topics.

> Freethinkers in Matilda's time and today
> Men who fought for women's suffrage
> The anti-suffrage movement
> A woman you are unfamiliar with from the first chapter of
> the *History of Woman Suffrage* (available online at Project
> Gutenberg and other sites)

Angelica Shirley Carpenter (right) with her mother, Jean Shirley, in 1993. *Carpenter Collection*

⁂ Author Interview

Q: When did you first realize you wanted to write nonfiction?

A: In the 1980s when I was the director of a small public library in South Florida, my mother, Jean Shirley, retired from her public relations job in Saint Louis and moved to live near me for the first time in many years. She had published several biographies for children, and she thought it would be fun for us to write together. I didn't consider myself a writer then, but I was always writing. When my daughter, Carey, was little and long-distance calls were expensive, I wrote Mother a letter about her almost every day. In library organizations, I volunteered to be secretary or newsletter editor.

Mother brought with her to Florida an autobiography called *The One I Knew the Best of All* by Frances Hodgson Burnett, author of *The Secret Garden*. This book described Burnett's childhood and told how she became a writer. Mother thought it would make a good basis for a young people's biography of Burnett. I resisted the idea at first, but I kept thinking about it. I knew that *The Secret Garden*, published in 1911, was still popular. I learned that the only other children's biography of Burnett, written by her daughter-in-law, omitted facts that embarrassed the family, such as Burnett's divorce and her second marriage. Finally I read *The One I Knew the Best of All*, admitted that "mother knows best," and we began work on what became our first joint book: *Frances Hodgson Burnett: Beyond the Secret Garden*.

Q: What is the most helpful resource or thing to remember when starting research?

A: For narrative nonfiction, the best resources are primary: letters, diaries, photographs, court documents, and other materials that provide firsthand accounts of the life or event I am studying. I especially like writing about writers because they write about themselves. When I track down their letters and diaries, I feel like a literary detective. Newspaper stories from the time also offer wonderful information and descriptions. Secondary sources, like books or articles written later, provide helpful overviews, and it is often through bibliographies or footnotes in these materials that I am able to locate the primary sources. I use Wikipedia or Google to check dates or gain an overview of a term or process I may not understand, but I verify information found there in known, reliable sources before believing it or using it.

Q: What made you interested in Matilda Joslyn Gage?

A: I discovered Matilda as Mother and I wrote our second book, *L. Frank Baum: Royal Historian of Oz*. We were both childhood Oz fans. Mother inherited her uncle's Oz books, and she passed them on to me. I became the family's third-generation Oz fan but the first Oz nut. In the 1970s I joined the International Wizard of Oz Club (ozclub.org), and I began reading the club's magazine, *The Baum Bugle*. At that time, not a lot had been published about L. Frank Baum and the books he wrote; now he is the subject of much scholarly study and, of course, huge amounts of information are available on the internet. Mother and I did most of our research in *The Baum Bugle*, which is where we discovered Baum's mother-in-law, Matilda Joslyn Gage. We learned that she was a famous women's rights advocate during her lifetime and that she had published many books and articles. She encouraged Baum to write, and she no doubt influenced the feminist ideas he wrote about in his fourteen Oz books.

In 2004 I was elected president of the Oz Club. In 2008 Dr. Sally Roesch Wagner, executive director of the Matilda Joslyn Gage Foundation, invited the club to meet in Fayetteville, New York. We visited Matilda's house, stepping carefully as it was still being restored. In 2010 I hosted a national Oz convention at California State University, Fresno, and Sally was a featured speaker. In 2011 I attended the opening of the Gage House as a museum and center for social justice dialogue. As I got to know Sally, I grew increasingly interested in Matilda. When I read Sally's books, I realized that Matilda had been written out of history. That is when I decided to write this book about her. Sally encouraged me and helped me along the way.

Q: Did you make any pilgrimages to the places Matilda visited or lived? If yes, which impacted you most?

A: I have been to lots of these places—her house, Independence Hall in Philadelphia, the grounds of the Chicago World's Fair—but the most exciting trip was to the Ontario County Court House in Canandaigua, New York, where Matilda attended Susan B. Anthony's trial for voting illegally. I went while on a driving trip with my best friend from eighth grade, Susan Linter James. We thought we had plenty of time to get there before the building closed at 5 p.m., but we had started to worry by the time we finally arrived at 4:30. Inside, three armed guards greeted us. I explained what we wanted to see, and an officer replied, "We don't let people into that courtroom unless there is a trial."

We must have looked very sad. "Oh, come on," he said, "but you'll have to put your things through security." When they scanned our purses, they saw cameras inside.

"I'm afraid we can't allow photography," another man said. This was disappointing news, but still we wanted to see the room.

The first guard led us through the empty building, up a beautiful flight of stairs. Then he unlocked the door to a large courtroom filled with green-cushioned benches and elegant woodwork. On the walls in a double row hung dozens of framed portraits, all men. We felt overwhelmed to be standing together, seeing what Matilda had seen when she stood with her friend (they were friends then). "Go ahead and take pictures," the guard urged, and we did.

Q: Do you share a quirk with Matilda? How was she like most girls and women of her time? How was she different?

A: I don't know if it's a quirk, but Matilda liked beautiful clothes and I do, too. She traveled often to big cities where she observed the latest fashions. Her letters to her three daughters and daughter-in-law in Dakota Territory included elaborate descriptions of hats, hairstyles, capes, sleeves, and fancy trim on dresses. Sometimes she even drew pictures to illustrate a new style for them. My experience reverses hers: when I visit Carey in San Francisco, she supervises my shopping and lets me know if something is too loud (I love Hawaiian prints) or "L.O.L." (little old lady).

Like many women of her time, Matilda cooked, cleaned, sewed, embroidered, gardened, canned, and put up preserves. She loved her children and doted on her grandchildren. Unusually, she traveled alone, spoke in public, took pride in getting her name into newspapers, and spoke frankly, even on controversial topics like birth control and prostitution.

Q: What do you think Matilda's superpower was? How did she further her cause?

A: Her intelligence and her lifelong desire to learn, coupled with her writing talent, were her strongest assets to the women's movement. She felt energized by opposition, considering it a sign that she was succeeding. She never gave up, working diligently until she died.

Q: How does the writing process make you feel closer to your subject?

A: Writing a biography is like time travel. By the time I finished *Born Criminal*, I had 380 pages of notes in my computer. These include quotations from letters, diaries, and newspapers. It took me several months to read Matilda's letters on borrowed microfilm. The film quality was poor, and her handwriting was often hurried and difficult to make out. Little by little, I got better at reading it. By arranging my notes in chronological order, sometimes I knew what Matilda had done day by day. I also found hundreds of photographs and illustrations from the period, mostly from online sources, and these, too, made me feel close to her. I know much more about Matilda than I do about my own great-great-grandmother, who lived at the same time. And through the Oz club, I have gotten to know some of Matilda's descendants, especially her great-great-grandchildren Bob Baum and Gita Dorothy Morena. Not all descendants of biographical subjects are pleased when unrelated writers publish books about their famous relatives, but Bob and Gita have offered encouragement, photos, and manuscripts. Bob even mailed me one of Matilda's silver spoons to be photographed for this book. Holding it in my hand, I could imagine eating dinner at Matilda's house. And hey, doesn't that griffin look a little like a winged monkey?

⁂ Index

See also Constitutional amendments; specific legislation

United States Constitution
and habeus corpus, 105, 107
and slavery, 64
See also specific amendments

United States Continental Congress, 100

"The United States on Trial, Not Susan B. Anthony" (MJG), 94–95

United States Patent Office, 91

United States Supreme Court, 113, 123

Universalist Church, 27

universal suffrage, 68–70, 74

"The Unthought-of Danger" (MJG), 159

Van Schaick, Mr., 50

Van Schurman, Anna Maria, 44, 261

Victoria (queen of England), 44, 261

A Vindication of the Rights of Women (Wollstonecraft), 78

Votes for Women Trail, 217

Voting. *See* Registering to vote; Right to vote

Wagner, Sally Roesch, 207, 215–16, 217, 222n5, 270

Washington Critic, 177

Washington *Evening Times*, 198

Watkins, N.Y., 122

Weaver, James B., 124

Weaver, Zebulon, 30–31

Weekly Recorder, 85

"Who Planned the Tennessee Campaign of 1862" (Carroll), 98

Wilbur, Dr., 192–93

Willard, Frances E., 129, 162–63, 165, 167, 167–68, 169, 262

Willard Hall, 177

Willard Hotel (Washington, D.C.), 176

Wilson, Woodrow, 219

Witches/witchcraft, 130, 186–87, 216–17

Wollstonecraft, Mary, 78

"Woman, Church, and State" (MJG), 129–30

Woman, Church and State (MJG), 155, 183–87, 189, 192, 199, 201, 212, 216

"Woman as Inventor" (MJG), 71–72, 84, 140

Woman in the Nineteenth Century (Fuller), 32

The Woman's Bible (ECS), 165–66
MJG and, 155, 195–96, 201
criticism of, 198

Woman's Bureau, 77–78

Woman's Christian Temperance Union (WCTU). *See* Temperance movement

"Woman's Declaration of Rights and Articles of Impeachment Against the Government of the United States" (MJG and ECS), 4, 9–11, 104–5, 109

"Woman's Demand for Freedom" (MJG), 205

Woman's National Indian Association, 162

Woman's National Liberal Union (WNLU), 174, 174–75, 177, 179, 211

"Woman's Rights Catechism" (Gage), 85–87

Woman's Tribune, 159, 169, 175, 176, 207

Woman suffrage. *See* Registering to vote; Right to vote

"Women in Ancient Egypt" (MJG), 91

"Women in Newspapers" (MJG), 129

"Women in the Early Christian Church" (MJG), 165–66, 168

Women of Ideas: And What Men Have Done to Them (Spender), 216

women's fashion
American Indian dress, 39–40
bloomers/reform dress, 39–41, 45, 50, 53, 55
bobbed hair, 40–41, 55
ensembles described, 3–4, 90–91
walking dresses, 77
wedding dress, 18, 31